Successful
Writing
at Work

Concise Edition

Successful Writing at Work

Concise Edition

Philip C. Kolin
University of Southern Mississippi

Houghton Mifflin Company   Boston   New York

To Kristin, Eric, Theresa, and Evan
Maureen
Julie and Loretta
and
MARY

Publisher: Patricia A. Coryell
Executive Editor: Suzanne Phelps Weir
Sponsoring Editor: Michael Gillespie
Development Editor: Julia Casson
Editorial Assistant: Lindsey Gentel
Project Editor: Shelley Dickerson
Manufacturing Coordinator: Renée Ostrowski
Senior Marketing Manager: Cindy Graff Cohen
Marketing Associate: Wendy Thayer

Cover image: © Ron Chan

Printed in the U.S.A.

Library of Congress Control Number: 2004114010

ISBN: 0-618-48111-7

123456789-CRW-09 08 07 06 05

Contents

Preface

Successful Writing at Work: Concise Edition is a practical introductory text for business, professional, and occupational writing courses. As readers of the full-length editions of this text have found, *Successful Writing at Work* can help students develop and master key communication skills essential for success in the workplace. Writing is a vital part of every job today, and this user-friendly, compact text will guide students to become better writers by teaching them to prepare essential job-related documents. The emphasis in the *Concise Edition* is on teaching the most necessary, useful skills and strategies for successful workplace writing.

This compact edition has been designed for a variety of educational settings where business and technical writing are taught. It is versatile enough for a full-semester or -quarter course, or it can be used successfully in a shorter 4-, 6-, or 8-week term. Written for the instructor who is looking for a brief, streamlined text, the *Concise Edition* can also meet the diverse goals of a variety of educational settings, including on-line, distance education, continuing education, and week-long intensive courses as well as in-house training programs, workshops, and conferences. Whereas the full-length edition includes seventeen chapters, this streamlined *Concise Edition* contains ten chapters and a Writer's Brief Guide focusing on only the most essential strategies and documents employees need.

Successful Writing at Work: Concise Edition provides students with easy-to-understand guidelines for writing and designing clear, well-organized, and readable documents and Web sites. The goal of this edition is to help students succeed not only in the classroom, but more importantly, in the workplace. Along with user-friendly guidelines, this edition provides students with realistic models of the precise kinds of documents they will be asked to write on the job. This text can also serve as a ready reference that readers can easily carry with them in the workplace.

Students will quickly find that this book is rich in practical applications as useful to individuals who have little or no job experience as to those with years of experience in the world of work. A wide range of diverse examples is drawn from e-mails, memos and letters, instructions and procedures, proposals, short and long reports, and Web sites. These examples—all bearing directly on practical issues in the business world—consistently portray effective writers as successful employees.

Viewing the Workplace Writer as a Problem Solver

The *Concise Edition* stresses that writing is a problem-solving activity that helps employees meet the needs of their employers, co-workers, customers, clients, community groups, and vendors. With its emphasis on the most up-to-date communication tools, the text shows students how to become better problem solvers, and hence better writers, by using the varied resources of an evolving, ever more complex technological workplace. In light of these expanding communication resources, and the needs of a global audience, *Successful Writing at Work: Concise Edition* features actual situations and problems that students writing in the workplace will encounter, such as complying with ethical writing standards, writing letters in the age of the Internet, and preparing for a job interview, and offers clear guidelines and proven strategies to address these challenges. Business-world contexts and examples give students clear and accurate information about format, style, content, scope, and audience needs.

Consistent with this overall view of writing as solving workplace problems, the *Concise Edition* includes writing for both print and on-line media. Easy-to-understand explanations cover the *hows* as well as the *whys* of writing for the digital world of work. Whether preparing for an on-line or print document, this *Concise Edition* teaches students how to develop the critical skills of brainstorming, searching (through print and on-line sources), drafting, revising, editing, formatting, and proofreading various business documents.

Emphasis on Audience Analysis

A key feature of the *Concise Edition* is its consistent emphasis on audience analysis, which determines what students write, when they write it, how they format it, and to whom it is addressed. The major concept of audience analysis, first defined and illustrated in Chapter 1, is carried throughout subsequent chapters with applications to audiences worldwide, whether they are co-workers, employers, clients, or representatives of various agencies and organizations. Accordingly, this edition stresses that careful audience analysis is essential to an employee's job performance. Each chapters shows students that audiences may have very different needs and expectations. For example, decision makers will want different kinds of feedback about a product or service than what a technician or consumer may need. Another vital part of audience analysis is the writer's obligation to make ethical decisions in meeting his or her readers' needs and fulfilling commitments to an employer. This edition also concisely describes and illustrates the legal and ethical implications of preparing business documents to meet the needs of non-native speakers of English, both in this country and abroad.

Focus on Students as Business Professionals

To encourage students in their job-related writing, the *Concise Edition* treats them as professionals seeking success at different phases of their business career. For example, they are addressed as recent hires who are new to the work force in Chapter 1; as employees who must communicate within and on behalf of an organization in Chapter 3; as representatives addressing the needs of customers and employers about specific requests, problems, and complaints in Chapter 4; as job seekers preparing a variety of documents in their searches in Chapter 5; as designers constructing, writing about, or evaluating key visuals and Web sites in Chapter 6; as competitive business-people preparing a persuasive proposal to win a customer's contract or to recommend a change in their own organization in Chapter 8; as employees having to submit a long company report in Chapter 9; and as members of a sales team making a Power-Point presentation in Chapter 10.

Key Features of the Concise Edition

The *Concise Edition* is a useful tool for instructors and a practical, useful resource for students because of the following key features:

Examples and guidelines reflect real-world business and practice.

- **The text concentrates on the most frequently written business messages**—practical examples and guidelines for preparing e-mail, memos, letters, instructions, proposals, reports, and Web sites are included along with crucial information, such as when, where, and how to send these common forms of business communication.
- **Examples of both effective and ineffective documents plus model reports,** many of them annotated and visually varied, help students to be more accomplished and confident writers at work. Examples not only serve as models of concise, clear, and well-organized business documents but also help students learn about the workings of a business culture.
- **Accurate and relevant coverage of instructions and procedures** illustrates the importance, preparation (in print and on-line), and implications of writing these common business documents. Also included are guidelines on how to use visuals effectively in instructions and procedures.
- **Coverage of essential methods of documentation** (both APA and MLA) in Chapter 9 offers easy-to-follow guidelines and clear examples of parenthetical documentation relevant for the world of work. Special attention is given to documenting Web sites. Moreover, a concisely written report on international workers illustrates how to incorporate and cite a variety of print and electronic sources. A discussion of plagiarism and how to avoid it is included in this key chapter to give students further guidelines and advice on this topic first covered in Chapter 1.
- **Checklists at the end of each chapter** allow students to review significant concepts and strategies and also assist them to revise and edit their assignments.
- **Useful, practical, and varied exercises** at the end of each chapter give students many opportunities to apply writing principles in creating business documents in real-life situations.

There is coverage of writing for and in the international workplace.

- **Emphasis on thinking globally and multiculturally** prepares students for the international world of work. To respect the cultural and communication needs and traditions of a global audience, various chapters (4, 7, and 9) include examples of multiculturalism in the workplace, such as a sales letter for an ethnic audience in Chapter 4; writing instructions and procedures for international readers in Chapter 7; and a long report on the needs and contributions of international employees in Chapter 9.

- **The impact of 9/11 is reflected** in sales letters, Web sites, and a report on the increasing importance of international employees in the workplace.

On-the-job writing is linked to communication technologies.

- **Coverage of how people communicate in the workplace electronically,** for example, through on-line résumés, PowerPoint presentations, instant messaging, WebCT, multitask printers/scanners, graphics software, and Web design—is highlighted throughout this edition.
- **There is emphasis on the latest technological information on how to prepare and send business messages.** The coverage of e-mail features carefully illustrated sections helping students recognize the differences between personal and business e-mail, privacy rights, format, style, and netiquette.
- **The importance of ethical and legal issues** involved in using the Web and related technologies, both in the classroom and the workplace, are consistently stressed throughout the text.
- **The interrelationship of visuals to text** teaches students about choosing and formatting the most effective visuals for their written work. Chapter 6, in particular, introduces the concept of document design and the use of visuals in job-related writing by progressing from a simple discussion of page layout to the much more complex topic of Web design. As the chapter progresses, students first learn about formats and then are shown how to identify, evaluate, write, design, and adapt visuals, and finally to prepare a professional-looking Web site.
- **Developing a PowerPoint presentation** in Chapter 10 includes examples and guidelines on how text and visuals are incorporated into a successful speech outline for a sales presentation.

Chapter 5 includes practical advice on searching for and securing a job.

- **A focus on how to look for, analyze, and assess job strengths** helps students recognize their qualifications and interests when searching for a job.
- **Business-savvy advice on how to prepare, write, and organize résumés and application letters** gives students the background and training they need to create professional and persuasive first impressions. Numerous examples of résumés and letters (on-line and in print) will assist job seekers with little or no experience as well as those who have been in the workforce for years.
- **Advice on how to succeed at a job interview** gives students frequently asked questions and proven techniques for a successful interview.

Supplements

- **Instructor's Guide.** The updated Instructor's Guide is broken into five sections. Part 1, "Some Suggestions on How to Teach Job-Related Writing," includes a discussion of writing for international/multicultural readers, guidance on using technology in the writing classroom, collaborative writing, and more. Part II, "Planning a Course with Successful Writing at Work," includes sample syllabi for using the book in short courses, full-semester courses, or on-line courses. Part III, "Some Teaching-Learning Resources," is an extensive categorized bibliography of resources. Part IV, "Answers to Exercises," includes author comments on the exercises and suggested answers. Part V, "Transparency and Photocopy Masters," includes transparency masters of the exercise answers for class discussion, additional examples of letters, abstracts, visuals, Web sites, news releases, policy regulations, and reports, to supplement those in the *Concise Edition,* and case studies.

- **Web site.** The Web site, accessible at *http://www.college.hmco.com,* supports the text by offering multimedia animated NetLabs, on-line quizzes, annotated Web links keyed to chapters in the book, chapter quick references, and additional student and instructor resources.

Acknowledgments

In a very real sense, the *Concise Edition* has profited from a collaboration of various reviewers with the author. I am, therefore, honored to thank the following reviewers who have helped me:

Brenda Eatman Aghahowa, Chicago State University

Arthur Khaw, Kirkwood Community College

Nevin K. Laib, College of Notre Dame of Maryland

Michael Piotrowski, University of Toledo

I am also deeply grateful to the following individuals at the University of Southern Mississippi for their help. I thank Beverly Ciko and Sherry Smith (Department of English); Mary Lux (Department of Medical Technology); and Kay Wall (Cook Library).

Several individuals from business and industry also gave me valuable assistance, for which I am thankful. They include Joycelyn Woolfolk at the Federal Reserve Bank at Atlanta; Sally Eddy at Georgia Pacific; John Krumpos at Gulf Paper Company; Hilary J. Englert at Rice's Potato Chips; Don McCarthy, an independent computer programmer; Russel Dukette at Petro Automotive Group; and Dr. Matt Fry and Dr. Michael O'Neal from the Hattiesburg Clinic.

I am also especially grateful to Father Michael Tracey for his counsel and his contributions to Chapter 6 on document design, especially on Web sites.

My thanks go to my editors at Houghton Mifflin for their assistance, encouragement, and friendship—Michael Gillespie, Bruce Cantley, Julia Casson, Charline Lake, and Shelley Dickerson.

Finally, I am grateful to my son Eric, my daughter-in-law Theresa, my grandson Evan Philip, and my granddaughter Megan Elise for their love and encouragement. My daughter Kristin merits extra praise for all the times she assisted me by doing various searches and revisions. To my wife Maureen goes my heart and my profound gratitude for her love.

P. C. K.

Successful Writing at Work

Concise Edition

Backgrounds

Getting Started: Writing and Your Career

Writing is a part of every job. In fact, your first contact with a potential employer is through posting your résumé and writing a letter of application, which determine a company's first impression of you. And the higher you advance in an organization, the more writing you will do. Promotions are often based on a person's writing skills.

The Associated Press reported in a recent survey that "most American businesses say workers need to improve their writing . . . skills." The same report cited a survey of 402 companies that identified writing as "the most valued skill of employees." Still, the employers polled in that survey indicated that 80 percent of their employees need to improve their writing skills. According to Don Bagin, a communications consultant, most people need an hour or more to write a typical business letter. If an employer is paying someone $30,000 a year, one letter costs $14 of that employee's time; for someone who earns $50,000 a year, the cost of the average letter jumps to $24. Clearly, writing is an essential skill for everyone in business—employers and employees alike.

This chapter gives you some basic information about writing and offers some questions you can ask yourself to make the writing process easier and the results more effective. It also describes the basic functions of on-the-job writing and introduces you to one of the most important requirements in the business world—writing ethically.

Four Keys to Effective Writing

Effective writing on the job is carefully planned, thoroughly researched, and clearly presented. Its purpose is always to accomplish a specific goal and be as persuasive as possible. Whether you send a routine e-mail to a co-worker or a special report to the president of the company, your writing will be more effective if you ask yourself four questions.

1. *Who* will read what I write? (Identify your *audience*.)
2. *Why* should they read what I write? (Establish your *purpose*.)
3. *What* do I have to say to them? (Formulate your *message*.)
4. *How* can I best communicate? (Select your *style* and *tone*.)

The questions *who? why? what?* and *how?* do not function independently; they are all related. You write (1) for a specific audience (2) with a clearly defined purpose in mind (3) about a topic your readers need to understand (4) in language appropriate for the occasion. Once you answer the first question, you are off to a good start toward answering the other three. Now let us examine each of the four questions in detail.

Identifying Your Audience

Knowing *who* makes up your audience is one of your most important responsibilities as a writer. Look for a minute at the American Heart Association posters reproduced in Figures 1.1, 1.2, and 1.3. The main purpose of all three posters is the same: to discourage people from smoking. The essential message in each poster—smoking is dangerous to your health—is also the same. But note how the different details—words, photographs, situations—have been selected to appeal to three different audiences.

The poster in Figure 1.1 emphasizes smoking problems that are especially troublesome to teenagers: red eyes, bad breath, discolored teeth, unattractive hair. The smiling teen pictured without a cigarette appears to have avoided those problems. The message at the top of the poster plays on two meanings of the word *heart:* (1) smoking can cause heart disease, and (2) smoking can be a deterrent to romance. Teenagers are particularly sensitive to the second meaning.

The poster in Figure 1.2 is aimed at an audience of pregnant women and appropriately shows a woman with a lit cigarette. The words at the top and bottom of the poster appeal to a mother's sense of responsibility as the reason to stop smoking, a reason to which pregnant women would be most likely to respond.

Figure 1.3 is directed toward fathers and appropriately shows a small child seated on his father's lap. The situation depicted appeals to a father's wish for his child's happiness. The words in the poster warn that a father who smokes may die prematurely and make his child's life unhappy.

The copywriters for the American Heart Association have chosen appropriate details—words, pictures, captions, and so on—to convince each audience not to smoke. With their careful choices, they successfully answered the question "How can we best communicate with each audience?" As an indication of their skill, note that details relevant for one audience (teenagers, for example) could not be used as effectively for another audience (such as fathers). Keep in mind:

- Members of each audience differ in backgrounds, experiences, needs, and opinions.
- How you picture your audience will determine what you say to them.
- Viewing something from the audience's perspective will help you select the most relevant details for that audience.

Some Questions to Ask About Your Audience

You can form a fairly accurate picture of your audience by asking yourself some questions *before* you write. For each audience for whom you write, consider the following questions.

FIGURE 1.1   Don't smoke poster aimed at teenagers.

© Reprinted with permission of the American Heart Association.

1. **Who is my audience?** What individual(s) will most likely be reading my work?

   If you are writing for individuals:

   - What is my reader's job? Co-worker? Supervisor?
   - What kind of job experience, education, and interests does my reader have?

   If you are writing for clients or consumers (a very large, sometimes fragmented audience):

   - How can I find out about their interest in my product or service?
   - How much will this audience know about my company? About me?

2. **How many people will make up my audience?**

   - Will just one individual read what I write (the nurse on the next shift, the production manager) or will many people read it (all the consumers of a product)?
   - Will my boss want to see my work?
   - Will I be sending my message to a large group of people sharing a similar interest in my topic, such as a listserv?
   - Will I be communicating with people all around the globe?

FIGURE 1.2   Stop smoking poster directed at pregnant women.

© Reprinted with permission of the American Heart Association.

3. How well does my audience understand English?

- Will some of my readers have less command of English than others and require extra sensitivity on my part to their needs as non-native speakers of English? (See Chapter 4, pp. 109–15, for guidelines about communication with this audience.)

4. How much does my audience already know about the writing topic?

- Will my audience know as much as I do about the particular problem or issue, or will they need to be briefed or updated?
- Are my readers familiar with, and do they expect me to use, technical terms and descriptions, or will I have to provide nontechnical summaries?

5. What is my audience's reason for reading my work?

- Is reading my communication part of their routine duties, or are they looking for information to solve a problem or make a decision?
- Am I writing to describe benefits that another writer or company cannot offer?
- Will my readers expect complete details or a short summary?

FIGURE 1.3   Stop smoking poster aimed at fathers.

© Reprinted with permission of the American Heart Association.

- Are they reading my work to take some action affecting a co-worker, a client, or a community official?
- What will my boss want from me—information alone, some analysis and conclusions drawn from the information, or a specific set of recommendations?

6. What are my audience's expectations about my written work?

- Do they want an e-mail or will they expect a formal letter?
- Will they expect me to follow a certain format and organization?
- Are they looking for a one-page memo or for a comprehensive report?

7. What is my audience's attitude toward me and my work?

- Will I be writing to a group of disgruntled and angry customers or vendors about a very sensitive issue—a product recall, a refusal of credit, a shipment delay?
- Will my readers—customers whose business I want to attract—be skeptical?
- Will my audience be eager and friendly, happy to read what I write?
- Will my readers feel guilty that they have not answered an earlier message of mine, not paid a bill now overdue, or not kept a promise or commitment?

8. **What do I want my audience to do after reading my work?**

- Do I want my reader to purchase something from me or my company or to approve my plan?
- Do I simply want my reader to get my message and not respond at all?
- Do I expect the reader to get my message, acknowledge it, save it for future reference, or review it and e-mail it to another individual or office?
- Does my reader have to take immediate action, or does he or she have several days or weeks to respond?

As your answers to these questions will show, you may have to communicate with many different audiences on your job. If you work for a large organization that has numerous departments, you may have to write to diverse readers such as accountants; office managers; engineers; public relations specialists; marketing specialists; programmers; and/or individuals who install, operate, and maintain equipment.

The advertisement in Figure 1.4 concisely illustrates how the writer for a manufacturer of heavy-duty equipment identified the priorities of five different audiences and selected appropriate information to communicate with each one.

Audience	Information to Communicate
Owner or principal executive	The writer appropriately stresses financial benefits: The machine is a "money-maker" and is compatible with other equipment so additional equipment purchases are unnecessary.
Production engineer	The writer emphasizes "state-of-the-art" transmissions, productivity, upkeep.
Operator	The writer focuses on how easy it is to run the machine—the pressurized cab keeps out environmental problems that interfere with a job.
Maintenance worker	Since this reader is concerned primarily about things such as "lube points" and "test ports," not costs or operations, the writer correctly selects appropriate information about making the worker's job easier and safer.
Production supervisor	The writer emphasizes the speed and efficiency the machine offers, thus zeroing in on this reader's needs and interests.

The lesson of this ad is clear: Give each reader the details he or she needs to accomplish a given job.

Establishing Your Purpose

By knowing *why* you are writing, you will communicate better and find writing itself to be an easier process. Make sure you follow the most important rule in occupational writing: **Get to the point right away.** At the start of your message, state your goal clearly.

I want to teach new employees the security code for logging on to the company computer.

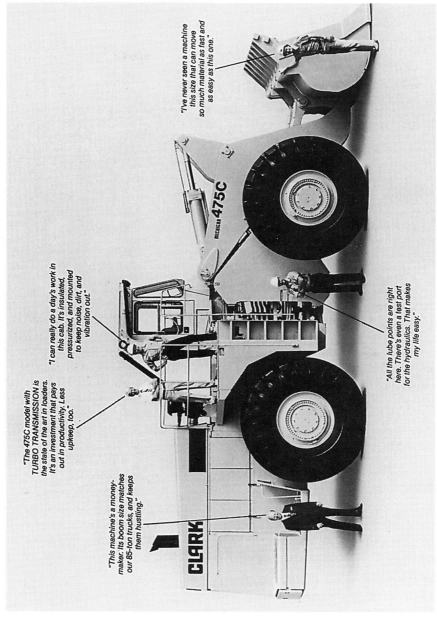

FIGURE 1.4   An advertisement aimed at the needs of five different audiences.

Courtesy of the Clark Company. Reprinted with permission.

Since your purpose controls the amount and order of information you include, state it clearly at the beginning of every e-mail, memo, letter, and report.

> This e-mail will acquaint new employees with the security measures they must take when logging on to the company computer.

In the opening purpose statement that follows, note how the author clearly informs the reader as to what the report will and will not cover.

> As you requested at last week's organizational meeting, I have conducted a study of our use of the Internet to advertise our services. This report describes, but does not evaluate, our current practices.

Formulating Your Message

Your message is the sum of *what* facts, responses, and recommendations you put into writing. A message includes the scope and details of your communication.

- *Scope* refers to how much information you give readers about the key details.
- The *details* are those key points you think readers need to know to perform their jobs.

Some messages will consist of one or two sentences: "Do not touch; wet paint." "Order #756 was sent this afternoon by Federal Express. It should arrive at your office on March 22." At the other extreme, messages may extend over twenty or thirty pages. Messages can carry good news or bad news. They may deal with routine matters; or they may handle changes in policy, special situations, or problems.

Keep in mind that you will adapt the message to fit your audience. For technical audiences, such as engineers or technicians, you may have to supply a complete report with every detail noted or contained in an appendix. For other readers—busy executives, for example—a short discussion or summary of the financial or managerial significance will be enough.

Selecting Your Style and Tone

Style

Style is *how* something is written rather than what is written. Style helps to determine how well you communicate with an audience, how well your readers understand and receive your message. It involves the choices you make about

- the construction of your paragraphs
- the length and patterns of your sentences
- your choice of words

You will have to adapt your style to take into account different messages, different purposes, and different audiences. The words, for example, will certainly vary with your audience. If all potential readers are specialists in your field, you may safely use the technical language and symbols of your profession. Nonspecialists, however, will be confused and annoyed if you write to them in the same way. The average consumer, for example, will not know what a *potentiometer* is; by writing "volume control on a radio," you will be using words that the general public can understand.

Tone

Tone in writing, like tone of voice, expresses your attitude toward a topic and toward your audience. In general, your tone can range from formal and impersonal (a scientific report) to informal and personal (e-mail to a friend or a how-to article for consumers). It can be unprofessionally sarcastic or diplomatically agreeable.

Tone, like style, is indicated in part by the words you choose. For example, saying that someone is "interested in details" conveys a more positive tone than saying the person is a "nitpicker." The word *economical* is more positive than *stingy* or *cheap*.

The tone of your writing is especially important in occupational writing because it reflects the image you project to readers and thus determines how they will respond to you, your work, and your company. Depending on your tone, you can appear sincere and intelligent or angry and uninformed. Of course, in all written work, you need to sound professional and knowledgeable about the topic and genuinely interested in your readers' opinions and problems.

Style and Tone Examples

A Description of Heparin for Two Different Audiences

To better understand the effects of style and tone on writing, read the two excerpts on page 12. In both, the message is basically the same, but because the audiences differ, so do the style and the tone. The two pieces are descriptions of *heparin*, a drug used to prevent blood clots.

Technical/Scientific Style and Tone   The first description appears in a reference work for physicians and other health care providers and is written in a highly technical style with an impersonal tone.

The writer made the appropriate stylistic choices for the audience, the purpose, and the message. Health care providers understand and need the technical vocabulary the writer uses; this audience also requires the sophisticated and lengthy explanations to prescribe and/or administer heparin correctly. The author's authoritative, impersonal tone is coldly clinical, which, of course, is also correct because the purpose is to convey the accurate, complete scientific facts about this drug, not the writer's or reader's opinions or beliefs. The author sounds both knowledgeable and appropriately objective.

HEPARIN SODIUM INJECTION, USP
STERILE SOLUTION
Description: Heparin Sodium Injection, USP, is a sterile solution of heparin sodium derived from bovine lung tissue, standardized for anticoagulant activity.

Each ml of the 1,000 and 5,000 USP units per ml preparations contains: heparin sodium 1,000 or 5,000 USP units; 9 mg sodium chloride; 9.45 mg benzyl alcohol added as preservative. Each ml of the 10,000 USP units per ml preparations contains: heparin sodium 10,000 units; 9.45 mg benzyl alcohol added as preservative.

When necessary, the pH of Heparin Sodium Injection, USP, was adjusted with hydrochloric acid and/or sodium hydroxide. The pH range is 5.0 to 7.5.
Clinical pharmacology: Heparin inhibits reactions that lead to the clotting of blood and the formation of fibrin clots both *in vitro* and *in vivo*. Heparin acts at multiple sites in the normal coagulation system. Small amounts of heparin in combination with antithrombin III (heparin cofactor) can inhibit thrombosis by inactivating activated Factor X and inhibiting the conversion of prothrombin to thrombin.
Dosage and administration: Heparin sodium is not effective by oral administration and should be given by intermittent intravenous injection, intravenous infusion, or deep subcutaneous (intrafrat, i.e., above the iliac crest or abdominal fat layer) injection. **The intramuscular route of administration should be avoided because of the frequent occurrence of hematoma at the injection site.**[1]

Nontechnical Style and Tone   The following description of heparin, on the other hand, is written in a nontechnical style and with an informal, caring tone. This description is similar to those found on information cards given to patients about the drugs they are receiving in a hospital.

Your doctor has prescribed a drug called *heparin* for you. This drug will prevent any new blood clots from forming in your body. Since heparin cannot be absorbed from your stomach or intestines, you will not receive it in a capsule or tablet. Instead, it will be given into a vein or the fatty tissue of your abdomen. After several days, when the danger of clotting has passed, your dosage of heparin will be gradually reduced. Then another medication you can take by mouth will be started.

The writer of the second description also made the appropriate choices for the readers and their needs. Familiar words rather than technical ones are suitable for nonspecialists such as patients. This audience does not need elaborate descriptions of the origin and composition of the drug. The tone is both personal and straightforward because the purpose is to win the patient's confidence and to explain the essential functions of the drug.

Characteristics of Job-Related Writing

Job-related writing characteristically serves six basic functions: (1) to provide practical information, (2) to give facts rather than impressions, (3) to provide visuals to clarify and condense information, (4) to give accurate measurements, (5) to state responsibilities precisely, and (6) to persuade and offer recommendations. These functions tell you what kind of writing you will produce after you successfully answer the *who? why? what?* and *how?*

Providing Practical Information

On-the-job writing requires a practical here's-what-you-need-to-do-or-to-know approach. One such practical approach is *action-oriented.* You instruct the reader to do something—assemble a ceiling fan, test for bacteria, perform an audit, create a Web site. Another practical approach is knowledge-oriented: to have someone understand something—why a procedure was changed, what caused a problem or solved it, how much progress occurred on a job site, why a new piece of equipment should be purchased. Examples of knowledge-oriented practical writing are a letter from a manufacturer to customers to explain a product recall and an e-mail to employees about changes in their group health insurance.

The following description of Energy Efficiency Ratio combines both the action-oriented and knowledge-oriented approaches of practical writing.

> Whether you are buying window air-conditioning units or a central air-conditioning system, consider the performance factors and efficiency of the various units on the market. Before you buy, determine the Energy Efficiency Ratio (EER) of the units under consideration. The EER is found by dividing the BTUs (units of heat) that the unit removes from the area to be cooled by the watts (amount of electricity) the unit consumes. The result is usually a number between 5 and 12. The higher the number, the more efficiently the unit will use electricity.[2]

Giving Facts, Not Impressions

Occupational writing is concerned largely with those things that can be seen, heard, felt, tasted, or smelled. The writer uses *concrete language* and specific details. The emphasis is on facts rather than on the writer's feelings or guesses.

The discussion on the next page by a group of scientists about the sources of oil spills and their impact on the environment is an example of writing with objectivity. It describes events and causes without anger or tears.

---

[2]Reprinted by permission of Entergy New Orleans.

Major oil spills occur as a result of accidents such as blowout, pipeline breakage, etc. Technological advances coupled with stringent regulations have helped to reduce the chances of such major spills; however, there is a chronic low-level discharge of oil associated with normal drilling and production operations. Waste oils discharged through the river systems and practices associated with tanker transports dump more significant quantities of oils into the ocean, compared to what is introduced by the offshore oil industry. All of this contributes to the chronic low-level discharge of oil into world oceans. The long-range cumulative effect of these discharges is possibly the most significant threat to the ecosystem.[3]

Providing Visuals to Clarify and Condense Information

Visuals are indispensable partners of words in conveying information to your readers. On-the-job writing makes frequent use of tables, charts, photographs, flow charts, diagrams, and drawings. Chapter 6 discusses the use of visuals.

Visuals play an important role in the workplace. Note how the drawing in Figure 1.5 from the National Safety Council's booklet, "Working Safely with Your Computer," can help computer users better understand and follow the accompanying written guidelines. A visual like this, reproduced in an employee handbook or displayed on a Web site, can significantly reduce stress and increase productivity.

Giving Accurate Measurements

Much of your work will depend on measurements—acres, bytes, calories, centimeters, degrees, dollars and cents, grams, percentages, pounds, square feet, units. Numbers are clear and convincing. The following discussion of mixing colored cement for a basement floor would be useless to readers if it did not supply accurate quantities.

The inclusion of permanent color in a basement floor is a good selling point. One way of doing this is by incorporating commercially pure mineral pigments in a topping mixture placed to a 1-inch depth over a normal base slab. The topping mix should range in volume between 1 part Portland cement, 1¼ parts sand, and 1¼ parts gravel or crushed stone and 1 part Portland cement, 2 parts sand, and 2 parts gravel or crushed stone. Maximum size gravel or crushed stone should be ⅜ inch.[4]

Stating Responsibilities Precisely

Job-related writing, because it is directed to a specific audience, must make absolutely clear what it expects of, or can do for, that audience. Misunderstandings waste time and cost money. Directions on order forms, for example, should indicate how and where information is to be listed and how it is to be routed and acted on. The following directions show readers how to perform a task and/or explain why.

Enter agency code numbers in the message box.

Items 1 through 16 of this form should be completed by the injured employee or by someone acting on his or her behalf, whenever an injury is sustained in the performance of duty. The term *injury* includes occupational disease caused by the employment. The form should be given to the employee's official superior within 24 hours following the injury. The official superior is that individual having responsible supervision over the employee.

---

[3] *The Offshore Ecology Investigation,* Galveston: Gulf Universities Research Consortium.

[4] Reprinted by permission from *Concrete Construction Magazine,* World of Concrete Center, 426 South Westgate, Addison, Illinois 60101.

FIGURE 1.5   Use of a visual to convey information.

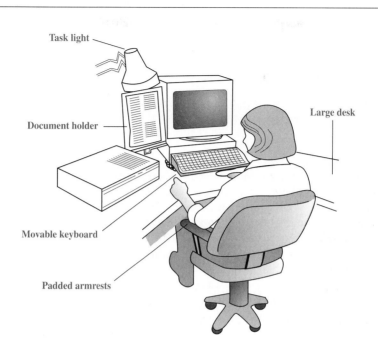

Task light

Document holder

Large desk

Movable keyboard

Padded armrests

Your working area

- ❏ Having a **desk** or other place to work that's big enough, and of the right size and height, is of first importance.

- ❏ **Keyboard** should be movable, non-glossy, and tilted slightly forward. Put a notebook under the back edge if it doesn't have built-in height adjustment pegs.

- ❏ **Padded wrist rests** for anyone who types a good deal. Or, use a chair with padded armrests. If the desk has a movable keyboard tray, adjust the height so that wrists are straight and forearms are parallel to the floor when fingers are on the keys.

- ❏ **Desk** large enough to hold computer monitor and keyboard, telephone, desk set, and all other needed accessories. It also should provide space for writing and doing other work comfortably.

- ❏ **Task light** adjustable so it can shine on a book or note pad without casting an annoying reflection on the screen.

- ❏ **Document holder** movable, upright, tilted, and at the same height as the video screen for easy reading.

- ❏ **Video monitors** at least four feet apart.

- ❏ **Muted desk top surface** doesn't reflect light into operator's eyes.

- ❏ **Screen** positioned so it won't reflect light from windows or overhead lights; also so operator won't be distracted by persons walking by.

Working Safely with Your Computer, 1991, National Safety Council. Reprinted by permission of the National Safety Council.

Other kinds of job-related writing deal with the writer's responsibilities rather than the reader's; for example, "Tomorrow I will meet with the district sales manager to discuss (1) July's sales, (2) the possibility of redesigning our Web site, and (3) next fall's production schedule. I will e-mail a short report of our discussion by August 5, 2006."

Persuading and Offering Recommendations

Persuasion is a vital part of writing on the job. In fact, persuasion is one of the most crucial skills you can learn. It determines how successful you and your company or agency will be.

Promoting Corporate Image

Much of your writing in the business world is to promote your company's image by persuading customers and clients (a) to buy a product or service or (b) to adopt a plan of action endorsed by your employer. Not only will you have to attract new customers but you will have to persuade previous ones to return and purchase your company's product and/or service again. You will have to convince readers that you (and your company) can save them time and money, increase efficiency, reduce risk, and improve their image.

To be persuasive, you will need to get your readers' attention, communicate clearly so that they understand your message, and make sure they remember it. A large part of persuasion is supporting claims with evidence. You will have to conduct research; provide logical arguments; supply concrete examples of appropriate data; and, especially important, identify the most relevant information for your audience. Notice how the advertisement in Figure 1.6 offers a bulleted list of persuasive reasons—based on cost, time, safety, efficiency, and convenience—to convince correctional officials that they should use General Medical's services rather than those of a hospital or clinic.

Writing Persuasively In-House

Writing for individuals you work for and with also requires you to develop your skills at persuading readers. You will be expected to make recommendations to your employer. In many of your memos, e-mails, letters, reports, and proposals, you will have to evaluate various products or options by studying, analyzing, and deciding on the most relevant one(s) for your boss. Your reader will expect you to offer clear-cut, logical, and convincing reasons for your choice.

On the job, you will also be asked to write memos, e-mails, and even letters to boost the morale of employees, encourage them to be more productive, and compliment them on jobs well done. You can also expect to write about (and explain and solve) problems your company faces, such as when a market has shrunk and your boss wants to know what can be done about it or when a service or product your company relies on becomes too costly.

Figure 1.7 (p. 18) contains a persuasive e-mail from an employee to a business manager to report a payroll mistake and to request a reimbursement. Note how the writer provides factual, not impressive, information; attaches a time sheet (a type of visual); gives accurate details; identifies her own and her immediate supervisor's responsibilities; and persuasively, and diplomatically, states her case.

FIGURE 1.6   An advertisement using arguments based on cost, time, efficiency, safety, and convenience to persuade a potential customer to use a service.

General Medical Services Corp.

A subsidiary of

Federal Medical Industries, Inc. O.T.C.
950 S.W. 12th Avenue, 2nd Floor Suite, Pompano, Florida 33069
(305) 942-1111   FL WATS: 1-800-654-8282

GENERAL MEDICAL WILL STOP THE UNNECESSARY TRANSPORTING OF YOUR INMATES.

- We'll bring our X-ray services to your facility, 7 days a week, 24 hours a day.
    We can reduce your X-ray costs by a minimum of 28%.
    X-ray cost includes radiologist's interpretation and written report.
    Same day service with immediate results telephoned to your facility.
- Save correctional officers' time, thereby saving your facility money.
- Avoid chance of prisoner's escape and possible danger to the public.
- Avoid long waits in overcrowded hospitals.
- Reduce your insurance liabilities.
- Other Services Available: Ultrasound, Two Dimensional Echocardiogram, C.T. Scan, EKG, Blood Lab and Holter Monitor.

General Medical Is Your On-Site Medical Problem Solver

Ethical Writing in the Workplace

On-the-job writing involves much more than conveying facts about products, equipment, costs, and the day-to-day operations of a business. Your writing also has to be ethical. Writing ethically means doing what is right and fair and being honest and just with your employer, co-workers, and customers. Your reputation and character plus your employer's corporate image will depend on your following an ethical course of action.

Many of the most significant bywords in the world of business reflect an ethical commitment to honesty and fairness: *accountability, public trust, equal opportunity employer, good faith effort, truth in lending, fair play, honest advertising, full disclosure, high professional standards,* and *community responsibility.*

Unethical business dealings, on the other hand, are stigmatized in *cover-ups, shady deals, spin doctors, foul play, misrepresentations, price gouging, bias,* and *unfair advantage.* Those are the activities that keep Better Business Bureaus active and make customers angry.

Eight Ethical Requirements on the Job

In the workplace, you will be expected to meet the highest ethical standards by fulfilling the following requirements.

- Supplying honest and up-to-date information about yourself in your résumé and job application. The résumé (see Chapter 5, pp. 126–40) is one key place where most people must make ethical decisions about candor and honesty.
- Maintaining accurate and current records at work. Remember: "If it isn't written, it didn't happen."
- Complying with all local, state, and federal regulations, especially those ensuring a safe, healthy work environment, products, and/or service.
- Adhering to your profession's code or standard of ethics, audits, or licensure requirements.
- Abiding by your company's policies and procedures.
- Honoring guarantees and warranties and meeting customer needs impartially.
- Cooperating fully and honestly with any collaborative team of which you are a member.
- Respecting all copyright obligations and privileges.

Following these guidelines may be not only an ethical requirement, but it could also be a legal one. For example, doing personal (or outside consulting) work on com-

FIGURE 1.7   A persuasive e-mail from an employee to a business manager.

Subject: **Mistake in October Paycheck**
Date: 19 October 2007 9:10 a.m. EST
From: rburke@starinstruments.com (R. Burke)
To: lgriffin@starinstruments.com (Lee Griffin)

My paycheck for the two-week period ending October 15 was $45.00 short. During this period I should have been paid $525.00. Instead, my check was for only $480.00. I think I know why there may have been a discrepancy. The $45.00 additional pay was the result of my having put in five hours of overtime on October 8 and October 12 (2½ hours each day @ $9.00 per hour). This overtime was not reflected on my current pay stub.

I have double-checked with my supervisor, Gloria Arrelo, who assured me that she recorded my overtime on the timesheets she sent to your office. She has kindly given me a copy that I have scanned and attached with the e-mail to verify my hours.

Thank you for correcting your records and crediting me with the additional $45.00 for my overtime.

FIGURE 1.8   The Ten Commandments of Computer Ethics.

1. Thou shalt not use a computer to harm other people.

2. Thou shalt not interfere with other people's computer work.

3. Thou shalt not snoop around in other people's computer files.

4. Thou shalt not use a computer to steal.

5. Thou shalt not use a computer to bear false witness.

6. Thou shalt not copy or use proprietary software for which you have not paid.

7. Thou shalt not use other people's computer resources without authorization or proper compensation.

8. Thou shalt not appropriate other people's intellectual output.

9. Thou shalt think about the social consequences of the program you are writing or the system you are designing.

10. Thou shalt always use a computer in ways that ensure consideration and respect for your fellow humans.

Computer Ethics Institute, London.

pany time, padding expense accounts, using company equipment for personal use, or accepting a bribe is unethical and illegal. It would also be neglectful and unethical to allow an unsafe product to stay on the market just to spare your company the expense of a product recall. It would be wrong, legally and ethically, to share information about your employer's patent plans on the Internet.

Computer ethics, especially when using the Internet, are essential in the world of work. It would be grossly unethical to erase a computer program intentionally, violate a software licensing agreement, or misrepresent (by fabrication or exaggeration) the scope of a database. Follow the Ten Commandments of Computer Ethics prepared by the Computer Ethics Institute and listed in Figure 1.8. (See also Chapter 3, pp. 64–66.)

Writing for the world of multinational corporations places additional ethical demands on you as a writer. You have to make sure you respect the ethics of the foreign countries where your firm does business. Some behavior regarded as normal or routine in the United States might be seen as highly unethical elsewhere. And you should be on your ethical guard not to take advantage of a host country, such as using pesticides or conducting experiments outlawed in the United States.

Some Guidelines to Help You Reach Ethical Decisions

The workplace presents all sorts of conflicts over who is right and who is wrong, what is best for the company and what is not, and whether a service or product should be changed and why. You will be asked to take a stand. Here are a few guidelines to help you respond ethically.

1. **Follow your conscience and "to thine own self be true."** You cannot authorize something that you believe is wrong, dangerous, unfair, contradictory, or incomplete. But don't be hasty. Leave plenty of room for diplomacy and for careful questioning. Don't blow a small matter out of proportion.

2. **Be suspicious of convenient (and false) appeals that go against your beliefs.** Watch out for the red flags that anyone places in the way of your conscience: "No one will ever know." "It's OK to cut corners every once in a while." "We got away with it last time." "Don't rock the boat." "No one's looking." "As long as the company makes money, who cares?" These rationalizations are traps you must avoid.

3. **Maintain good faith in meeting your obligations to your employer, your co-workers, your customers, and your community.** It is unethical to lie, exaggerate, or even dodge an issue. Keeping information from a co-worker who needs it, using a password belonging to someone else, omitting a fact, justifying unnecessary expenses—all are unethical acts, just as cheating on an examination or plagiarizing are unethical in your schoolwork.

4. **Take responsibility for your actions.** Saying "I do not know" when you do know can constitute a serious ethical violation. Keep up-to-date and accurate records. Sign and date your work. Never backdate a document to delete information or to fix an error that you committed. Such action constitutes a cover-up and a serious breach of ethics.

5. **Weigh all sides before you commit to a conclusion.** Research what you write and communicate orally. Rely on hard evidence: documentation, testimony, valid precedents. Do your homework by studying code books and agency handbooks; confer with a customer or a co-worker when you are in doubt about a major issue. Familiarize yourself with company protocols and specifications about the procedures, methods, and materials of your job.

Writing Ethically

Your writing as well as your behavior must be ethical. Words, like actions, have implications and consequences. If you slant your words to conceal the truth or to gain an unfair advantage, you are not being ethical. False advertising is false writing. In your written work, strive to be fair, reliable, and accurate, in reporting events and figures honestly and without bias or omissions.

Unethical writing is usually guilty of one or more of the following faults, which can conveniently be listed as the three *M*'s: misquotation, misrepresentation, and manipulation. Here are seven examples.

1. **Plagiarism** is stealing someone else's words (work) and claiming it as your own. At work, plagiarism is unethically claiming a co-worker's ideas, input, or report as your contribution. In a research report or paper, you are guilty of plagiarism if you use another person's words (or even a rough paraphrase) without documenting the source. Do not think that by changing a few words here and there you are not plagiarizing. Copying someone else's software is also an act of plagiarism. Give proper credit to your source, whether in print, in person (through an interview), or on-line.

The penalties for plagiarism are severe—a reprimand or even the loss of your job. At school, you run the risk of failing the course or, worse, being expelled.

2. Selective misquoting deliberately omits damaging or unflattering comments to paint a better (but untruthful) picture of you or your company. By picking and choosing words from a quotation, you unethically misrepresent what the speaker or writer originally intended.

> Full Quotation: I've enjoyed at times our firm's association with Technology, Inc., although I was troubled by the uneven quality of their service. At times, it was excellent while at others it was far less so.
>
> Selective Misquotation: I've enjoyed . . . our firm's association with Technology, Inc. The quality of their service was . . . excellent.

The dots, called *ellipses,* unethically suggest that only extraneous or unimportant details were omitted.

3. Arbitrary embellishment of numbers unethically misrepresents, by increasing or decreasing percentages or other numbers, statistical or other information. It is unethical to stretch the differences between competing plans or proposals to gain an unfair advantage or to express accurate figures in an inaccurate way.

> Embellishment: Our competitor's sales volume increased by only 10 percent in the preceding year while ours doubled.
>
> Ethical: Our competitor controls 90 percent of the market, yet we increased our share of that market from 5 percent to 10 percent last year.

4. Manipulation of data or context, closely related to #3, is the misrepresentation of events, usually to "put a good face" on a bad situation. The writer here unethically uses slanted language and intentionally misleading euphemisms to misinterpret events for readers.

> Manipulation: Looking ahead to 2007, the United Funds Group is exceptionally optimistic about its long-term prospects in an expanding global market. We are happy to report steady to moderate activity in an expanding sales environment last year. The United Funds Group seeks to build on sustaining investment opportunities beneficial to all subscribers.
>
> Ethical: Looking ahead to 2007, the United Funds Group is optimistic about its long-term prospects in an expanding global market. Though the market suffered from inflation this year, the United Funds Group hopes to recoup its losses in the year ahead.

The writer minimizes the negative effects of inflation by calling it "an expanding sales environment."

5. Using fictitious benefits to promote a product or service seemingly promises customers advantages but delivers none.

> False Benefit: Our bottled water is naturally hydrogenated from clear underground springs.
>
> Truth: All water is hydrogenated because it contains hydrogen.

6. Unfairly characterizing (by exaggerating or minimizing) hiring or firing conditions is unethical.

> Unethical: Our corporate restructuring will create a more efficient and streamlined company, benefiting management and workers alike.
> Truth: Downsizing has led to 150 layoffs.

7. Misrepresenting through distorting or slanted visuals is one of the most common types of unethical communication. Making a product look bigger, better, or more professional is all too easy with graphics software packages. Making warning or caution statements the same size and type font as ingredients or directions or enlarging advertising hype (Double Your Money Back) is unethical if major points are reduced to small print.

Because ethics are such an important topic in writing for the workplace, they will be stressed throughout this book. (See, for example, Chapter 3, p. 64, and Chapter 8, p. 227.)

✓ Revision Checklist

At the end of each chapter is a checklist you should review before you submit the final copy of your work, either to your instructor or to your boss. The checklists include the types of research, planning, drafting, editing, and revising you should do to ensure the success of your work. Regard each checklist as a summary of the main ideas in the chapter as well as a handy guide to quality control. You may find it helpful to check each box as you verify that you have performed the necessary revision and review. Effective writers are also careful editors.

❑ Identified my audience—their background, knowledge of English, reason for reading my work, and likely response to my work and me.

❑ Made it clear what I want my audience to do after reading my work.

❑ Tailored the message to my audience's needs and background, giving them neither too little nor too much information.

❑ Pushed to the main point right away; did not waste my reader's time.

❑ Selected the most appropriate language, technical level, tone, and level of formality.

❑ Did not waste my audience's time with unsupported generalizations or opinions; instead gave them accurate measurements, facts, and carefully researched material.

❑ Used appropriate visuals to make my work easier for my audience to follow.

❑ Used persuasive reasons and data to convince my reader to accept my plan or work.

❑ Ensured that my writing is ethical—accurate, fair, honest, a true reflection of the situation or condition I am explaining or describing.
❑ Followed the Ten Commandments of Computer Ethics.
❑ Gave full and complete credit to any sources I used, including resource people.
❑ Avoided plagiarism and unfair or dishonest use of copyrighted materials, both written and visual, including all electronic media.

Exercises

1. Write a memo (see Chapter 3, pp. 58–59 for format) addressed to a prospective supervisor to introduce yourself. Your memo should have four headings: **education**—including goals and accomplishments; **job information**—where you have worked and your responsibilities; **community service**—volunteer work, church work, youth groups; and **writing experience**—your strengths and what you would like to see improved.

2. Bring to class a set of printed instructions from a memo, a sales letter, or a brochure. Comment on how well the printed material answers the following questions.
   a. Who is the audience?
   b. Why was the material written?
   c. What is the message?
   d. Are the style and tone appropriate for the audience, the purpose, and the message? Why?
   e. Discuss the use of color in the document. How does color (or the lack of it) affect an audience's response to the message?

3. Cut out a newspaper ad that contains a drawing or photograph. Bring it to class together with a paragraph of your own (75–100 words) describing how the message of the ad is directed to a particular audience and commenting on why the illustration was selected for that audience.

4. Pick one of the following topics and write two descriptions of it. In the first description, use technical vocabulary; in the second, use language suitable for the general public.
   a. spark plug
   b. blood pressure cuff
   c. carburetor
   d. computer chip
   e. camera
   f. legal contract
   g. electric sander
   h. cyberspace
   i. muscle
   j. protein
   k. high-definition TV
   l. DVD
   m. bread
   n. money
   o. color scanner
   p. soap
   q. calculator
   r. X-Box game
   s. AIDS
   t. thermostat
   u. trees
   v. food processor
   w. earthquake
   x. recycling

5. Select one article from a newspaper and one article from either a professional journal in your major field or one of the following journals: *Advertising Age, American Journal of Nursing, Business Marketing, Business Week, Computer, Construction Equipment, Criminal Justice Review, E-Commerce, Food Service Marketing, Journal of Forestry, Journal of Soil and Water Conservation, National Safety News, Nutrition Action, Office Machines, Park Maintenance, Scientific American.* State how the two articles you selected differ in terms of audience, purpose, message, style, and tone.

6. Assume that you work for Appliance Rentals, Inc., a company that rents TVs, microwave ovens, stereo components, and the like. Write a persuasive letter to the members of a campus organization or civic club urging them to rent an appropriate appliance or appliances. Include details in your letter that might have special relevance to members of this specific organization.

7. Evaluate how well the advertisement on the next page illustrates the technique of occupational writing described in this chapter. Specifically comment on what your evaluation of the ad reveals about the copywriter's analysis of the intended audience when the product was available. Pay attention to advertising copy (words), the images of people and equipment (visuals), and the situation depicted. Also explain how the ad illustrates the six functions of on-the-job writing.

8. Write a letter to an Internet service provider that has mistakenly billed you for caller ID equipment that you never ordered, received, or needed.

9. The following statements contain embellishments, selected misquotations, false benefits, and other types of unethical tactics. Revise each statement to eliminate the unethical aspects.
   a. Storm damage done to water filtration plant #3 was minimal. While we had to shut down temporarily, service resumed to meet residents' needs.
   b. All customers qualify for the maximum discount available.
   c. The service contract . . . on the whole . . . applied to upgrades.
   d. We followed the protocols precisely with test results yielding further opportunities for experimentation.
   e. All of our costs were within fair-use guidelines.
   f. Customers' complaints have been held to a minimum.
   g. All of the lots we are selling offer easy access to the lake.

10. Your company is regulated and inspected by the Environmental Protection Agency. In ninety days, the EPA will relax a particular regulation about dumping industrial waste. Your company's management is considering cutting costs by relaxing the standard now, before the new, easier regulation is in place. You know that the EPA inspector probably will not return before the ninety-day period elapses. What do you recommend to management?

2

The Writing Process at Work

In Chapter 1 you learned about the different functions of writing for the world of work and also explored some basic concepts all writers must master. To be a successful writer, you need to

- identify your audience's needs
- determine your purpose in writing to that audience
- make sure your message meets your audience's needs
- use the most appropriate style and tone for your message
- format your work to clearly reflect your message for your audience

Just as significant to your success is knowing how effective writers actually create their work for their audiences. This chapter gives you some practical information about the strategies and techniques careful writers use when they work. These procedures are a vital part of what is known as the *writing process*. This process involves matters such as how writers gather information, how they transform their ideas into written form, and how they organize and revise what they have written to make it suitable for their audiences.

What Writing Is Not and Is

As you begin your study of writing for the world of work, it might be helpful to identify some notions about what writing is and what it is not.

What Writing Is Not

- **Writing is not something mysterious done according to a magical formula known only to a few.** Even if you have not done much writing before, you can learn to write effectively.
- **Writing is not simply a hit-or-miss affair, left up to chance.** Successful writing requires hard work and thoughtful effort. It is not done well by simply going through an ordered set of steps as if you were painting by number. You cannot

sit down for fifteen minutes and expect to write the perfect memo, letter, or short report straight through. Writing does not proceed in some predictable way, in which introductions are always written first and conclusions last.

- **Just because you put something on paper or on a computer screen does not mean it is permanent and unchangeable.** Writing means *re*writing, *re*vising, *re*thinking. The better a piece of writing is, the more the writer has reworked it.

What Writing Is

- **Writing is a fluid process**—it is dynamic, not static. It enables you to discover and evaluate your thoughts.
- A piece of **writing changes as your thoughts and information change** and as your view of the material changes.
- **Writing takes time.** Some people think that revising and polishing are too time consuming. But poor writing actually takes more time and costs more money in the end. It can lead to misunderstandings, lost sales, product recalls, and even damage to your and your company's reputations.
- **Writing means making a number of judgment calls.**
- **Writing grows sometimes in bits and pieces and sometimes in great spurts.** It needs many revisions; an early draft is never a final copy.

Researching

Before you start to compose any e-mail, memo, letter, or report, you'll need to do some research. Research is crucial to obtain the right information for your audience. Information must be factually correct and intellectually significant. The world of work is based on conveying information—the logical presentation and sensible interpretation of facts.

Don't ever think you are wasting time by not starting to write your report or letter immediately. Actually, you will waste time and risk doing a poor job if you do not find out as much as possible about your topic (and your audience's interest in it).

First, find out as much as you can about the nature of your assignment and your readers, and what they expect from your written work. Next, determine the exact kind of research you must do to gather and interpret the information your audience needs. Your research can include

- interviewing people inside and outside your company
- doing fieldwork or performing lab studies
- preparing for conferences to ask the right questions
- collaborating with colleagues in person or by e-mail
- distributing a questionnaire and conducting a survey
- belonging to a chat room
- reading current periodicals, reports, and other documents
- evaluating reports, products, and services
- getting briefings from sales or technical staff
- contacting customers

Keep in mind that research is not confined to just the beginning of the writing process; it goes on throughout.

Planning

At this stage in the writing process, your goal is to get something—anything—down on paper or on your computer screen. For most writers, many of whom are fearful of writer's block, getting started is the hardest part of the job. But you will feel more comfortable and confident once you begin to see your ideas before your eyes. It is always easier to clarify and criticize something you can see.

Getting started is also easier if you have researched your topic, because you have something to say and to build on. Each part of the process relates to and supports the next. Careful research prepares you to begin writing.

Still, getting started is not easy. Take advantage of a number of widely used strategies that can help you to develop, organize, and tailor the right information for your audience. Use any one of the following techniques, alone or in combination.

1. Clustering. In the middle of a sheet of paper, write the word or phrase that best describes your topic, then start writing other words or phrases that come to mind. As you write, circle each word or phrase and connect it to the word from which it sprang. Note the clustered grouping in Figure 2.1 for a report encouraging a manager to switch to **flextime**—a system in which employees can work on a flexible time schedule within certain limits. The resulting diagram gives the writer a rough sense of some of the major divisions of the topic and where they may belong in the report.

2. Brainstorming. At the top of a sheet of paper or your computer screen, describe your topic in a word or phrase and then list any information you know or found out about that topic—in any order and as quickly as you can. Brainstorming is like thinking aloud except that you are recording your thoughts.

- Don't stop to delete, rearrange, or rewrite anything, and don't dwell on any one item.
- Don't worry about spelling, punctuation, grammar, or whether you are using words and phrases instead of complete sentences.
- Keep the ideas flowing. The result may well be an odd assortment of details, comments, and opinions.
- After ten to fifteen minutes, take a short break. When you come back to your list, you will no doubt want to make some changes. Some of your points will be irrelevant, so strike them.
- Expect to add some ideas or combine or rearrange others as you start to develop them in more detail.

Figure 2.2 (p. 30) shows Marcus Weekley's initial brainstormed list for a report

FIGURE 2.1   Clustering on the topic of flextime.

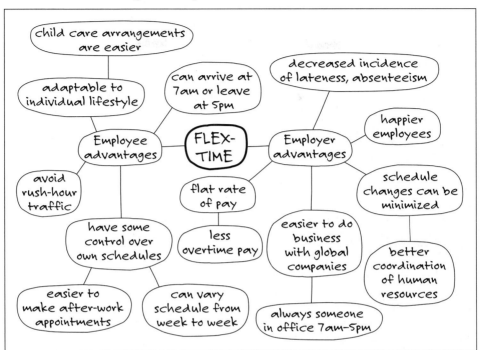

to his boss on purchasing a new color laser printer. After he began to revise it, he realized that some items were not relevant for his audience (6, 8, and 13) and that another was pertinent but needed to be adapted for his reader (5). He also recognized that some items were repetitious (1, 2, and 11). Further investigation revealed that his company could purchase a printer for far less than his initial high guess (17). As Weekley continued to work on his list, other important points came to mind that were not part of his original brainstorming.

   3. Outlining. For most writers, outlining may be the easiest and most comfortable way to begin or to continue planning their report or letter. Outlines can go through stages, so don't worry if your first attempt is brief and messy. It does not have to be formal (with roman and arabic numerals), complete, or pretty. It is intended for no one's eyes but yours. Use your preliminary outline as a quick way to sketch in some ideas, a convenient container into which you can put information. You might simply jot down a few major points and identify a few subpoints. Note that Marcus Weekley organized his revised brainstormed list into an outline (Figure 2.3, p. 31).

FIGURE 2.2   Marcus Weekley's initial, unrevised brainstormed list.

1. combines four separate pieces of equip—printer, copier, fax, and scanner

2. more comprehensive than our current configuration of four pieces of equip

3. would coordinate with office furniture

4. energy efficiency increased due to fewer machines being used

5. more scalable fonts

6. one machine interfaces with all others in same-case housing

7. scanner makes photographic-quality pictures

8. print capabilities are a real contribution to technology

9. increase communication abilities through fax machine

10. new scanner picture quality better than current scanner

11. only have to buy one machine as opposed to four

12. speed of fax allows quick response time

13. stock is doing better on Wall Street compared to other stocks

14. reducing our advertising costs through use of color printer

15. increase work area available

16. would help us do our work better

17. top of line models can be bought for $4,500

FIGURE 2.3   Marcus Weekley's early outline after revising his brainstormed list.

I. Convenience/Capabilities

    A. Would reduce number of machines required to service

    B. Can be configured easily for our network system

    C. Easy to install and operate

    D. 33.6 Kbps fax machine would increase our communication

    E. 300 × 600 dpi copier means better copy quality

    F. 2,400 × 2,400 dpi scanner means higher quality pictures than current scanner

II. Time/Efficiency

    A. 50 ppm printer is nearly twice as fast as current printer

    B. 33.6 Kbps speed fax allows quick response time

    C. Greater graphics capability—90 scalable fonts

    D. Scanner compatible with our current PhotoEdit imaging/graphics software

    E. 60,000-page monthly duty cycle means less maintenance

III. Money

    A. Costs less for multitasking printer than combined four machines

    B. Reduced monthly power bill by using one machine rather than four

    C. Included ScanText and WordPort software means not buying new software to network office computers

    D. Save on service costs

    E. Reduced advertising costs through printer 50–1,000% enlargement/ reduction options, which allows for production of more ads in-house

Drafting

If you have done your planning carefully, you will find it easier to start your first draft. When you draft, you convert the words and phrases from your outlines, brainstormed lists, or clustered groups into paragraphs. Think of your earlier jottings as the material out of which the basic building blocks (paragraphs) of your drafts will come. During drafting, as elsewhere in the writing process, you will see some overlap as you look back over your lists or outlines to shape your text.

Don't expect to wind up with a polished, complete version of your paper after working on only one draft. In most cases, you will have to work through many drafts, but each draft should be less rough and more acceptable than the preceding one.

Key Questions to Ask as You Draft

As you work on your drafts, ask yourself the following questions about your content and organization.

- Am I giving my readers too much or too little information?
- Is my information too technical for my audience?
- Does this point belong where I have it, or would it more logically follow or precede something else?
- Is this point necessary and relevant?
- Am I repeating myself?
- Have I contradicted myself?
- Have I ended appropriately for my audience?

To answer the questions successfully, you may have to continue researching your topic and reexamining your audience's needs. But, during the process, new and even better ideas may come to you.

Guidelines for Successful Drafting

The following are some suggestions to help your drafting go more smoothly and efficiently.

- In an early draft, write the easiest part first, regardless of where in the paper it may finally end up. Some writers feel more comfortable drafting the body (or middle) of their work first. See the differences between the memo in Figures 2.4 and 2.5, pages 34–35.
- As you work on a later draft, write straight through. Do not worry about spelling, punctuation, or the way a word or sentence sounds. Save those concerns for later stages.
- Allow enough time between drafts so that you can evaluate your work with fresh eyes and a clear mind.
- Get frequent outside opinions. Show, e-mail, or fax a draft to a fellow student, a co-worker, or maybe a supervisor for comment. A new pair of eyes will see things you missed.
- Start considering if visuals would enhance the quality of your work and where they might best be positioned.

Revising

Revision is an essential stage in the writing process. It requires more than giving your work another quick glance. Do not be tempted to skip the revision stage just because you have written the required number of words or sections or because you think you have put in too much time already. Revision is done *after* you produce a draft that you think conveys the appropriate message for your audience. The quality of your memo, letter, or report depends on the revisions you make now.

Allow Enough Time to Revise

Like planning or drafting, revision is not done well in one big push. It evolves over a period of time. Budget enough time to do it carefully.

- Avoid drafting and revising in one sitting. If possible, wait at least a day before you start to revise. (In the busy work world, waiting a couple of hours may suffice.)
- Ask a co-worker or friend familiar with your topic to comment on your work.
- Plan to read your revised work more than once.

Revision Is Rethinking

When you revise, you *re*see, *re*think, and *re*consider your entire document. You ask questions about the major issues of content, organization, and tone. Revision involves going back and repeating earlier steps in the writing process.

Revision means asking again the questions you have already asked and answered during the planning and drafting stages. During the process, you will discover gaps to fill, points to change, and errors to correct in your draft. Revision gives you a second (or third or fourth) chance to get things right for your audience.

Key Questions to Ask as You Revise

Content

1. Is it accurate? Are my facts (figures, names, dates, costs, references, statistics) correct?
2. Is it relevant for my audience and purpose? Have I included information that is unnecessary, too technical, not appropriate?
3. Have I given enough evidence to explain things adequately and to persuade my readers? (Too little information will make readers skeptical about what you are describing or proposing.) Have I left anything out?

Organization

1. Have I clearly identified my main points and shown readers why those points are important?
2. Is everything in the right, most effective order? Should anything be switched or moved closer to the beginning or the end of my document?
3. Have I spent too much (or too little) effort on one section? Do I repeat myself? What can be cut?

4. Have I grouped related items in the same part of my report or letter, or have I scattered details that really need to appear together in one paragraph or section?

Tone

1. How do I sound to my readers—professional and sincere, or arrogant and unreliable? What attitude do my words or expressions convey?
2. How will my readers think I perceive them—honest and intelligent or unprofessional and uncooperative?

A "Before" and "After" Revision

Figures 2.4 and 2.5 show a "before" and "after" revision. The writer, Mary Fonseca, an employee at Seacoast Labs, was asked by her supervisor to prepare a short report for the general public on the lab's most recent experiments. One of her later drafts begins with the paragraphs in Figure 2.4.

When starting to revise Figure 2.4, Fonseca realized that it lacked focus. It jumped back and forth between *drag* on ships and on an airplane. Since Seacoast Labs did not work on planes, she wisely decided to drop that idea. She also realized that the information on the effects of drag, something Seacoast was working on, was so important it deserved a separate paragraph. In light of this key idea, she realized

FIGURE 2.4   Opening, unorganized paragraphs of Mary Fonseca's draft.

Drag is an important concept in the world of science and technology. It has many implications. Drag occurs when a ship moves through the water and eddies build up. Ships on the high seas have to fight the eddies, which results in drag. In the same way, an airplane has to fight the winds at various altitudes at which it flies; these winds are very forceful, moving at many knots per hour. All these forces of nature are around us. Sometimes we can feel them, too. We get tired walking against a strong wind. The eddies around a ship are the same thing. These eddies form various barriers around the ship's hull. They come from a combination of different molecules around the ship's hull and exert quite a force. Both types of molecules pull against the ship. This is where the eddies come in.

Scientists at Seacoast Labs are concerned about drag. Dr. Karen Runnels, who joined Seacoast about three years ago, is the chief investigator. She and her team of highly qualified experts have constructed some fascinating multilevel water tunnels. These tunnels should be useful to ship owners. Drag wastes a ship's fuel.

FIGURE 2.5   A revision of Mary Fonseca's draft in Figure 2.4.

What is drag?

We cannot see or hear many of the forces around us, but we can certainly detect their presence. Walking or running into a strong wind, for example, requires a great deal of effort and often quickly leaves us feeling tired. When a ship sails through the water, it also experiences these opposing sources known as **drag**. Overcoming drag causes a ship to reduce its energy efficiency, which leads to higher fuel costs.

How drag works

It is not easy for a ship to fight drag. As the ship moves through the water, it drags the water molecules around its hull at the same rate the ship is moving. Because of the cohesive force of those molecules, other water molecules immediately outside the ship's path get pulled into its way. All the molecules become tangled rather than simply sliding past each other. The result is an eddy, or small circling burst of water around the ship's hull, which intensifies the drag. Dr. Charles Hester, a noted engineer, explains it using an analogy: "When you put a spoon in honey and pull it out, half the honey comes out with the spoon. That's what is happening to ships. The ship is moving and at the same time dragging the ocean with it."

At Seacoast Labs, scientists are working to find ways to reduce drag on ships. Dr. Karen Runnels, the principal investigator, and a team of researchers have constructed water tunnels to simulate the movement of ships at sea. The drag a ship encounters is measured from the tiny air bubbles emitted in the water tunnel. Dr. Runnels's team has also developed the use of polymers, or long carbon chain molecules, to reduce drag. The polymers act like a slimy coating for the ship's hull to help it glide through the water more easily. When asbestos fibers were added to the polymer solutions, the investigators measured a 90 percent reduction in drag. The team has also experimented with an external pump attached to the hull of a ship, which pushes the water away from a ship's path.

that her explanation of molecules, eddies, and drag needed to be made more reader-friendly. Researching further, she decided to add a new paragraph on the causes and effects of drag, which became paragraph 2 in Figure 2.5.

Yet by pulling ideas about drag and its effects from her longish first paragraph in Figure 2.4, Fonseca was left with the job of finding an opening for her report. Buried in her original opening paragraph was the idea that we cannot always see the forces of nature but "we can feel them." She thought this analogy of walking against the wind and drag would work better for her audience of nonspecialists than the original wooden remarks she had started with.

Although her original draft organization and ideas were now far better than those in Figure 2.4, she realized she had said very little about her employer Seacoast Labs. Doing more research, she found information about Seacoast's experiments and why they were so important in saving money. This information was far more important and relevant than saying Dr. Runnels had been at Seacoast for three years.

Through revision and further research, then, Mary Fonseca transformed two poorly organized and incomplete paragraphs into three separate yet logically connected ones that highlighted her employer's work. Thanks to her revision, too, she came up with two very helpful headings—"What is drag?" and "How drag works"—for her nonspecialist readers (see Figure 2.5).

Editing

Editing is quality control for your reader. This last stage in the writing process might be compared to detailing an automobile—the preparation a dealer goes through to ready a new car for prospective buyers. Editing is done only after you are completely satisfied that you have made all the big decisions about content and organization—that you have said what you wanted to, where and how you intended, for your audience.

When you edit, you will check your work for

- sentences
- word choices
- punctuation
- spelling
- grammar and usage

As with revising, don't skip or rush through the editing process, thinking that once your ideas are down, your work is done. Your style, punctuation, spelling, and grammar matter a great deal to readers. If your work is hard to read or contains mistakes in spelling or punctuation, readers will think that your ideas and your research are also faulty.

The following sections give you some basic guidelines about what to look for when you edit your sentences and words. The appendix, "A Writer's Brief Guide to Paragraphs, Sentences, and Words" (pp. 313–331), contains helpful suggestions on correct spelling and punctuation.

Guidelines for Writing Lean and Clear Sentences

Here are three of the most frequent complaints readers voice about poorly edited writing in the world of work:

- The sentences are too long. I could not follow the writer's meaning.
- The sentences are too complex. I could not understand what the writer meant the first time I read the work; I had to reread it several times.
- The sentences are unclear. Even after I reread them, I am not sure I understood the writer's message.

Wordy, unclear sentences frustrate readers and waste their time. Writing clear, readable sentences is not always easy. It takes effort, but the time you spend editing will pay off in rich dividends for you and your readers. The guidelines that follow should help with the editing phase of your work.

Avoid Needlessly Complex or Lengthy Sentences

Do not pile words on top of words. Instead, edit one overly long sentence into two or even three more manageable ones.

> **Too Long:** The planning committee decided that the awards banquet should be held on May 15 at 6:30, since the other two dates (May 7 and May 22) suggested by the hospitality committee conflict with local sports events, even though one of those events could be changed to fit our needs.
>
> **Edited for Easier Reading:** The planning committee has decided to hold the awards banquet on May 15 at 6:30. The other dates suggested by the hospitality committee—May 7 and May 22—conflict with two local sports events. Although the date of one of those sports events could be changed, the planning committee still believes that May 15 is our best choice.

Combine Short, Choppy Sentences

Don't shorten long, complex sentences only to turn them into choppy, simplistic ones. A memo, e-mail, or letter written exclusively in short, staccato sentences sounds immature and makes for boring reading.

When you find yourself looking at a series of short, blunt sentences, as in the following example, combine them where possible and use connective words similar to those italicized in the edited version.

> **Choppy:** Medical transcriptionists have many responsibilities. Their responsibilities are important. They must be familiar with medical terminology. They must listen to dictation. Sometimes physicians talk very fast. Then the transcriptionist must be quick to transcribe what is heard. Words could be missed. Transcriptionists must also prepare final reports. This will take a great deal of time and concentration. These reports are copied and stored properly for reference.
>
> **Edited:** Medical transcriptionists have many important responsibilities. *These* include transcribing physicians' orders using correct medical terminology. *When*

physicians talk rapidly, transcriptionists have to keyboard accurately *so* that no words are omitted. *Among the most demanding* of their duties are preparing final transcriptions *and then* making and storing those copies properly for future reference.

Edit Sentences to Tell Who Does What to Whom or What

The clearest sentence structure in English is the subject-verb-object (s-v-o) pattern.

> s   v   o
> Sue mowed the grass.

>   s   v   o
> Our Web site contains a link to key training software programs.

Readers find this pattern easiest to understand because it provides direct and specific information about the action. Hard-to-read sentences obscure or scramble information about the subject, the verb, or the object. In the following unedited sentence, subjects are hidden in the middle rather than being placed in the most crucial subject position.

> **Unclear:** The control of the ceiling limits of glycidyl ethers on the part of the employers for the optimum safety of workers in the workplace is necessary. (Who is responsible for taking action? What action must they take? For whom is such action taken?)
>
> **Edited:** Employers must control the ceiling limits of glycidyl ethers for the workers' safety.

Use Strong, Active Verbs Rather Than Verb Phrases

In trying to sound important, many bureaucratic writers avoid using simple, graphic verbs. Instead, these writers use a weak verb phrase (for example, *provide maintenance of* instead of *maintain, work in cooperation with* instead of *cooperate*). Such verb phrases imprison the active verb inside a noun format and slow a reader down. Note how the edited version here rewrites the weak verb phrase.

> **Weak:** The city provided the employment of two work crews to assist the strengthening of the dam.
>
> **Strong:** The city employed two work crews to strengthen the dam.

Avoid Piling Modifiers in Front of Nouns

Putting too many modifiers (words used as adjectives) in the reader's path to the noun will confuse the reader, who cannot decipher how one modifier relates to another modifier or to the noun. To avoid that problem, edit the sentence to place some of the modifiers after or before the nouns they modify.

> **Crowded:** The vibration noise control heat pump condenser quieter can make your customer happier.
>
> **Readable:** The quieter on the condenser for the heat pump will make your customer happier by controlling noise and vibrations.

Replace Wordy Phrases or Clauses with One- or Two-Word Synonyms

Wordy: The college has parking zones for different areas for people living on campus as well as for those who do not live on campus and who commute to school.

Edited: The college has different parking zones for resident and commuter students. (Twenty words of the original sentence—everything after "areas for"—have been reduced to four words: "resident and commuter students.")

Combine Sentences Beginning with the Same Subject or Ending with an Object That Becomes the Subject of the Next Sentence

Wordy: I asked the inspector if she were going to visit the plant this afternoon. I also asked her if she would come alone.

Edited: I asked the inspector if she were going to visit the plant alone this afternoon.

Wordy: Homeowners want to buy low-maintenance bushes. These low-maintenance bushes include the ever-popular holly and boxwood varieties. These bushes are also inexpensive.

Edited: Homeowners want to buy low-maintenance and inexpensive bushes such as holly and boxwood. (This revision combines three sentences into one, condenses twenty-four words into fourteen, and joins three related thoughts.)

Guidelines for Cutting Out Unnecessary Words

Too many people in business think the more words, the better. Nothing could be more self-defeating. Your readers are busy; unnecessary words slow them down. Make every word work. Cut out any words you can from your sentences. If the sentence still makes sense and reads correctly, you have eliminated wordiness. For example, the phrases on the left should be replaced with the precise words on the right.

Wordy	Concisely Edited
at a slow rate	slowly
at this point in time	now
be in agreement with	agree
bring to a conclusion	conclude, end
come to terms with	agree, accept
due to the fact that	because
express an opinion that	affirm
for the length of time that	while
for the period of	for
in such a manner that	so that
in the area / case / field of	in
in the neighborhood of	approximately
look something like	resemble
serve the function of	function as
show a tendency to	tend
with reference to	regarding, about
with the result that	so

Another kind of wordiness comes from using redundant expressions—saying the same thing a second time, in different words. "Fellow colleague," "component parts," "corrosive acid," and "free gift" are phrases that contain this kind of double speech; a fellow *is* a colleague, a component *is* a part, acid *is* corrosive, and a gift *is* free. The suggested changes on the right are preferable to the redundant phrases on the left.

Redundant	Concise
absolutely essential	essential
advance reservations	reservations
basic necessities	necessities, needs
close proximity	proximity, nearness
end result	result
final conclusions/final outcome	conclusions/outcome
first and foremost	first
full and complete	full, complete
personal opinion	opinion
over and done with	over
tried and true	tried, proven

Watch for repetitious words, phrases, or clauses within a sentence. Sometimes one sentence or one part of a sentence needlessly duplicates another.

Redundant: To provide more room for employees' cars, the security department is studying ways to expand the employees' parking lot.

Edited: The security department is studying ways to expand the employees' parking lot. (Since the first phrase says nothing that the reader does not know from the independent clause, cut it.)

Adding a prepositional phrase can sometimes contribute to redundancy. The italicized words in the next list are redundant because of the unnecessary qualification they impose on the word they modify. Be on the lookout for the italicized phrases and delete them.

audible *to the ear*	hard *to the touch*
bitter *in taste*	honest *in character*
fly *through the air*	light *in weight*
orange *in color*	soft *in texture*
rectangular *in shape*	tall *in height*
second *in sequence*	twenty *in number*
short *in duration*	visible *to the eye*

Figure 2.6 shows an e-mail that Trudy Wallace wants to send to her boss about issuing cell phones to the entire sales force. Her unedited work is bloated with unnecessary words, expendable phrases, and repetitious ideas.

After careful editing, Wallace streamlined her e-mail to Lee Chadwick. Note how, in Figure 2.7 (p. 42), she pruned wordy expressions and combined sentences to

FIGURE 2.6   Wordy, unedited e-mail.

Subject: **Issuing cell phones**
Date: 5/19/2006 2:45 PM Eastern Standard Time
From: twallace@transtech.org (Trudy Wallace)
To: lchadwick@transtech.org (Lee Chadwick)

Due to the amount of time our sales force spends traveling the roads each day, it strikes me as beneficial to look into the distinct possibility of issuing cellular phones to our work force. Such an addition would benefit our sales force in a variety of multiple ways. The sales force could increase their efficiency and morale with these phones. With the aid of cellular phones we could bring together our customers and our sales force a lot easier. Our salespeople could have a shortened period of time to respond using their cellular phones. The response rate of returning a call could be markedly reduced and dropped down. Moreover, by having cellular phones at work salespeople would minimize the problems of returning calls to people and then finding out they are out and then having to call them back. It is difficult to catch people this way. Cellular phones would increase both the convenience and the ease by which we operate our business. Sophisticated keying codes would allow us to track all employee calls and to make sure employees are where they are supposed to be by calling them. I think it would be absolutely essential to the ongoing operation of our company's business today to respond fully and completely to the possibility such a proposal affords us. It would therefore appear safe to conclude that with reference to the issue of cellular phones that every means at our disposal should be brought to bear on issuing such phones to our employees.

cut out duplication. The revised version is only 92 words, as opposed to the 251 words in the draft. Not only has Wallace shortened her message, she has made it easier to read.

Guidelines for Eliminating Sexist Language

Editing involves far more than just making sure your sentences are readable. It also reflects your professional style—how you see and characterize the world of work and the individuals in it, not to mention how you want your readers to see you. Your words should reflect a high degree of ethics and honesty, free from bias and offense.

FIGURE 2.7   The e-mail in Figure 2.6 edited for conciseness.

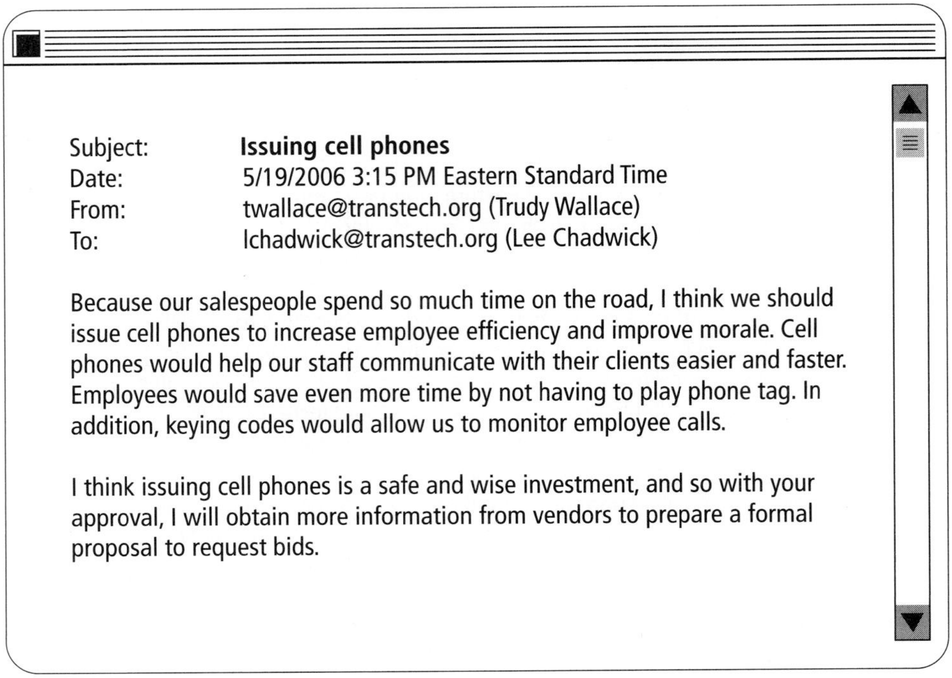

Subject:	**Issuing cell phones**
Date:	5/19/2006 3:15 PM Eastern Standard Time
From:	twallace@transtech.org (Trudy Wallace)
To:	lchadwick@transtech.org (Lee Chadwick)

Because our salespeople spend so much time on the road, I think we should issue cell phones to increase employee efficiency and improve morale. Cell phones would help our staff communicate with their clients easier and faster. Employees would save even more time by not having to play phone tag. In addition, keying codes would allow us to monitor employee calls.

I think issuing cell phones is a safe and wise investment, and so with your approval, I will obtain more information from vendors to prepare a formal proposal to request bids.

Sexist language offers a distorted view of our society and discriminates in favor of one sex at the expense of another, usually women. Using sexist language offends and demeans female readers by depriving them of their equal rights. You may cost your company business. Escape displaying gender bias by using inclusive language for women and men alike.

Sexist language is often based on sexist stereotypes that depict men as superior to women. For example, calling politicians *city fathers* or *favorite sons* follows the stereotypical picture of seeing politicians as male. Such phrases discriminate against women who do or could hold public office at all levels of government.

Sexist language also prejudiciously labels some professions as masculine and others as feminine. For example, sexist phrases assume engineers, physicians, and pilots are male (*he, his,* and *him* are often linked with these professions in descriptions) while social workers, nurses, and secretaries are female *(she, her),* although members of both sexes work in all those professions. Sexist language also wrongly points out gender identities when such roles do not seem to follow biased expectations—*lady lawyer, male nurse, female surgeon,* or *female astronaut.* Such offensive distinctions reflect prejudiced attitudes that you should eliminate from your writing.

Always prune the following sexist phrases: *every man for himself, gal Friday, little woman, lady of the house, the best man for the job, the weaker sex, woman's work, working wives,* and *young man on the way up.* Sexist terms will not only offend but also exclude many of the members of the audience you want to reach.

Ways to Avoid Sexist Language

1. Replace sexist words with neutral ones. Neutral words do *not* refer to a specific sex; they are genderless. The sexist words on the left in the following list can be replaced by the neutral nonsexist substitutes on the right.

Sexist	Neutral
alderman; assemblyman	representative
businessman	businessperson
cameraman	photographer
chairman	chair, chairperson
congressman	representative
divorcée	divorced person
fireman	firefighter
foreman	supervisor
janitress	cleaning person
landlord, landlady	owner
maiden name	family name
mailman/postman	mail carrier
man-hours	work-hours
manmade	synthetic, artificial
manpower	strength, power
man to man	candidly
policeman	police officer
repairman	repair person
salesman	salesperson
stewardess	flight attendant
woman's intuition	intuition
workman	worker

2. Watch masculine pronouns. Avoid using masculine pronouns *(he, his, him)* when referring to a group that includes both men and women.

> Every worker must submit his travel expenses by Monday.

Workers may include women as well as men, and to assume that all workers are men is misleading and unfair to women. You can edit such sexist language in several ways.

a. Make the subject of your sentence plural and thus neutral.

> Workers must submit their travel expenses by Monday.

b. Replace the pronoun *his* with *the* or *a* or drop it altogether.

> Every employee is to submit a travel expense report by Monday.
> Every worker must submit travel expenses by Monday.

  c. Use *his or her* instead of *his*.

  Every worker must submit his or her travel expenses by Monday.

  d. Reword the sentence using the passive voice.

  All travel expenses must be submitted by Monday.

3. Eliminate sexist salutations. Never use the following salutations when you are unsure of who your readers are:

- Dear Sir
- Gentlemen
- Dear Madam

Any woman in the audience will surely be offended by the first two and may also be unhappy with the pompous and obsolete *madam*. It is usually best to write to a specific individual, but if you cannot do that, direct your letter to a particular department or office: *Dear Warranty Department* or *Dear Selection Committee*.

  Be careful, too, about using the titles *Miss, Mr.,* and *Mrs.;* sexist distinctions are unjust and insulting. It would be preferable to write *Dear Ms. McCarty* rather than *Dear Miss or Mrs. McCarty.* A woman's marital status should not be an issue. If you are in doubt, write *Dear Indira Kumar.* (Review Chapter 4, page 78, about acceptable salutations in your letters.)

4. Never single out a person's physical appearance. Sexist physical references negatively draw attention to a woman's gender. Even sexist writers would not describe a male manager this way.

  The manager is a tall blonde who received her training at Mason Technical Institute.

Collaborative Writing and the Writing Process

The writing process just described also applies to collaborative writing. Groups use the same strategies and confront the same problems as individual writers—brainstorm, plan, research, draft, revise, and edit, as the team of workers does in Figure 2.8. Like the individual writer, too, a team moves through the writing process only by identifying its audience, following a common purpose, defining the problem, and deciding on the best ways to solve that problem.

  A brief rundown of how groups move through the writing process follows.

1. Groups plan before they write. The planning phase includes brainstorming on the group scale with each member contributing to the overall discussion. Members should be encouraged to express ideas freely and without fear of criticism at an early planning session. During this early phase, the group must also establish the ground rules by which it will operate, including making individual assignments, establishing schedules, and selecting a facilitator.

2. Groups do research. Researching entails more than chitchat or a casual pooling of undocumented opinions. It requires searching, interviewing, and reading.

FIGURE 2.8   A collaborating team at work.

© Royalty-Free/CORBIS.

Some tasks may be undertaken by individuals working alone or each member may be assigned to research one part of a subject. *Never hoard information;* always share for the benefit of the group. As a team member, you may even be called on to distribute copies of documents you retrieved from the Internet or other sources or to report on an interview you conducted.

3. Groups prepare drafts. While it is possible for a group to draft a document together, requiring everyone to sit down together and write word for word is not always feasible or justifiable. Individuals are more likely to draft sections of a document on their own and then present their work for group discussion and revision.

4. Groups revise and edit. Group interaction can spot and resolve problems—omissions, difficulties in organization (a section out of order), length, inconsistencies in content, and so on. Discussion also helps groups agree on a final style and accepted rules of usage. It often makes sense to appoint someone who has the most writing ability to give the group document a final editing for style.

Each stage of the writing process just outlined can be modified to account for group activities. Flexibility is as important to a group of writers as it is to an individual writer.

✓ Revision Checklist

- ❑ Investigated the research, drafting, revising, and editing benefits available through the computer.
- ❑ Researched my topic carefully to obtain enough information to answer all my readers' questions. Used appropriate means such as library research, on-line data search, interviews, questionnaires, personal observations, or a combination of methods.
- ❑ Before writing, determined how much and what kind of information was needed to complete writing task.
- ❑ Spent enough time planning—brainstorming, outlining, clustering, or a combination of those techniques. Produced enough substantial material from which to shape a draft.
- ❑ Prepared enough drafts to decide on major points in message to readers. Made major changes and deletions if necessary in drafts.
- ❑ Revised drafts carefully to successfully answer readers' questions about content, organization, and tone.
- ❑ Made time to edit work so that style is clear and concise and sentences are readable and varied. Checked words to make sure they are spelled correctly and are appropriate for audience.
- ❑ Eliminated sexist language.
- ❑ Attended all group meetings and understood responsibilities of the group and my own obligations.
- ❑ Finished research, planning, and drafting expected of me.

Exercises

1. Write a short report (2–3 pages) to the manager of the small company you work for on a topic of your choice. Prepare an outline similar to that on flextime in Figure 2.1 (p. 29). Add, delete, or rearrange anything in this clustered grouping to complete your outline. Submit your final outline along with your report to your instructor.

2. Assume you have been asked to write a short report, as Marcus Weekley did (see Figure 2.2), to a decision maker (the manager of a business you work for or have worked for; the director of your campus union, library, or security force; a city official) about one of the following topics.
   a. recruitment of international work force
   b. Internet resources
   c. security lighting
   d. food service

e. insurance plans
f. public transportation
g. sporting events/activities
h. team building
i. morale
j. hiring more part-time student workers

Do some research and planning about one of those topics and the audience for whom it is intended by answering the following questions.

- What is my precise purpose in writing to my audience?
- What do I know about the topic?
- What information will my audience expect me to know?
- Where can I obtain relevant information about my topic to meet my audience's needs?

3. Using one or more of the planning strategies discussed in this chapter (clustering, brainstorming, outlining), generate a group of ideas for the topic you chose in Exercise 2. Work on your planning activities for about 15 to 20 minutes or until you have about 10 to 15 items. At this stage do not worry about how appropriate the ideas are or even if some of them overlap. Just get some thoughts down on paper.

4. The following paragraphs are wordy and full of awkward, hard-to-read sentences. Edit these paragraphs to make them more readable by using clear and concise words and sentences.

a. It has been verified conclusively by this writer that our institution must of necessity install more bicycle holding racks for the convenience of students, faculty, and staff. These parking modules should be fastened securely to walls outside strategic locations on the campus. They could be positioned there by work crews or even by the security forces who vigilantly patrol the campus grounds. There are many students in particular who would value the installation of these racks. Their bicycles could be stationed there by them, and they would know that safety measures have been taken to ensure that none of their bicycles would be apprehended or confiscated illegally. Besides the precaution factor, these racks would afford users maximized convenience in utilizing their means of transportation when they have academic business to conduct, whether at the learning resource center or in the instructional facilities.

b. On the basis of preliminary investigations, it would seem reasonable to hypothesize that among the situational factors predisposing the Smith family toward showing pronounced psychological identification with the San Francisco Giants is the fact that the Smiths make their domicile in the San Francisco area. In the absence of contrariwise considerations, the Smiths' attitudinal preferences would in this respect interface with earlier behavioral studies. These studies, within acceptable parameters, correlate the fan's domicile with athletic allegiance. Yet it would be counterproductive to establish domicility as the sole determining factor for the Smiths' preference. Certain sociometric studies of the Smiths disclose a factor of atypicality which enters into an analysis of their determinations. One of these factors is that a younger Smith sibling is a participant in the athletic organization in question.

5. Following are very early drafts of memos that businesspeople have sent to their bosses or fellow workers. Revise and edit each draft, referring to the revising and editing checklists. Turn in your revision and the final, reader-ready copy. As you revise, keep in mind that you may have to delete and add information, rearrange the order of information, and make the tone suitable for the reader. As you edit, make sure your sentences are clear and concise and your words well chosen.

a. DATE: April 29, 2006
   TO: All workers
   FROM: B.J. Blackwell
   RE: Parking

The parking violations around here have gotten very very bad. And the administration is provoked and wants some action taken. I don't blame them. I have been late for meetings several times in the last month because inconsiderate folks from other divisions have parked their cars in our zone. That just is not fair, and so I must not be the only one who is upset. No wonder the management finds things so bad they have asked me to prepare this memo.

A big part of the problem it seems to me is that employees just cannot read signs. They park in the wrong zones. They also park in visitors' spots. The penalties are going to be stiff. The administration, or so I was led to believe, is thinking of fining any employee who does not obey the parking policies. I know for a fact that I saw someone from the research department pull right into a visitor parking area last week just because it was 8:55 and he did not want to be late for work. That gives our business a bad name. People will not want to do business with us if they cannot even find a parking spot in the area that the company has reserved for them.

Ms. Watson has laid the law down to me about all this and told me to let each and every one of you know that things have to improve. One of the other big problems around here is that some employees have even parked their cars in loading zones, and security had to track them down to move.

As part of the administration's new policy, each employee is going to be issued a company parking policy and will have to come in and sign for it verifying that he received it. I think things really have gotten out of hand and that some drastic action has to be taken. We will all have to shape up around here.

b. DATE: February 20, 2006
    TO: All Employees
    FROM: George Holmes
    RE: Travel

Every company has its policies regarding travel and vouchers. Ours strike me as important and fairly straightforward. Yet for the life of me I cannot fathom why they are being ignored. It is in everyone's best interest. When you travel, you are on company time, company business. Respect that, won't you. Explain your purpose, keep your receipts, document your visits, keep track of meals.

If you see more than one client per day, it should not be too hard or too much to ask you to keep a log of each, separate, individual visit. After all, our business does depend on these people, and we will never know your true contributions on company trips unless you inform us (please!) of whom you see, where, why, and how much it costs you. That way we can keep our books straight and know that everything is going according to company policy.

Please review the appropriate pages (I think they are pages 23–25) about travel procedures. Thanks. If you have questions, give me a call, but check your procedures book or with your office/section manager, first. That will save everyone more time. Good luck.

Correspondence

Writing Memos, Faxes, and E-Mails

Memos, faxes, and e-mail messages are the types of writing you can expect to prepare most frequently on the job. These three forms of business correspondence are quick, easy, and effective ways for a company to communicate internally as well as externally. You will find yourself preparing one or more of these types of writing each day to co-workers in your department, to colleagues in other departments and divisions of your company, and to decision makers at all levels.

What Memos, Faxes, and E-Mails Have in Common

1. Each of these forms of writing is streamlined for the busy world of work. Memos are far less formal in tone than letters; e-mails can be even more informal than a memo. Memos, faxes, and e-mails also require you to follow different formats than you do for letters.

2. They give busy readers information fast. While these messages can be about any topic in the world of work, most often they focus on the day-to-day activities and operations at your company—sales and product information, policy and schedule changes, progress reports, orders, personnel decisions, and so on.

3. Even though routine, they still demand a great deal of thought and time. Which one you use—memo, fax, or e-mail—depends on your company policy, the nature of your message, and your audience's needs and expectations. While some individuals believe we are moving toward a paperless office, most companies will still want to see a paper or electronic trail documenting what has been done when and by whom. Your success as an employee can depend as much on your preparing a readable and effective memo, fax, or e-mail as it will on your technical expertise.

Memos

Memorandum, from which the term *memo* comes, is a Latin word for "something to be remembered." The Latin meaning points to the memo's chief function: to record information of immediate importance and interest in the busy world of work. **Memos** are brief in-house correspondence sent up and down the corporate ladder. Employees send memos to their supervisors, and workers send memos to one another. Figure 3.1 shows a memo sent from one worker to another. Figure 3.2 illustrates a memo sent

FIGURE 3.1   Standard memo format.

MEMO

TO: Lucy
FROM: Roger
DATE: November 11, 2006
SUBJECT: Review of Successful Web Site Seminar

As you know, I attended the "How to Build a Successful Web Site" seminar on November 7 and learned the "rules and tools" we will need to redesign our own site.

Here is a review of the major topics covered by the director, Jackie Lowery.

1. Keep your Web site content-based—hit your target audience.
2. Visualize and "map out" your site's ad links.
3. Design your Web site to look the way you envision it—make it aesthetically pleasing.
4. Make your site easy to navigate.
5. Maintain your page outline; make changes when necessary.
6. Create hot links and image maps to usher users from page to page.
7. Complete your site with sound and animation.

Could we meet in the next day or two to discuss recreating our own Web site in light of these guidelines? I would really like your suggestions about this project. Thanks.

FIGURE 3.2   Memo with a clear introduction, discussion, and conclusion.

Dearborn Equipment Company

To: Machine Shop Employees
From: Janet Hempstead, Shop Supervisor
Date: September 27, 2006
Subject: Cleaning Brake Machines

Introduction

During the past two weeks I have received several reports that the brake machines are not being cleaned properly after each use. Through this memo I want to emphasize and explain the importance of keeping these machines clean for the safety of all employees.

Discussion

When the brake machines are used, the cutter chops off small particles of metal from brake drums. These particles settle on the machines and create a potentially hazardous situation for anyone working on or near the machines. If the machines are not cleaned routinely before being used again, these metal particles could easily fly into an individual's face when the brake drum is spinning.

To prevent accidents like this from happening, please make sure you vacuum the brake machines after each use.

You will find two vacuum cleaners for this purpose in the shop—one of them is located in work area 1-A and the other, a reserve model, is in the storage area. Vacuuming brake machines is quick and easy: it should take no more than a few seconds. This is a small amount of time to make the shop safer for all of us.

Conclusion

Thanks for your cooperation. If you have any questions, please call me at Extension 324 or come by my office.

204 South Mill St., South Orange, NJ 02341-3420 (609) 555-9848 JHEMP@dearco.com

from the top down; Figure 3.3 shows a memo sent from an employee to management. Memos are not as formal as letters and contain the terms and abbreviations familiar to employees of your company. They can be on paper, or sent through e-mail as in Figure 1.7 (p. 18) or Figures 3.4 and 3.5 (pp. 62 and 63).

Memo Protocol and Company Politics

Memos reflect a company's image—its politics, policies, and organization. Note how Janet Hempstead's memo in Figure 3.2 reminds workers about a crucial safety policy at Dearborn Equipment Company. A company's logo may even appear on the top, as in Figures 3.2 and 3.3. Memos reflect the company's leadership skills and the ways in which it builds employee morale and encourages productivity.

Regardless of where you work, your employer will expect memos to be timely (don't wait until the day of a meeting to announce it), professional, and tactful. Just because a memo is an informal in-house communication does not mean you can be gruff, curt, or bossy. Politeness and diplomacy count a lot at work. Learning effective memo writing is vital to your success in any organization.

Most companies have their own memo *protocol*—accepted ways in which in-house communications are formatted, organized, written, and routed. In fact, some companies offer protocol seminars on how employees are to prepare communications. In the corporate world, protocol determines where your memo will go. Don't send copies of your memos (or your e-mails for that matter) to individuals who don't need them, however. You will only increase the paper inflation or electronic traffic in your company. For example, it would be presumptuous to send copies of all your memos to the vice president. You would offend your immediate supervisor, who might think that you are trying to avoid going through proper channels.

Functions of Memos

Memos serve a variety of functions, including

- announcing a company policy or plan
- changing a policy or procedure
- offering information (FYI)
- making a request
- explaining a procedure or giving instructions
- clarifying or summarizing an issue
- alerting readers to a problem or to a deadline
- confirming the outcome of a conversation
- calling a meeting
- providing documentation necessary for business
- providing suggestions or recommendations
- documenting, for your own protection, something you did or did not do
- summarizing a long report or proposal

Memos are valuable written records used for a variety of purposes. They are used for a number of short reports; see Chapter 8 for examples of periodic, field trip, or progress reports in memo format. Many internal proposals (pp. 243–49) also are written as memos. In fact, the memo in Figure 3.3 is an example of such a proposal.

FIGURE 3.3   A memo that uses headings to highlight organization.

RAMCO INDUSTRIES

Where Technology Shapes Tomorrow
ramco@gem.com   http://www.Ramcogem.com

TO: Rachel Mohler, Vice President
                 Harrison Fontentot, Public Relations
FROM: Mike Gonzalez *MG*
SUBJECT: Ways to Increase Ramco's Community Involvement
DATE: March 2, 2006

At our planning session in early February, our division managers stressed the need to generate favorable publicity for our new Ramco facility in Mayfield. Knowing that such publicity will highlight Ramco's visibility in Mayfield, I think the company's image might be enhanced in the following ways.

CREATE A SCHOLARSHIP FUND
Ramco would receive favorable publicity by creating a scholarship at Mayfield Community College for any student interested in a career in technology. A one-year scholarship would cost $4,800. The scholarship could be awarded by a committee composed of Ramco executives and staff. Such a scholarship would emphasize Ramco's support for technical education at a local college.

OFFER SITE TOURS
Guided tours of the Mayfield facility would introduce the community to Ramco's innovative technology. The tours might be organized for community and civic groups. Individuals would see the care we take in production and equipment choice and the speed with which we ship our products. Of special interest to visitors would be Ramco's use of industrial robots alongside its employees. Since these tours would be scheduled well in advance, they should not conflict with our production schedules.

PROVIDE GUEST SPEAKERS
Many of our employees would be excellent guest speakers at civic and educational meetings in the Mayfield area. Possible topics include the technological advances Ramco has made in designing and engineering and how these advances have helped consumers.

Thanks for giving me your comments as soon as possible. If we are going to put one or more of the suggestions into practice before the facility opens, we'll need to act before the end of the month.

Memo Format

Memos vary in format and the way they are sent. Some companies use standard, printed forms (Figure 3.1), while others (as in Figure 3.2) have their names (letterhead) printed on their memos. You can also make a memo by including the necessary parts in an e-mail, as in Figures 3.4 and 3.5, which appear later in this chapter.

As you can see from looking at Figures 3.1 through 3.3, memos look different from letters, and they are less formal. Because they are often sent to individuals within your company, memos do not need the formalities necessary in business letters, such as an inside address, salutation, complimentary close, or signature line, as discussed in Chapter 4 (see pp. 76–80).

Basically, the memo consists of two parts: the identifying information at the top and the message itself. The identifying information includes these easily recognized parts: **To, From, Date,** and **Subject** lines.

TO: Aileen Kelly, Chief Computer Analyst
FROM: Stacy Kaufman, Operator, Level II
DATE: January 30, 2006
SUBJECT: Progress report on the fall schedule

You can use a memo template in your word processing program that will list these headings, as follows, to save time.

TO:
FROM: Linda Cowan
DATE: October 4, 2006
RE: (Enter subject here.)

On the **To** line, type the name and job title of the individual(s) who will receive your memo or a copy of it. If your memo is going to more than one reader, make sure you list your readers in the order of their status in your company or agency, as Mike Gonzalez does in Figure 3.3 (according to company policy the vice president's name appears before that of the public relations director). If you are on a first-name basis with the reader, use just his or her first name, as in Figure 3.1. Otherwise, include the reader's first and last names.

On the **From** line, type your name (use your first name only if your reader refers to you by it) and your job title (unless it is unnecessary for your reader). Some writers handwrite their initials after their typed name to verify that the message comes from them.

On the **Subject** line, type the purpose of your memo. The subject line serves as the title of your memo; it summarizes your message. Vague subject lines, such as "New Policy," "Operating Difficulties," or "Shareware," do not identify your message precisely and may suggest that your message is not carefully restricted or developed. "Shareware," for example, does not tell readers if your memo will discuss new equipment, corporate arrangements, or vendors; offer additional or fewer benefits; or warn employees about abusing the system. Note how Mike Gonzalez's subject line in Figure 3.3 is so much more precise than just saying "Ramco's Community Involvement."

On the **Date** line, do not simply name the day of the week—Friday. Give the full calendar date—June 4, 2007.

Memo Style and Tone

The style and tone of your memos will be controlled by the audience within your company or agency. When writing to a co-worker whom you know well, you can adopt a casual, conversational tone. You want to be seen as friendly and cooperative. In fact, to do otherwise would make you look self-important, stuffy, or hard to work with. Consider the friendly tone appropriate for one colleague writing to another in Roger's memo to Lucy in Figure 3.1. Note how he ends in a polite but informal way.

When writing a memo to a manager, though, you want to use a more formal tone than when communicating with a co-worker or peer. Your boss will expect you to show a more respectful, even official, posture. See how formal yet conversationally persuasive Mike Gonzalez's memo to his bosses is in Figure 3.3. His tone and style are a reflection of his hard work as well as his courtesy to his employer. Here are two ways of expressing the same message, the first more suitable when writing to a co-worker and the second more appropriate for a memo to the boss.

> **Co-worker:** I think we should go ahead with Marisol's plan for reorganization. It seems like a safe option to me, and I don't think we can lose.
>
> **Boss:** I think that we should adopt the organizational plan developed by Marisol Vega. Her recommendations are carefully researched and persuasively answer all the questions our department has about solving the problem.

When a boss writes to workers informing them about policies or procedures, as Janet Hempstead does in Figure 3.2, the tone of the memo is official and straightforward. Yet even so, Hempstead takes into account her readers' feelings (she does not blame) and safety, which are at the forefront of her rhetorical purpose.

Finally, remember that your employer and co-workers deserve the same clear and concise writing and attention to the "you attitude" (see Chapter 4, pp. 80–85) that your customers do. Memos require the same care and should follow the same rules of effective writing as letters do.

Strategies for Organizing a Memo

Organize your memos so that readers can find information quickly and act on it promptly. For longer, more complex communications, such as the memos in Figures 3.2 and 3.3, your message might be divided into three parts: (1) introduction, (2) discussion, and (3) conclusion. Regardless of how short or long your memo is, recall the three *P*'s for success—*p*lan what you are going to say; *p*olish what you wrote before you send it; and *p*roofread everything.

Introduction

The introduction of your memo should do the following:

- Tell readers clearly about the problem, procedure, question, or policy that prompted you to write.
- Explain briefly any background information the reader needs to know.
- Be specific about what you are going to accomplish in your memo.

Do not hesitate to come right out and say: "This memo explains new e-mail security procedures" or "This memo summarizes the action taken in Evansville to reduce air pollution."

Discussion

In the discussion section (the body) of your memo, help readers in these ways:

- State why a problem or procedure is important, who will be affected by it, and what caused it and why.
- Indicate why changes are necessary.
- Give precise dates, times, locations, and costs.

See how Janet Hempstead's memo in Figure 3.2 carefully describes an existing problem and explains the proper procedure for cleaning the brake machines.

Conclusion

In your conclusion, state specifically how you want the reader to respond to your memo. To get readers to act appropriately, you can do one or more of the following:

- Ask readers to call you if they have any questions, as in Figure 3.2.
- Request a reply—in writing, over the telephone, via e-mail, or in person—by a specific date, as in Figures 3.1 and 3.3.
- Provide a list of recommendations that the readers are to accept, revise, or reject, as in Figures 3.1 and 3.3.

Organizational Markers

Throughout your memo use the following organizational markers, where appropriate:

- **Headings** organize your work and make information easy for readers to follow, as in Figure 3.3.
- **Numbered** or **bulleted lists** help readers see comparisons and contrasts readily and thereby comprehend your ideas more quickly, as in Figure 3.1.
- **Underlining** or **boldfacing** emphasize key points (see Figure 3.2). Do not overuse this technique; draw attention only to main points and those that contain summaries or draw conclusions.

Organizational markers are not limited to memos; you will find them in e-mail, letters, and reports as well. (See Chapter 6, pp. 160–69.)

Faxes

Even though you may use e-mail extensively, fax (facsimile) machines are still in widespread use in the world of work. A fax machine sends copies of letters, memos, reports, graphs, blueprints, and artwork over ordinary phone lines. You also can send graphics that resemble actual photos. Faxes are especially effective if you have to make a few changes in a detailed document (for example, a contract or a boilerplate) and do not want to rekey or transmit the entire work. Unlike e-mails, faxes provide a signature authorization and give recipients a hard copy.

When you send a fax, be sure to use a fax cover sheet, which lists the persons sending and receiving the fax; their addresses, and phone and fax numbers; and the total number of pages being faxed. This last information is essential so that the recipient will know when the transmission is complete and can alert the sender of any interruption or omission during transmission.

Be aware that, unless the recipient has her or his own secured fax machine, your confidentiality is not easily protected when communicating by fax. If your fax is sent to a machine available to the entire office staff, anyone can read it.

Fax Guidelines

When you send a fax, observe the following guidelines:

1. As a courtesy, e-mail or call your reader ahead of time to let him or her know you are sending a fax.
2. Because the type size of a document generally is reduced during transmission, print your fax message in a larger point size (12 or 14).
3. Avoid writing any comments at the very top or bottom of a fax. Your notes might be cut off or blurred in transmission.
4. Make sure the document you are faxing is clear, but always include your phone and fax numbers in case the recipient needs to verify your message or has questions about it.
5. Be careful about sending anything longer than three to four pages. You might tie up the recipient's phone line. For a longer document, call before you fax to see whether the recipient will allow you to fax or would prefer that you send it another way.

E-Mails

E-mail is the most common workplace communication. It is the lifeblood of almost any business or organization because it expedites communications within your firm as well as communications with those outside it. Professionals in the world of work may receive hundreds of e-mails a day from supervisors, colleagues, clients, and a host of vendors and suppliers. Moreover, you can send a variety of documents via e-mail, including memos; pictures; video clips; soundbites; and various tables, lists, and statistical files.

Business E-Mail versus Personal E-Mail

E-mail is the most informal, relaxed type of business correspondence, far more so than a printed memo, letter, short report, or proposal. (However, as we shall see in Chapter 4, e-mail should never be sent in place of a formal letter.) Think of business e-mail as a polite, informative, and professional phone conversation—friendly, to the point, and always accessible. Yet, even though business e-mail is basically informal and casual, its informality does not mean you can forget about your responsibilities as a careful, cautious, and courteous writer.

The e-mail you write on the job will require things from you as a writer that your personal e-mail may not. You cannot be a sloppy, unorganized writer. You will have to follow all of the rules of proper spelling, capitalization, punctuation, and word choice, plus those guidelines spelled out specifically for e-mail in the next section. Proofread your e-mail and make sure all names are spelled correctly; use your spell-checker. Business e-mail should be much more professional than the instant messaging you may do with friends.

Unlike your personal e-mail, your business e-mail must take into account the impact such a communication will have on your company and on your career. When you send a business e-mail, you are representing more than just yourself and your preferences, as you do in a personal e-mail. You are speaking on behalf of your employer.

The workplace has rules that govern what you can put in an e-mail and to whom you can send it. Employers own their internal e-mail systems and thus have the right to monitor what you write and to whom. Any e-mail at work can be saved, stored, forwarded, and, most significantly, intercepted. You could even be fired for writing an angry or abusive e-mail. Always remember your e-mail could be forwarded to people you did not intend to send it to. Figures 3.4 and 3.5 are examples of effectively written business e-mails. Notice that e-mail can be cordial without being unprofessional.

FIGURE 3.4   An example of an effectively written business e-mail.

Subject:	**Status of Hinson-Davis Order**
Date:	Tuesday, 27 July 2006 9:38:35-0400
From:	peter.zacharias@craftworks.com
To:	marge.parish@craftworks.com

At last the Hinson-Davis Company received its order, and they are very pleased with our service. Victor Arana, their district manager, just called me to say the order came in at 9:00 a.m. and by 9:15 it was up on their systems.

Things could not have gone smoother. Congrats to all.

I am going to send Arana a thank you letter today to keep up the goodwill.

FIGURE 3.5   E-mail sent to a distribution list of co-workers.

Subject: **Collaboration on annual report**
Date: 19 June 2006 13:18:33-0400
From: melinda.bell@netech.com
To: annulla.cranston@netech.com; peter.hwang@netech.com;
          margaret.habermas@netech.com; a.pena@netech.com

To follow up on our conversation yesterday regarding working together on
this year's annual report, I'm glad our schedules are flexible. I've checked our
calendars and we are all available next Tuesday the 24th at 10:30 a.m. Let's
meet in Conference Room 410.

Don't forget we have to draft a two- to three-page overview first that
explains Northeast's strategic goals and objectives for fiscal year 2007. Not
an easy assignment, but we can do it, gang.

It would be a big help if Annulla would bring copies of the reports for the last
three years. Would Peter call Ms. Jhandez in Engineering for a copy of the
speech she gave last month to the Powell Chamber of Commerce? If memory
serves me correctly, she did a first-rate job summarizing Northeast's
accomplishments for 2005. Thanks for all your splendid work, team.

Melinda Bell
Director, Marketing
New Tech
melinda.bell@netech.com
FAX: (603) 555-2162
Voice: (603) 555-1505

Guidelines for Using E-Mail

Using e-mail technology at work obligates you to prepare and organize your messages carefully with your specific reader's needs in mind as well as those of his or her company and your own. Your e-mail at work must be professional, clear, concise, and well written. Following the guidelines here will help you to write effective e-mail messages.

1. **Make sure your e-mail is confidential, ethical, and safe.**

   a. Do not use business e-mail for personal messages.
   b. Never attack your employer, a customer, or a colleague.
   c. Do not spread gossip.
   d. Avoid *flaming,* that is, using strong, angry language that mocks, attacks, or insults your reader, as in Figure 3.6 (p. 67). Abusive and obscene language has no place in the world of work.
   e. Send nothing through e-mail that you would not want to see on the front page of your newspaper.
   f. Always use an anti-virus program.

2. **Observe all of the legal (proprietary) requirements when using e-mail.**

   a. Use quotation marks to indicate words that are not yours and give a source.
   b. Do not forward a co-worker's or boss's e-mail unless they approve.
   c. Do not refer readers to another document and ask them to copy it without the writer's permission.
   d. Do not change the wording of a message that you are expected simply to read and then forward.
   e. Print e-mails that are necessary for further use in a talk or report, those that contain specific directions that you may have to refer to again, or those where you have to establish or maintain a paper trail.

3. **Use an acceptable format.**

   Since most e-mail is read on-line rather than in hard copy, take into account how your message will look on a screen and what special considerations your on-line reader deserves.

   a. Make your e-mail easy to read.

   - Do not send e-mail in all capital letters. It's hard to read and looks as if you are shouting. It also looks unprofessional.
   - Break your message into paragraphs. A screen filled with one long unbroken paragraph is intimidating. Consider numbering your paragraphs.
   - Watch the length of your paragraphs. Keep them to three or four lines and double-space between them.
   - Avoid using boldface, asterisks, italics, and underlining, which may not be readable by your recipient's e-mail, thus potentially garbling or distorting your message.

b. Make your e-mail easy to process.

- Include all parts of your message—correct address, subject line, date, and so on.
- Get to the point right away. Because your readers receive vast amounts of e-mail, they may look only at the first few lines you write.
- Use a concise (three- or four-word), direct subject line. Avoid vague one-word subjects. A subject line like "Bill" would leave your reader wondering if your e-mail is about a person, an unpaid account, or a notice just sent.
- Include a *signature block* with your name, company affiliation, title, address, and phone numbers, especially on e-mails sent outside your company.

Marsala Cooper
Senior Sales Rep.
RTS Technologies
Mcooper@RTS.com
Voice (708) 555-1970 Fax (708) 555-1997

4. Follow all of the rules of netiquette when answering e-mail.

a. Respond promptly to your e-mail.

- Check your mail several times each day—don't let it build up in your in-box.
- Reply the same day, if possible. Let correspondents know you received their messages and when you will respond if you can't do so immediately.
- If you receive a lot of messages, prioritize them so that you reply to the boss first and to others later.
- If you expect a delay in getting information, tell the correspondent how long it will be before you can respond.
- If you are off-line, use your e-mail software's **auto-reply feature** to send back a message to that effect (and indicate when you will return) to each correspondent.
- Keep your address book up to date.

b. Identify your audience correctly.

- Send your e-mail to the right address (is it an individual or a group?).
- Verify if your reader wants unsolicited mail, or **spam**—people do not like spam. (Never e-mail an advertisement, story, or joke unless the recipient welcomes them.)
- Learn all you can about your reader to facilitate shaping the tone of your mail to his or her needs; judge how much information the reader needs.
- Do not inflate your distribution list. Send messages only to readers who need them (e.g., scheduling a meeting, as in Figure 3.5). Managers dislike being included on unnecessary distribution lists because it wastes their time.

c. Be courteous to your reader.

- Don't send the same message over and over (just as you would not send hard copies or faxes of the same information repeatedly).

- Respect the cultural traditions of non-native speakers of English. (See Chapter 4, pp. 106–12.) Do not use first names unless the reader approves, and avoid jokes and slang.
- Delete long lists of previous messages that may appear when you reply to a message so that the reader won't have to waste time scrolling to find your message, or put your message first if you are forwarding something.
- Choose the NewMessage option to avoid sending old news again and again.
- Do not send long attachments or graphics files without obtaining recipients' permission. Such messages may be difficult to read onscreen or use a lot of memory. If your message is long, consider sending it as an attachment.

5. **Follow a professional style.**

   a. Keep your message concise.

   - Cut wordy phrases. See how many words you can eliminate without distorting your message.
   - Don't turn your e-mail into a telegram. "Report immediately: need for meeting" makes you sound discourteous and demanding. Likewise, responding with only a "Yes" or "No" is discourteous. Save "Yeah," "Nope," and "Huh" for your personal e-mails.
   - Send only the information needed to answer the reader's questions or concerns. Exclude nonessential details and chatter

   b. Avoid abbreviations (e.g., BAK, back at keyboard; OTOH, on the other hand), catchwords, or phrases people outside your office might not understand or appreciate.

   c. Do not use slang or jargon unless it is appropriate for the context and your audience.

   d. Be careful about including **emoticons** (e.g., happy [:-)], or sad [:-( ] faces) made with punctuation marks and letters to indicate the emotional response you want to convey to the reader. When you use such notations, you run the risk of the reader not understanding your humor or not approving of it.

   e. End your message politely. Let the reader know you appreciate and welcome his or her help.

Figure 3.6 shows an example of a poorly written e-mail that violates many of the preceding guidelines. Figure 3.7 (p. 68) contains an effective revision that reflects the professional and courteous way the writer and his company do business.

E-Mail versus Other Types of Business Communications

Table 3.1 compares and contrasts the function, scope, and format of e-mail with memos and letters. Note that e-mails are brief, informal, and to-the-point messages that should never take the place of far more formal and official documents. Keep this table in mind as you learn more about various types of letters, including business letters and job application letters, in the following chapters.

FIGURE 3.6   A poorly written e-mail, with annotations.

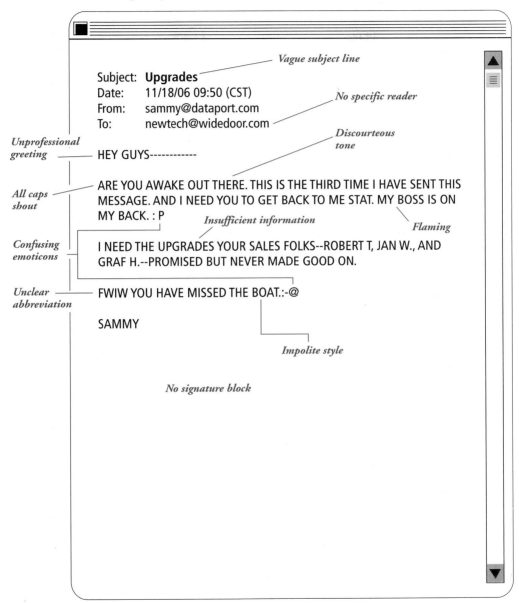

FIGURE 3.7   A revised, effective version of the poor e-mail in Figure 3.6.

Subject: **Upgrades for service contract #4552**
Date: 11/18/06
From: sammy@dataport.com
To: MWood@widedoor.com

Hello, Mary:

I would appreciate your delivering the upgrades for our service contract
#4552 by Monday afternoon, the 22nd of November, if at all possible.

We need to proceed to the next phase of our operation and the upgrades are
crucial to that task.

I am attaching a copy of our service agreement with NewTech for your
convenience.

If you run into any problem with the delivery date, please give me a call this
afternoon or e-mail me.

Thanks,

Sammy

                    Samuel Atherton
                    Operations Assistant
                    Data Port
                    4300 Morales Highway
                    San Padre, CA 95620-0326
                    Voicemail: 723-555-1298
                    http://dataport.com

TABLE 3.1   The Uses of E-Mail versus Memos or Letters

	E-Mail	Memo	Letter
Brief messages	X	X	
Informal	X	X	
Formal			X
Legal record		X	X
Relaxed tone	X	X	
Confidential material		X	X
Multiple pages			X
Reports		X	X
In-house messages	X	X	
Proofreading	X	X	X

✓ Revision Checklist

Memos

❑ Used appropriate and consistent format.
❑ Announced purpose of memo early and clearly.
❑ Organized memo according to reader's need for information, with main ideas up front; supplied clear conclusion.
❑ Made style and tone of memo suitable for audience.
❑ Included bullets, lists, underscoring where necessary to reflect logic and organization of memo and for ease of reading.
❑ Refrained from overloading reader with unnecessary details.

Faxes

❑ Verified reader's fax number.
❑ Sent cover sheet with number of pages faxed and phone number to call in the event of transmission trouble.
❑ Enlarged font to minimize reduction of type in transmission.
❑ Excluded anything confidential or sensitive if reader's fax machine is not secure.
❑ Promptly returned any calls regarding transmission difficulties with fax.

E-Mails
- ❑ Did not send unsolicited mail.
- ❑ Sent to reader's correct address.
- ❑ Formatted e-mail with acceptable margins and spacing.
- ❑ Observed netiquette, especially by avoiding flaming.
- ❑ Wrote a message rather than returning sender's message with a short reply.
- ❑ Kept paragraphs short but used full—not telegraphic—sentences.
- ❑ Avoided unfamiliar abbreviations or terms that would cause reader confusion.
- ❑ Received permission to repeat or incorporate another person's e-mail.
- ❑ Observed all legal obligations in using e-mail.
- ❑ Safeguarded employer's confidentiality and security by excluding sensitive or privileged information.
- ❑ Included enough information for reader's purpose.
- ❑ Honored reader by observing proper courtesy.
- ❑ Began with friendly greeting; ended politely.

Exercises

1. Write a memo to your boss saying that you will be out of town two days next week and three days the following week for **one** of the following reasons: (a) to inspect some land your firm is thinking of buying, (b) to investigate some claims, (c) to look at some new office space for a branch your firm is thinking of opening in a city five hundred miles away, (d) to attend a conference sponsored by a professional society, or (e) to pay calls on customers. In your memo, be specific about dates, places, times, and reasons.

2. Write an e-mail to a business that provides daily or weekly information to interested customers and submit its response along with your e-mail request to your instructor. Choose one of the following:
   a. an airline: an up-to-date schedule along a certain route and information about any bonus-mile or discount programs
   b. a catalog order company: information about any weekly specials for Net users
   c. a stock brokerage firm: free quotes or research about a particular stock
   d. a resort: special rates for a given week

3. Write an e-mail with one of the following messages, observing the guidelines discussed in this chapter.
   a. You have just made a big sale and you want to inform your boss.
   b. You have just lost a big sale and you have to inform your boss.
   c. Tell a co-worker about a union meeting.

d. Notify a company to cancel your subscription to one of its publications because you find it to be dated and no longer useful in your profession.

e. Request help from a listserv about research for a major report you are preparing for your employer.

f. Advise your district manager to discontinue marketing one of the company's products because of poor customer acceptance.

g. Send a short article (about 200 words) to your company newsletter about some accomplishment your office, department, or section achieved during the last month.

h. Write to a friend studying finance at a German, Korean, or South American university about the biggest financial news in your town or neighborhood in the last month.

4. Rewrite the following e-mail to make it more suitable.

Hi——

This new territory is a pain. Lots of stops; no sales. Ughhhh. People out here resistant to change. Could get hit by a boulder and still no change. Giant companies ought to be up on charges. Will sub. reports asap as long as you care rec.

The long and short of it is that market is down. No news=bad news.

5. Send your instructor an e-mail message about the project you are now working on for class, outlining your progress and describing any difficulties you are having.

6. You have just missed work or a class meeting. E-mail your employer or your instructor explaining the reason and indicate how you intend to make up the work.

Writing Letters

Letters are among the most important and official writing you will do on your job. Businesses take letter writing very seriously, and employers will expect you to prepare and respond to your correspondence effectively. Your signature on a letter tells readers you are accountable for everything in it. The higher up the corporate ladder you climb, the more letters you will be expected to write. Because letter writing is so significant to your career, this chapter introduces you to the entire process, provides guidelines and problem-solving strategies, and shows you how to prepare the most frequent types of business letters. It also shows you how to write for international readers.

Letters in the Age of the Internet

Even in this age of electronic communications, letters are still vital for the following reasons.

1. Letters represent your company's public image and your competence. A firm's corporate image is on the line when it sends a letter. Carefully written letters can create goodwill; poorly written letters can anger customers, cost your company business, and project an unfavorable image of you.

2. Letters are far more formal—in tone and structure—than any other type of business communication. Memos and e-mail are the least formal communications.

3. Letters constitute an official legal record of an agreement. They state, modify, or respond to a business commitment. When sent to a customer, a signed letter constitutes a legally binding contract. Be absolutely sure that what you put in a letter about prices, warranties, equipment, delivery dates, and/or other issues is accurate. Your reader can hold you and your company to such written commitments.

4. Unlike e-mail, many businesses require letters to be routed through channels before they are sent out. Because they convey how a company looks and what it offers to customers, letters often must be approved at a variety of corporate levels.

5. Letters are more permanent than e-mails. They provide a documented hard copy. Unlike e-mails that can be erased, letters are often logged in, filed, and bear a written authorized signature; they are far more confidential.

6. A letter is still the official and expected medium through which important documents and attachments (contracts, specifications, proposals) are sent to readers. Sending such attachments via e-mail or with a memo lacks the formality and respect readers deserve.

7. A letter is still the most formal and approved way to conduct business with many international audiences. These readers see a letter as more polite and honorable than an e-mail for initial contacts and even for subsequent business communications.

Letter Formats

Letter format refers to the way in which you print a letter—where you indent and where you place certain kinds of information. Several letter formats exist. Two of the most frequently used business letter formats are full-block and modified.

Full-Block Format

In the full-block format all information is flush against the left margin, with spaces between paragraphs. Figure 4.1 (p. 75) shows a full-block letter. Use this format only when your letter is on **letterhead stationery** (specially printed giving a company's name and logo, business and Web addresses, fax and telephone numbers, and sometimes the names of executives).

Modified Format

The modified style (Figure 4.2, p. 76) positions the writer's address (if it is not imprinted on a letterhead), date, complimentary close, and signature to the right side of the letter. The date aligns with the complimentary close, and notations of any enclosures with the letter are flush left below the signature. Paragraphs in the modified style can be indented as in the figure, or not.

Continuing Pages

To indicate subsequent pages if your letter runs beyond one page, use one of these conventions. Note the use of the recipient's name.

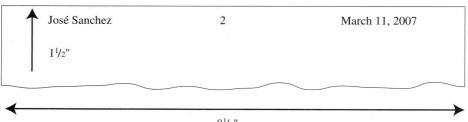

2
A.D. Smith
October 15, 2007

Guidelines on Printing Your Letters

Here are a few general hints about laying out and printing your letters.

- Single-space within each paragraph but always double-space between paragraphs.
- Leave margins of approximately 1 inch all around your type area (set 1-inch margins as the default on your PC). Leave more white space at the top of your letter than at the bottom, and watch the right margin in particular, since it is easy to exceed that limit. Shorter letters may require wider margins than longer letters, but generally don't exceed a margin of 1 inch on the right.
- Choose a type font that is inviting to the eye. Crowding too many letters on a line makes your letter difficult to read. You will not win any points from your readers if your letter looks cramped. Avoid script or other fancy type fonts (see Chapter 6, pp. 165–67).

Parts of a Letter

A letter contains many parts, each of which contributes to your overall message. The parts and their placement in your letter form the basic conventions of effective letter writing. Readers look for certain information in key places.

In the following sections, those parts of a letter marked with an asterisk should appear in every letter you write. Figure 4.3 (p. 77) is a sample letter containing all the parts discussed here. Note where each part is placed in the letter.

*Date Line

Spell out the name of the month in full—"September" or "March" rather than "Sept." or "Mar." The date line is usually keyboarded this way: November 12, 2005.

*Inside Address

The inside address, the same address as you put on the envelope, is always placed against the left margin, two lines below the date line. It contains the name, title (if any), company, street address, city, state, and ZIP code of the person to whom you are writing. Single-space the inside address and do not use any punctuation at the end of the lines.

Dr. Mary Petro
Director of Research
Midwest Laboratories
1700 Oak Drive
Rapid City, SD 56213-3406

FIGURE 4.1   Full-block letter format.

Nevada Insurance Research Agency
7500 South Maplewood Drive, Las Vegas, NV 89152-0026
(702) 555-9876 **http://www.NIRA.org**

April 6, 2006

Ms. Molly Georgopolous, C.P.A.
Business Manager
Meyers, Inc.
3400 South Madison Rd.
Reno, NV 89554-3212

Dear Ms. Georgopolous:

As I promised in our telephone conversation this afternoon, I am enclosing a study of the Nevada financial responsibility law. I hope that it will help you prepare your report.

I wish to emphasize again that probably 95 percent of all individuals who are involved in an accident do obtain reimbursement for hospital and doctor bills and for damages to their automobiles. If individuals have insurance, they can receive reimbursement from their own carrier. If they do not have insurance and the other driver is uninsured and judged to be at fault, the State Bureau of Motor Vehicles will revoke that party's driver's license and license plates until all costs for injuries and damages are paid.

Please call me again if I can help you.

Sincerely yours,

Carmen Tredeau

Carmen Tredeau, President

CT/IMB

Encl.

All printing lined up against the left-hand margin

Bradley Fuller, CPCU	Carmen Tredeau, CPCU	Theodore Kendrick	Iping Li, CPCU	Dora Salinas-Diego, CPCU
Chairperson	President	Vice President	Vice President	Vice President
		Public Affairs	Research	Actuary

FIGURE 4.2   Modified letter format.

Arthur T. McCormack

7239 East Daphne Parkway, Mobile, AL   36608-1012

Date is indented.   September 30, 2007

Mr. Travis Boykin, Manager
Scandia Gifts
703 Hardy St.
Hattiesburg, MS 39401-4633

Dear Mr. Boykin:

I would appreciate knowing if you currently stock the Crescent
pattern of model 5678 and how much you charge per model
number. I would also like to know if you have special prices per
box order.

The name of your store is listed in the Annual Catalog as the
closest distributor of Copenhagen products in my area. Would you
please give me directions to your shop from Mobile and the hours
you are open?

I look forward to hearing from you.

                                        Sincerely yours,

Complimentary
close and writer's
name are indented.   Arthur T. McCormack

Arthur.McCormack@Widedor.com

FIGURE 4.3   A sample letter, full-block format, with all parts labeled.

M& **Madison and Moore, Inc.**
Professional Architects

7900 South Manheim Road   *Letterhead*
Crystal Springs, NE 71003-0092
Phone 402-555-2300   **http://www.MMI.com**

Date line   March 12, 2007

Inside   Ms. Paula Jordan
address   Systems Consultant
                Broadacres Development Corp.
                12 East River Street
                Detroit, MI 48001-0422

Salutation   Dear Ms. Jordan:

                Thank you for your letter of March 6, 2007. I have discussed your request
                with the officials in our planning department and have learned that the
                design modules we used are no longer available.

Body of   In searching through my files, however, I have come across the enclosed
letter   catalog from a California firm that might be helpful to you. This firm,
                California Concepts, offers plans very similar to the ones you are interested
                in, as you can tell from the design I checked on page 23 of their catalog.

                I hope this will help you and I wish you every success in your project.

Complimentary   Sincerely yours,
close

Company name   MADISON AND MOORE, INC.

Signature   *William Newhouse*

Writer's name   William Newhouse
and title   Office Manager

Enclosure   Encl.: Catalog
Copy to   cc: Planning Department

Always try to write to a specific person rather than just "Sales Manager" or "President." To find out the person's name, check previous correspondence, e-mail lists, the company's or individual's Web site, or call the company. Abbreviate only courtesy titles (Mr., Dr., Ms.).

The last line of the inside address contains the city, state, and ZIP code. Table 4.1 lists the official U.S. Postal Service abbreviations—two capital letters without periods—for the states and territories.

*Salutation

Begin with *Dear,* and then follow with a courtesy title, the reader's last name, and a colon (Dear Mr. Brown:). **Never use a comma for a formal letter.** Never use the sexist "Dear Sir," "Gentlemen," or "Dear Madam," and avoid the stilted "Ladies and Gentlemen" or "Dear Sir/Madam." (For a discussion of sexist language and how to avoid it, see Chapter 2, pp. 41–44.)

TABLE 4.1   U.S. Postal Service Abbreviations

U.S. State/ Territory	Abbreviation	U.S. State/ Territory	Abbreviation
Alabama	AL	Montana	MT
Alaska	AK	Nebraska	NE
American Samoa	AS	Nevada	NV
Arizona	AZ	New Hampshire	NH
Arkansas	AR	New Jersey	NJ
California	CA	New Mexico	NM
Colorado	CO	New York	NY
Connecticut	CT	North Carolina	NC
Delaware	DE	North Dakota	ND
District of Columbia	DC	Ohio	OH
Florida	FL	Oklahoma	OK
Georgia	GA	Oregon	OR
Guam	GU	Pennsylvania	PA
Hawaii	HI	Puerto Rico	PR
Idaho	ID	Rhode Island	RI
Illinois	IL	South Carolina	SC
Indiana	IN	South Dakota	SD
Iowa	IA	Tennessee	TN
Kansas	KS	Texas	TX
Kentucky	KY	Utah	UT
Louisiana	LA	Vermont	VT
Maine	ME	Virginia	VA
Maryland	MD	Virgin Islands	VI
Massachusetts	MA	Washington	WA
Michigan	MI	West Virginia	WV
Minnesota	MN	Wisconsin	WI
Mississippi	MS	Wyoming	WY
Missouri	MO		

Sometimes you may not be sure of the sex of the reader. There are women named Stacy, Robin, and Lee, and men named Leslie, Kim, and Kelly. If you aren't certain, you can use the reader's full name: "Dear Terry Banks." If you know the person's title, you might write "Dear Credit Manager Banks."

*Body of the Letter

The body of the letter contains your message. Some of your letters will be only a few lines long, while others may extend to three or more paragraphs. Keep your sentences short and try to hold your paragraphs to under six or seven lines.

In organizing the body of your letter, follow this plan:

- In your first paragraph tell readers why you are writing and why your letter is important to them. Acknowledge any previous correspondence or telephone calls early in the paragraph (see Figures 4.1 and 4.3).
- Put the most significant point of each paragraph first to make it easier for the reader to find. Never bury important ideas in the middle or at the end of your paragraph.
- In a second (or subsequent) paragraph, develop your message with factual support, the key details, and descriptions readers need.
- In your last paragraph, thank readers and be very clear and precise about what you want them to do. Let them know what will happen next, and when they will hear from you again, or any combination of those messages. Don't leave readers hanging.

*Complimentary Close

For most business correspondence, use one of these standard closes:

Sincerely,

Respectfully,

Sincerely yours,

Yours sincerely,

If you and your reader know each other well, you can use

Cordially,

Warmest regards,

Best wishes,

Regards,

But avoid flowery closes, such as

Forever yours,

Devotedly yours,

Faithfully yours,

Admiringly yours,

which belong in a romance novel, not a business letter.

*Signature

Allow four spaces so that your signature will not look squeezed in. Always sign your name in ink. An unsigned letter indicates carelessness or, worse, indifference toward your reader. A stamped signature tells readers you could not give them personal attention

Some firms prefer using their company name along with the employee's name in the signature section. If so, type the company name in capital letters two line spaces below the complimentary close and then sign your name. Add your title underneath your typed name. Here is an example:

Sincerely yours,

THE FINELLI COMPANY

Helen Stravopoulos

Helen Stravopoulos
Cover Coordinator

*Enclosure(s) Line

The enclosure line informs the reader that additional materials (such as brochures, diagrams, forms, contract(s), a proposal) accompany your letter.

Enclosure

Enclosures (2)

Encl.: 2000 Sales Report

*Copy Notation

The abbreviation *cc:* (carbon copy) or *pc:* (photocopy) informs your reader that a copy of your letter has been sent to one or more individuals.

cc: Service Dept.

cc: Janice Tukopolous
    Ivor Vas

Letters are copied and sent to third parties for two reasons: (a) to document a paper trail and (b) to indicate to other readers who else is involved. Professional courtesy dictates that you tell the reader if others will receive a copy of your letter.

Making a Good Impression on Your Reader

You have just learned about formatting and printing your letters. Now we turn to the content of your letter—what you say and how you say it. Writing letters means communicating to influence your readers, not to alienate or antagonize them. Keep in mind that writers of effective letters are like successful diplomats in that they represent both their company and themselves. You want readers to see you as courteous, credible, and professional.

First, put yourself in the reader's position. What kinds of letters do you like to receive: vague, impersonal, sarcastic, pushy, or condescending; or polite, businesslike, and considerate? If you have questions, you want them answered honestly, courteously, and fully.

To send such effective letters adopt the **you attitude;** in other words, signal to readers that they and their needs are of utmost importance. Incorporating the "you attitude" means you should be able to answer "Yes" to these two questions:

1. Will my readers receive a positive image of me?
2. Have I chosen words that convey both my respect for the readers and my concern for their questions and comments?

Figures 4.4 (p. 82) and 4.5 (p. 83) contain two versions of the same letter. Which one would you rather receive?

Guidelines for Achieving the "You Attitude"

As you draft and revise your work, pay special attention to the following four guidelines for making a good impression on your reader.

1. Never forget that your reader is a real person. Avoid writing cold, impersonal letters that sound as if they were form letters or voice mail instructions. Let the readers know that you are writing to them as individuals. This letter violates every rule of personal and personable communications.

> It has come to our attention that policy number 342q-765r has been delinquent in payment and is in arrears for the sum of $302.35. To keep the policy in force for the duration of its life, a minimum payment of $50.00 must reach this office by the last day of the month. Failure to submit payment will result in the cancellation of the aforementioned policy.

The example displays no sense of one human being writing to another, of a customer with a name, personal history, or specific needs. Revised, this letter contains the necessary personal (and human) touch.

> We have not yet received your payment for your insurance policy (#342q-765r). By sending us your check for $50.00 within the next two weeks, you will keep your policy in force and can continue to enjoy the financial benefits and emotional security it offers you.

The benefits to an individual reader are stressed, and the reader is addressed directly as a valued customer.

Don't be afraid of using "you" in letters. Readers will feel more friendly toward you and your message. Of course, no amount of "you's" will help if they appear in a condescending context, such as the letter in Figure 4.4.

2. Keep the reader in the forefront of your letter. Make sure the reader's needs control the tone, message, and organization of your letter—the essence of the "you attitude." Stress the "you," not the "I" or the "we." At the top of page 84 is a paragraph from a letter that forgets about the reader.

FIGURE 4.4   A letter lacking the "you attitude."

Brown County • Office of the Tax Assessor

County Building, Room 200, Ventura, Missouri 56780-0101

712-555-3000

February 5, 2006

Mr. Ted Ladner
451 West Hawthorne Lane
Morris, MO 64507-3005

Dear Mr. Ladner:

You have written to the wrong office here at the County Building. There
is no way we can attempt to verify the kinds of details you are demanding
from Brown County.

Simply put, by carefully examining the 2005 tax bill you said you
received, you should have realized that it is the Tax Collector's Office, not
the Tax Assessor's, that will have to handle the problem you claim exists.

In short, call or write the Tax Collector of Brown County.

Thank you!

Tracey Kowalski

Tracey Kowalski

http://www.browncounty.gov

FIGURE 4.5   A you-centered revision of Figure 4.4.

Brown County • Office of the Tax Assessor

County Building, Room 200, Ventura, Missouri 56780-0101

712-555-3000

February 5, 2006

Mr. Ted Ladner
451 West Hawthorne Lane
Morris, MO 64507-3005

Dear Mr. Ladner:

Thank you for writing about the difficulties you encountered with your
2005 tax bill. I wish I could help you, but it is the Tax Collector's Office
that issues your annual property tax bill. Our office does not prepare
individual homeowners' bills.

If you will kindly direct your questions to Paulette Sutton at the Brown
County Tax Collector's Office, County Building, Room 100, Ventura,
Missouri 56780-0100, I am sure that she will be able to assist you.
Should you wish to call her, the number is 458-3455, extension 212.

Respectfully,

Tracey Kowalski

Tracey Kowalski

http://www.browncounty.gov

Draft

```
I think that our rug shampooer is the best on the market. Our
firm has invested a lot of time and money to ensure that it is
the most economical and efficient shampooer available today.
We have found that our customers are very satisfied with the
results of our machine. We have sold thousands of these sham-
pooers, and we are proud of our accomplishment. We hope that
we can sell you one of our fantastic machines.
```

The draft spends its time on the machine, the company, and the sales success. Readers are interested in how *they* can benefit from the machine, not in how much profit the company makes from selling it.

To win the readers' confidence, show how and why they will find the product useful, economical, and worthwhile at home or at work. Here is a reader-centered revision.

Revision

```
Our rug shampooer would make cleaning your Comfort Rest Motel
rooms easier for you. It is equipped with a heavy-duty motor
that will handle your 200 rooms with ease. Moreover, that
motor will give frequently used areas, such as the lobby or
hallways, a fresh and clean look you want for your motel.
```

3. Be courteous and tactful. However serious the problem or the degree of your anger at the time, refrain from turning your letter into a punch sent through the mail. Don't inflame your letter or e-mail readers. (Review Figures 3.5 and 3.6.)

Be careful that you do not use your letter to vent your feelings. Do not fall victim to letter rage. A letter that insults, nags, or threatens is best left unsent. Follow the overnight rule: Let such letters sit until the next day, when you can rewrite them diplomatically. You and your boss will be happier with the revised letter, and your purpose will be better served.

Compare the following discourteous sentences with the courteous revisions.

Discourteous	Courteous Revision
We must discontinue your service unless payment is received by the date shown.	Please send us your payment by November 4 so that your service will not be interrupted.
The rotten sound card you installed caused all my trouble.	The trouble may be caused by a malfunctioning sound card.
You are sorely mistaken about the contract.	We are sorry to learn about the difficulty you experienced over the service terms in our contract.
The new laptop you sold me is third-rate and you charged first-rate prices.	Since the laptop is still under warranty, I hope you can make the repairs easily and quickly.
Needless to say, you have misread your warranty agreement.	Clause 17 of your warranty agreement does not cover the problem you have called to our attention.

It goes without saying that your suggestion is not worth considering.	It was thoughtful of you to send me your suggestion, but unfortunately we cannot implement it right now.

4. Don't sound pompous or bureaucratic. Write to your reader as if you were carrying on a professional conversation with her or him. A business letter should be upbeat, simple, and to the point. It needs to be reader-friendly and believable, not stuffy and overbearing.

Don't resort to using phrases that remind readers of "legalese"—language that smells of contracts, deeds, and stuffy rooms. In the following list, the words and phrases on the left are pompous expressions that have crept into letters for years; the ones on the right are contemporary equivalents.

Pompous	Contemporary
aforementioned	previously mentioned
as per your request	as you requested
at this present writing	now
I am in receipt of	I have
attached herewith	enclosed
I am cognizant of	I know
endeavor	try
forthwith	at once
henceforth	after this
hereafter, heretofore, hereby	(drop these three "h's" entirely)
immediate future	soon
in lieu of	instead of
pursuant	concerning
pending your reply	until I hear from you
per our conversation	when we spoke
remittance	payment
your letter arrived and I have same	I have your letter
under separate cover	I'm also sending you
the wherewithal	the way
this writer	I
we regret to inform you that	we are sorry that

Types of Business Letters

The following section discusses the common types of business correspondence that you will be expected to write on the job.

1. inquiry letters
2. special request letters
3. sales letters
4. customer relations letters
   a. follow-up letters
   b. complaint letters
   c. adjustment letters
   d. collection letters

These letter types involve a variety of formats, writing strategies, and techniques. Business letters can be classified as **positive, neutral,** or **negative,** depending on their message and the anticipated reactions of your audience. Inquiry and special request letters are examples of neutral letters. They carry neither good nor bad news; they simply inform, responding to routine correspondence.

- Neutral letters request specific information about a product or service, place an order, or respond to some action or question.
- Sales letters promoting a product carry good news, according to the companies that spend millions of dollars a year preparing them.
- Customer relations letters can be positive (responding favorably to a writer's request or complaint) or negative (refusing a request, saying no to an adjustment, denying credit, seeking payment, critiquing poor performance, or announcing a product recall).

Inquiry Letters

An inquiry letter asks for information about a product, service, or procedure. Businesses frequently exchange such letters. As a customer, you too have occasion to ask in a letter about a special line of products, the price, the size, the color, and delivery arrangements. The clearer your letter, the quicker and more helpful your answers are likely to be.

Figure 4.6 illustrates a letter of inquiry from Michael Ortega to a real-estate office managing a large number of apartment complexes. Note that it follows these five rules for an effective inquiry letter:

- states exactly what information the writer wants
- indicates clearly why the writer must have the information
- keeps questions short and to the point
- specifies when the writer must have the information
- thanks the reader

Had Michael Ortega simply written the following very brief letter to Acme, he would not have received information he needed about size, location, and price of apartments: "Please send me some information on housing in Roanoke. My family and I plan to move there soon."

Special Request Letters

Special request letters make a special demand, not a routine inquiry. For example, these letters can ask a company for information that you as a student will use in a paper, an individual for a copy of an article or a speech, or an agency for facts that your company needs to prepare a proposal or sell a product. The person or company being asked for help stands to gain no financial reward for supplying the information; the only reward is the goodwill a response creates.

FIGURE 4.6   A letter of inquiry.

Michael Ortega
403 South Main Street Kingsport, TN 37721-0217
mortega@erols.com

March 1, 2007

Mr. Fred Stonehill
Property Manager
Acme Property Corporation
Main and Broadway
Roanoke, VA 24015-1100

Dear Mr. Stonehill:

States precise request

Explains need for information

Please let me know if you will have any two-bedroom furnished apartments available for rent during the months of June, July, and August. I am willing to pay up to $650 a month plus utilities. My wife, one-year-old son, and I will be moving to Roanoke for the summer so I can take classes at Virginia Western Community College.

If possible, we would like to have an apartment that is within two or three miles of the college. We do not have any pets.

Specifies exact date when a reply is needed

I would appreciate hearing from you within the next two weeks. My e-mail address is mortega@erols.com, or you can call me at home (606-555-8957) any evening from 6 to 10 p.m.

Offers to confer with reader

If you have any suitable vacancies, we would be happy to drive to Roanoke to look at them and give you a deposit to hold an apartment. Thanks for your help.

Sincerely yours,

Michael Ortega

Michael Ortega

Make your request clear and easy to answer. Supply readers with an addressed, postage-paid envelope, an e-mail address, and fax and telephone numbers in case they have questions. But don't ask a company to fax a long document to you. It is discourteous to ask someone else to pay the fax charges for something you need. If you request information via e-mail, don't expect your reader to tie up computer lines by sending a lengthy attachment.

Follow these seven points when asking for information in a special request letter.

1. Make sure you address your letter to the right person.
2. State who you are and why you are writing—student doing a paper, employee compiling information for a report, and so on.
3. Indicate clearly your reason for requesting the information. Mention any individuals who may have suggested you write for help and information.
4. State precisely and succinctly the questions you want answered; list, number, and separate the questions.
5. Specify exactly when you need the information. Allow sufficient time—at least three weeks. Be reasonable; don't ask for the impossible.
6. Offer to forward a copy of your report, paper, or survey in thanks of the anticipated help.
7. Thank the reader for helping.

Figure 4.7 gives an example of a letter that uses the guidelines.

Sales Letters

A sales letter is written to persuade the reader to buy a product, try a service, support some cause, or participate in some activity. No matter what profession you have chosen, there will always be times you have to sell a product, a service, a community or charitable program, a point of view, or yourself!

The Four A's of Sales Letters

Successful sales letters follow a time-honored and workable plan—what can be called the "Four A's":

1. It gets the reader's *attention*—with a question or a how-to statement (e.g., we can show you how to save $1,000 on your next credit card purchase).

2. It highlights the product's *appeal*—emotionally or financially, or both.

3. It shows the customer the product's *application*—descriptions, special features, guarantees.

4. It ends with a specific request for *action*—call, visit, participate, return an order card.

These four goals can be achieved in fewer than four or five paragraphs. Look at the sales letter in Figure 4.8 in which these parts are labeled.

Do I Mention Costs?

As a general rule, do not bluntly state the cost. Relate prices, charges, or fees to the benefits provided by the services or products to which they apply. Let customers see how much they are getting for their money, as Cory Soufas does in paragraph 3

FIGURE 4.7   A special request letter.

1505 West 19th Street
Syracuse, NY 13206

phone 315-555-1214

February 5, 2007

Ms. Sharonda Aimes-Worthington
Research Director
Creative Marketing Associates
198 Madison Ave.
New York, NY 10016-0092

Dear Ms. Aimes-Worthington:

I am a sophomore at Monroe College in Syracuse and am writing a report on the topic "Internet Marketing Strategies for the Finger Lakes Region of New York" for my Marketing 340 class. I have learned a great deal from reading your article on Web designs and local economies that appeared in *Marketing for the Electronic Age* two years ago.

Given your extensive experience in using the Internet to promote regional businesses and tourism, I would be most grateful if you would share your responses to the following three questions with me:

1. What have been the most effective ways to design Web sites for a regional marketplace such as the Finger Lakes?

2. How can area chambers of commerce best provide links to area businesses to benefit both the local municipalities and businesses in the Finger Lakes area?

3. Which other regional area do you see having the same or very similar marketing goals and challenges as the Finger Lakes?

jkawatsu@webnet.com

Continued

FIGURE 4.7   (Continued)

Page 2

Even a few sentences for each question would be a big help. I would be happy to send you a copy of my report and will, of course, cite you and Creative Marketing Associates in my work.

Many thanks for any help. Because my paper is due by April 2, I would deeply appreciate having your answers within the next month so that I can include them. If you have any questions about my request, I would be happy to answer them.

Sincerely yours,

Julie Kawatsu

Julie Kawatsu

---

in Figure 4.8. Similarly, a dealer who installs steel shutters did not tell readers the exact price of the product but indicated in her sales letter that they will save money by buying it: "Virtually maintenance free, your Reel Shutters also offer substantial savings in energy costs by reducing your heat loss through radiation by as much as 65% . . . and that lowers your utility bills by 35%."

Customer Relations Letters

Much business correspondence deals explicitly with establishing and maintaining friendly working relations. Such correspondence, known as **customer relations letters,** sends readers good news or bad news, acceptances or refusals. Good news tells customers one or more of the following:

- You agree with them about a problem they brought to your attention.
- You are solving their problem exactly the way they want.
- You are approving their loan.
- You are grateful to them for their business.

Thank you letters, congratulations letters, and adjustment letters saying "Yes" with these messages are all examples of good news messages.

Bad news messages, however, inform readers that:

- You do not like their work or the equipment they sold you.
- You do not have the equipment or service they want or you cannot provide it at the price they want to pay.

FIGURE 4.8   A sales letter sent to a business reader.

Workwell Software
3700 Stewart Avenue   Chicago IL 60637-2210
Phone: (312) 555-3720 **Fax:** (312) 555-7601 **E-mail:** sales@workwell.com
http://www.workwell.com

October 1, 2006

Ali Jen
Circuit Systems
7 Tyler Place
Oklahoma City, OK 73101

Dear Ali Jen:

Gets reader's attention with a question Do you know how much money your company loses from repetitive strain injury? Each year employers spend millions of dollars on employee insurance claims because of back pains, fatigue, eye strain, and carpal tunnel syndrome.

Emphasizes the product's appeal **Workwell** can solve your problems with its easy-to-use Exercise Program Software that will automatically monitor the time employees spend at their computers and also measure keyboard activity. After each hour (or the specified number of keystrokes), **Workwell** software will take your employees through a series of exercises that will help prevent carpal tunnel syndrome and strains.

Shows specific application of the product **Workwell's Exercise Program Software** will not interfere with busy schedules. Each of the 27 exercises is demonstrated on screen with audio instructions. The entire program takes less than 3 minutes and *Links costs to benefits* is available for Windows 2000 and Windows XP. For only $1499.00, you can provide a networked version of this valuable software to all of your employees.

Ends with a call for action To make sure your employees stay at peak efficiency in a safe work environment, please call us at 1-800-555-WELL or contact us at **http://www.workwell.com** to order your software today.

Thank you,

Cory Soufas
Manager, Sales

- You cannot refund their purchase price or perform a service.
- You are raising their rent or not renewing their lease.
- You want them to pay what they owe you now.

Bad news messages often come to readers through complaint letters, adjustment letters that say "No," and collection letters.

Being Direct or Indirect

Not every customer relations letter starts by giving the reader the writer's main point, judgment, conclusion, or reaction. Whether you are sending good news or bad news, determine what to say and where. *Where you place your main idea is determined by the type of letter you are writing.* Good news messages require one tactic; bad news ones, another.

Good News Message

If you are writing a good news letter, use the direct approach. Start your letter with the welcome, pleasant news that the reader wants to hear. Don't postpone the opportunity to put your reader in the right frame of mind. Then provide any relevant supporting details, explanations, or commentary. Being direct is advantageous when you have good news to convey.

Bad News Message

If you have bad news to report, do *not* open your letter with it. Be indirect. Prepare your reader for the bad news; keep the tension level down. If you throw the bad news at your reader right away, you jeopardize the goodwill you want to create and sustain. Consider how you would react to a letter that begins with these slaps:

- "Your order cannot be filled."
- "Your application for a loan has been denied."
- "It is our unfortunate duty to report . . ."

Having been denied, disappointed, or even offended in the first sentence or paragraph, the reader is not likely to give you his or her attentive cooperation thereafter.

Notice how A. J. Griffin's bad news letter in Figure 4.9 curtly starts off with the bad news of a rent increase. Receiving such a letter, the owner of Flowers by Dan certainly could not be blamed for looking for a new place of business.

Compare the curt version of Griffin's letter in Figure 4.9 with his revised message in Figure 4.10 (p. 94). In the revised version, Griffin begins tactfully with pleasant, positive words designed to put his reader in a good frame of mind. Then Griffin gives some background information that the owner of Flowers by Dan can relate to. Griffin makes one more attempt to encourage Sobol to recall his good feelings about the Mall—last year they did not raise rents—before introducing the bad news of a rent increase. Even after giving the bad news, Griffin softens the blow by saying that the Mall knows it is bad news. Griffin's tactic here is to defuse some of the anger that Sobol will inevitably feel. Griffin then ends on a positive, upbeat note: a prosperous future for Flowers by Dan.

FIGURE 4.9   An ineffective bad news letter.

River Road Mall

December 1, 2005

Mr. Daniel Sobol
Flowers by Dan
Lower Level
River Road Mall

Dear Mr. Sobol:

This is to inform you of a rent increase. Starting next month your new rent will be $2,500.00, resulting in a 15 percent increase.

Please make sure that your January rent check includes this increase.

Sincerely yours,

A.J. Griffin

A. J. Griffin
Manager
ajg@rrdmall.com

300 First Street
Canton, Ohio 44701
(216) 555-6700
www.RRMall.com

FIGURE 4.10   A diplomatic revision of the bad news letter in Figure 4.9.

River Road Mall

December 1, 2005

Mr. Daniel Sobol
Flowers by Dan
Lower Level
River Road Mall

Dear Mr. Sobol:

It has been a pleasure to have you as a tenant at the Mall for two years, and we look forward to serving you in the future.

Over these last two years we have experienced a dramatic increase in costs at River Road Mall for security, maintenance, landscaping, pest control, utilities, insurance, and taxes. Last year we absorbed those increases and so did not have to raise your rent. Unfortunately, we find we cannot do it again for 2006, so regretfully we must increase your rent by 15 percent, to $2,500, effective January 1.

Although we do not like to raise rents, we also know that you do not want us to compromise on the quality of service that you and your customers expect and deserve.

Please let us know how we can assist you in the future. We wish you a very successful and profitable 2006. If you have any questions, please call or visit my office.

Cordially,

A. J. Griffin

A. J. Griffin
Manager
ajg@rrdmall.com

300 First Street
Canton, Ohio 44701
(216) 555-6700
www.RRMall.com

Follow-Up Letters

A follow-up letter is sent by a company after a sale to thank the customer for buying a product or using a service and to encourage the customer to buy more products and services in the future. A follow-up letter is a combination thank you note and sales letter. The letter in Figure 4.11 (p. 96) shows how an income tax preparation service attempts to obtain repeat business by doing the following:

1. begins with a brief and sincere expression of gratitude
2. discusses the benefits (advantages) already known to the customer and then transfers the firm's dedication to the customer from service to a continuing sales area
3. ends with a specific request for future business

Complaint Letters

Each of us, either as customers or businesspeople, at some time has been frustrated by a defective product, inadequate or rude service, or incorrect billing. When we get no satisfaction from calling an 800 number and are routed through a series of menu options, our frustration level goes up. Usually our first response is to write a letter dripping with juicy insults. But a hate letter, like a piece of flaming e-mail (see Figure 3.6, p. 67), rarely gets positive results.

A complaint letter is a delicate one to write. First off, avoid the following:

- name calling
- sarcasm
- insults
- threats
- anger
- unflattering clip art
- intimidating type fonts (e.g., all capital letters)

The key thing to keep in mind is that you can disagree without being disagreeable. Be rational, not hostile. Just to let off steam, you might want to write an angry letter but then tear it up, replacing all the heat with courteous and diplomatic language.

Establishing the Right Tone

A complaint letter is written for more reasons than just blowing off steam. You want some specific action taken. The "you attitude" is especially important here to maintain the reader's goodwill. An effective complaint letter can be written by an individual consumer or by a company. Figure 4.12 (p. 97) shows Michael Trigg's complaint about a defective fishing reel; Figure 4.13 (p. 98) expresses a restaurant's dissatisfaction with an industrial dishwasher.

Writing an Effective Complaint Letter

To increase your chances of receiving a speedy settlement, follow these five steps in writing your letter of complaint. They will help you build your case.

   1. **Begin with a detailed description of the product or service.** Give the appropriate model and serial numbers, size, quantity, color, and cost. Specify check and invoice numbers. Indicate when and where (specific address) you purchased it and also the

FIGURE 4.11   A follow-up letter to encourage repeat business.

Taylor Tax Service
Highway 10
North Jennings, TX 78326
phone (888) 555-9681 e-mail taylor@aol.com
http://www.taylor.com

December 3, 2005

Ms. Laurie Pavlovich
345 Jefferson St.
Jennings, TX 78326

Dear Ms. Pavlovich:

Thank you for using our services in February of this year. We were pleased to help you prepare your 2004 federal and state income tax returns. Our goal is to save you every tax dollar to which you are entitled. If you ever have questions about your return, we are open all year long to help you.

We are looking forward to serving you again next year. Several new federal tax laws, which go into effect January 1, will change the types of deductions you can declare. These changes might appreciably increase your refund. Our consultants know the new laws and are ready to apply them to your return.

Another important tax matter influencing your 2005 returns will be any losses you may have suffered because of the hailstorms and tornadoes that hit our area three months ago. Our consultants are specially trained to assist you in filing proper damage claims with your federal and state returns.

To make using our services even easier, we can help you file your tax return electronically to speed up any refund to which you are entitled. Please call us at (888) 555-9681 or e-mail us at **taylor@aol.com** in order to set up an appointment as soon as you have received all your forms. We are waiting to serve you six days a week from 9:00 a.m. to 9:00 p.m.

Sincerely yours,

TAYLOR TAX SERVICE

Demetrius Taylor

Demetrius Taylor

FIGURE 4.12   A complaint letter from a consumer.

17 Westwood Drive

Magnolia, MA 01930

mtrigg@roof.com

September 15, 2006

Mr. Ralph Montoya
Customer Relations Department
Smith Sports Equipment
P.O. Box 1014
Tulsa, OK 74109-1014

Dear Mr. Montoya:

On August 22, 2006, I purchased a Smith reel, model 191, at the Uni-Mart Store on Marsh Avenue in Magnolia. The reel sold for $54.95 plus tax. The reel is not working effectively, and I am returning it to you under separate cover by first-class mail.

I had made no more than five casts with the reel when it began to malfunction. The button that releases the spool and allows the line to cast will not spring back into position after casting. In addition, the gears make a grinding noise when I try to retrieve the line. Because of these problems, I was unable to continue my participation in the Gloucester Fishing Tournament last week.

I am requesting that a new reel be sent to me free of charge in place of the defective one I returned. I would also like to know what was wrong with the defective reel.

I would appreciate your processing my claim within the next two weeks.

Sincerely yours,

Michael Trigg

Michael Trigg

FIGURE 4.13   A complaint letter from a business.

Camerson and Dale, Sunnyside, California 91793-4116   213-555-7500

June 21, 2007

Priscilla Dubrow
Customer Relations Department
Superflex Products
San Diego, CA 93141-0808

Dear Ms. Dubrow:

On September 15, 2006, we purchased a Superflex industrial dishwasher, model 3203876, at the Hillcrest store at 3400 Broadway Drive in Sunnyside, for $5,000. In the last three weeks, our restaurant has had repeated problems with this machine. Three more months of warranty remain on the unit.

The machine does not complete a full cycle; it stops before the final rinsing and thus leaves the dishes dirty. It appears that the cycle regulators are not working properly because they refuse to shift into the next necessary gear. Attempts to repair the machine by the Hillcrest crew on June 3, 10, and 16 have been unsuccessful.

The Loft has been greatly inconvenienced. Our kitchen team has been forced to sort, clean, and sanitize utensils, dishes, pans and pots by hand, resulting in additional overtime. Moreover, our expenses for proper detergents have increased.

We want your main office to send another repair crew at once to fix this machine. If your crew is unable to do this, we want a discount worth the amount of the warranty life on this model to be applied to the purchase of a new Superflex dishwasher. This amount would come to $1,000, or 20 percent of the original purchase price.

So that our business is not further disrupted, we would appreciate your resolving this problem promptly within the next week.

Sincerely yours,

Emily Rashon

Emily Rashon
Manager

▼ Browse our menu, which changes daily, at www.theloft.com

remaining warranty. If you are complaining about a service, give the name of the company, the date of the service, the personnel providing it, and their exact duties.

2. State exactly what is wrong with the product or service. Precise information will enable the reader to understand and act on your complaint.

- How many times did the product work before it stopped?
- What parts were malfunctioning?
- What parts of a job were not done or were done poorly?
- When did all this happen?
- Where and how were you inconvenienced?

Stating that "the brake shoes were defective" tells very little about how long they were on your car, how effectively they may have been installed, or what condition they were in when they ceased functioning safely.

3. Briefly describe the inconvenience you have experienced. Show that your problems were directly caused by the defective product or service. To build your case, give precise details about the time and money you lost. Don't just say you had "numerous difficulties." Did you have to pay a mechanic to fix your car when it was stalled on the road? Did you have to buy a new printer or recording machine? Where appropriate, refer to any previous telephone calls, e-mails, or letters. Give the names of the people you have written to or spoken with and the dates.

4. Indicate precisely what you want done. Do not simply write that you "want something done." Indicate precisely that you want one or more of the following:

- your purchase price refunded
- your model repaired or replaced
- a completely new repair crew provided
- an apology from the company for discourteous treatment

5. Ask for prompt handling of your claim. Ask that an answer be provided to any question you may have (such as finding out where calls came from that you were billed for but did not make). You might even specify a reasonable time by which you want to hear from the reader or need the problem fixed. Note the last paragraph in Figure 4.13.

Adjustment Letters

Adjustment letters respond to complaint letters by telling customers dissatisfied with a product or service how their claim will be settled. Adjustment letters should reconcile the differences that exist between a customer and a firm and restore the customer's confidence in that firm.

Adjustment Letters That Tell the Customer "Yes"

It is easy to write if you remember a few useful suggestions. As with a good news message, start with the favorable news the customer wants to hear; that will put him or her in a positive frame of mind to read the rest of your letter. Let the customer know that you sincerely agree with him or her—don't sound as if you are reluctantly honoring the request.

The two examples of adjustment letters saying "Yes" show you how to write this kind of correspondence. The first example, Figure 4.14, says "Yes" to Michael Trigg's letter in Figure 4.12. You might want to reread the Trigg complaint letter to see what problems Ralph Montoya faced when he had to write to Mr. Trigg. The second example of an adjustment letter that says "Yes" is in Figure 4.15. It responds to a customer who has complained about an incorrect billing.

Writing a "Yes" Letter
The following four steps will help you write a "Yes" adjustment letter.

   1. Admit immediately that the customer's complaint is justified and apologize. Briefly state that you are sorry and thank the customer for writing to inform you.

   2. State precisely what you are going to do to correct the problem. Let the customer know that you will

- extend warranty coverage
- credit account with funds, more air miles, and soon
- offer discount on next purchase
- cancel a bill
- repair a damaged camera
- give the customer credit toward another purchase
- upgrade software

In Figure 4.14 Michael Trigg is told right away that he will receive a new reel; in Figure 4.15 Kathryn Brumfield learns in the first paragraph that she will not be charged for parts or service.

   3. Tell customers exactly what happened. They deserve an explanation for the inconvenience they suffered. Note that the explanations in Figures 4.14 and 4.15 (p. 101) give only the essential details; they do not bother the reader with side issues or petty remarks about who was to blame. Assure customers that the mishap is not typical of your company's operations.

   4. End on a friendly—and positive—note. Leave your customers with a good feeling about your company.

Adjustment Letters That Tell the Customer "No"
Writing to tell customers "No" is obviously more difficult than agreeing with them. You are faced with the sensitive task of conveying bad news, while at the same time convincing the reader that your position is fair, logical, and consistent. Do not bluntly start off with a "No." Do not accuse or argue. Avoid remarks that blame, scold, or remind customers of a wrongdoing.

How to Say "No" Diplomatically
The following five suggestions will help you say "No" diplomatically. Practical applications of these suggestions can be found in Figures 4.16 (p. 104) and 4.17 (p. 105). Contrast the refusal of Michael Trigg's complaint in Figure 4.16 with the favorable response to it in Figure 4.14.

FIGURE 4.14   An adjustment letter saying "Yes."

Smith Sports Equipment
P.O. Box 1014   Tulsa, Oklahoma 74109-1014
(918) 555-0164 ▪ www.smithsport.com

September 21, 2006

Mr. Michael Trigg
17 Westwood Drive
Magnolia, MA 01930

Dear Mr. Trigg:

Thank you for alerting us in your letter of September 15 to the problems
you had with one of our model 191 spincast reels. I am sorry for the
inconvenience the reel caused you. A new Smith reel is on its way to you.

We have examined your reel and found the problem. It seems that a
retaining pin on the button spring was improperly installed by one of our
new soldering machines on the assembly line. We have thoroughly
inspected, repaired, and cleaned the soldering machine to eliminate the
problem.

Since we began making quality reels in 1955, we have taken pride in
helping our customers who use a Smith reel. We hope that your new Smith
reel brings you years of pleasure and many good catches, especially next
year at the Gloucester Fishing Tournament.

Thank you for your business. Please let me know if I can assist you again.

Respectfully,

SMITH SPORTS EQUIPMENT

Ralph Montoya

Ralph Montoya, Manager
Customer Relations Department

FIGURE 4.15   An adjustment letter saying "Yes."

Brunelli Motors
- -
Route 3A, Giddings, Kansas 62034-8100 (913) 555-1521

October 5, 2007

Ms. Kathryn Brumfield
34 East Main
Giddings, KS 62034-1123

Dear Ms. Brumfield:

We appreciate your notifying us, in your letter of September 30, about the problem you experienced regarding warranty coverage on your new Phantom Hawk GT. The bills sent to you were incorrect, and I have canceled them. Please accept my apologies. You should not have been charged for a shroud or for repairs to the damaged fan and hose, since all those parts, and labor on them, are covered by warranty.

The problem was the result of an error in the way the charges were listed. Our firm has begun using new software to give customers better service, and the mechanic apparently entered the wrong code for your account. I have instructed our mechanics to double-check code numbers before submitting them to the Billing Department. We hope that this policy will help us serve you and our other customers more efficiently.

We value you as a customer of Brunelli Motors. When you are ready for another Phantom, I hope that you will once again visit our dealership.

Sincerely yours,

Susan Chee-Saafir

Susan Chee-Saafir
Service Manager

- -
Experience virtual reality: Drive a new Phantom at
http://www.brunelli.com

1. **Thank customers for writing.** Make a friendly start by putting them in a good frame of mind. Don't put readers on the defensive by starting off with "We regret to inform you." The letter writers in Figures 4.16 and 4.17 thank the customers for bringing the matter to their attention. As with other bad news letters, never begin with a refusal. You need time to calm and convince customers. Telling them "No" in the first sentence or two will negatively color their reactions to the rest of the letter. Use the indirect approach discussed earlier in the chapter (p. 92).

2. **State the problem so that the customer realizes you understand the complaint.** You thereby prove that you are not trying to misrepresent or distort what the customer has told you.

3. **Explain what happened with the product or service before you give the customer a decision.** Provide a factual explanation to show the customer that he or she is being treated fairly. Rather than focusing on the customer's misunderstanding the instructions or a failure to observe details of a service contract, state the proper ways of handling a piece of equipment.

> **Poor:** "By reading the instructions on the side of the paint can, you would have avoided the streaking condition that you claim resulted."
> **Better:** "Hi-Gloss Paint requires two applications, four hours apart, for a clear and smooth finish."

The better version reminds the customer of the right way to apply the paint without pointing an accusing finger. Note how the explanations in Figures 4.16 and 4.17 emphasize the right way of using the product.

4. **Give your decision without hedging.** Do not say, "Perhaps some type of restitution could be made later" or "Further proof would have been helpful." Indecision will infuriate customers who believe that they have already presented a sound, convincing case. Never apologize for your decision.

5. **Leave the door open for better and continued business.** Whenever possible, help customers solve their problem by offering to send them a new product or part and quote the full sales price. Note how the second-to-last paragraph in Figure 4.16 and the last paragraph in 4.17 do that diplomatically.

Collection Letters

Collection letters require the same tact and fairness as do complaint and adjustment letters. Each nonpayment case should be evaluated separately. A nasty collection letter sent to a customer who is a good credit risk after only one month's nonpayment can send the customer elsewhere. On the other hand, three easygoing letters to a customer who is a poor credit risk may encourage that individual to postpone payment, perhaps indefinitely.

Many businesses send several letters to customers before turning matters over to a collection agency. Each letter in the series employs a different technique, ranging from giving compliments and offering flexible credit terms to issuing demands for immediate payment and threats of legal consequences. One hospital uses the collection letters illustrated in Figures 4.18 (p. 107) and 4.19 (p. 108) to encourage ex-patients to pay their bills. Figure 4.18 is a letter sent early in the collection process when a client is

FIGURE 4.16   An adjustment letter saying "No."

Smith Sports Equipment

P.O. Box 1014   Tulsa, Oklahoma 74109-1014
(918) 555-0164 ▪ www.smithsport.com

September 21, 2006

Mr. Michael Trigg
17 Westwood Drive
Magnolia, MA 01930

Dear Mr. Trigg:

Thank you for writing to us on September 15 about the trouble you experienced with our model 191 spincast reel. We are sorry to hear about the difficulties you had with the release button and gears.

We have examined your reel and found the trouble. It seems that a retaining pin in the button spring was pushed into the side of the reel casing, thereby making the gears inoperable. The retaining pin is a vital yet delicate part of your reel. In order to function properly, it has to be pushed gently. Since the pin was not used in this way, we are not able to refund your purchase price.

We will be pleased, however, to repair your reel for $29.98 and return it to you for hours of fishing pleasure. Please let us know your decision.

I look forward to hearing from you.

Respectfully,

SMITH SPORTS EQUIPMENT

Ralph Montoya

Ralph Montoya, Manager
Customer Relations Department

FIGURE 4.17   Another adjustment letter saying "No."

Health AIR

4300 Marshall Drive
Salt Lake City, Utah 84113-1521
(801) 555-6028
www.healthair.com

August 19, 2007

Ms. Denise Southby, Director
Bradley General Hospital
Bradley, IL 60610-4615

Dear Director Southby:

Thank you for your letter of August 10 explaining the problems you have encountered with our Puritan MAII ventilator. We were sorry to learn that you were unable to get the high-volume PAO_2 alarm circuit to work.

Our ventilator is a high-volume, low-frequency machine that can deliver up to 40 ml of water pressure. The ventilator runs with a center of gravity attachment on the right side of the diode. The trouble you had with the high oxygen alarm system is due to an overload on your piped-in oxygen. Our laboratory inspection of the ventilator you returned indicated that the high-pressure system had blown a vital adaptor in the machine. Our company cannot be responsible for any overload caused by an oxygen system. We cannot, therefore, send you a replacement ventilator free of charge. Your ventilator is being returned to you by National Express.

We would, however, be pleased to send you another model of the adaptor, which would be more compatible with your system, as soon as we receive your order. The price of the adaptor is $600, and our factory representative will be happy to install it for you at no charge. Please let me know your decision.

Sincerely yours,

R. P. Gifford

R. P. Gifford
Customer Service Department

only a month or two late. The collection letter in Figure 4.19 is sent much later to a client who has ignored earlier notices.

The tone of Figure 4.18 is cordial and sincere—now is not the time to say "pay up or else." It stresses how valuable the person is and underscores how pleased the hospital is to have provided the care he needed. The last paragraph makes a request for payment, offering: (1) a flexible payment schedule and (2) an escape from the inconvenience (or embarrassment) of receiving past due notices. The bottom of the letter conveniently lists payment options available to the patient.

The late collection letter in Figure 4.19, on the other hand, points out that the time for concessions is over, and reminds the patient of all the efforts that the hospital has expended to collect its bills. Then it announces what consequences will result if he still does not pay.

Writing for International Readers

Electronic communications have made the world so compact that, in effect, we live and work in a global village. Companies today depend on international trade to stay in business. Many U.S. businesses are multinational corporations with sales branches, plants, and customers throughout the world. In fact, many businesses in the United States are themselves branches of international firms. To be successful in the workplace, you have to understand and respect cultural diversity.

As a result, don't presume that you will be writing to only those who speak English. As part of your job, you will very likely write to readers for whom English is not their first (or native) language; these individuals constitute a large and important audience of **non-native speakers of English,** and writing for them requires you to broaden your sense of audience analysis. Such an audience may reside in a foreign country or in the United States.

Companies frequently offer seminars to educate their employees to be sensitive to an audience's multicultural and multilingual background. Study Terri Ruckel's long report (pp. 272–90) to see how advantageous such training programs are to both the firms and their employees and clients who are non-native speakers of English.

Assessing Readers' Knowledge of English

Expect your international readers to have varying degrees of proficiency in English. Some readers will have an excellent command of American (or British) English; others will have only basic literacy in English. Do not necessarily conclude, however, that all your international contacts are non-native speakers of English. Many readers in Singapore, Malaysia, and India, for example, know English as their first language. They simply speak a dialect different from American Standard English. Keep in mind, too, that your reader may not speak any English at all but will rely on an English grammar book and a foreign language dictionary to translate your work.

You can expect to write a variety of documents to and for these readers—e-mails, reports, Web sites, product descriptions, proposals, even operating instructions. If you find the set of directions accompanying your computer or a software package confusing, imagine how much more intimidating such a document would be to a non-native speaker of English.

FIGURE 4.18   A first, or early, collection letter.

Sabine County Hospital
432 Washington St.
Sabine, TX 77231
512-555-6734
www.sabine.org

May 15, 2005

Re: Inpatient Services
Date of Hospitalization: March 11–12, 2005
Balance Due: $3,725.48

Dear Mr. Peterson:

We are grateful that we were able to serve your health care needs during your recent stay at Sabine County Hospital. It is our continuing goal to provide the best possible hospital care for residents of Sabine County and its vicinity. To do so we must keep our finances up to date.

Our records indicate that your account is now overdue, and that we have not received a payment from you for two months. If you have recently sent one in, kindly disregard this letter.

If for any reason you are unable to pay the full amount at this time, we will be happy to set up a payment schedule that is convenient for you. Just fill in the appropriate blanks below, and return this letter to us. That will enable us to avoid billing you on a "Past Due" basis. Thank you for your cooperation.

Sincerely,

Morris T. Jukes

Morris T. Jukes
Accounts Receivable Department

( ) I will pay $ _____ ( ) monthly; ( ) quarterly, on my account.

( ) Enclosed is a check for full payment in the amount of $ _____.

Signature

_____

FIGURE 4.19   A late, or final, collection letter.

Sabine County Hospital
432 Washington St.
Sabine, TX 77231
512-555-6734
www.sabine.org

September 21, 2005

Re: Inpatient Services
Date of Hospitalization: March 11–12, 2005
Balance Due: $3,725.48

Dear Mr. Peterson:

During the past few months we have written to you several times about your balance of $3,725.48 for services you received on March 11 and 12. Your account is now more than 190 days overdue, and we cannot allow any further extensions in receiving a payment from you.

As you will recall, we have tried to help you in any way we could to meet your obligations by offering several options for paying your bill. You could have arranged for installment payments that would be due each month or each quarter, whichever would be more convenient. Because you have not replied, we must ask for full payment at this time.

If we do not hear from you within ten days, we will have no alternative but to turn your account over to our collection agency, which will hurt your credit rating. Neither of us would find this a welcome alternative.

Sincerely,

Morris T. Jukes

Morris T. Jukes
Accounts Receivable Department

Guidelines for Communicating with International Readers

It would be impossible to give you information about how best to communicate with every audience; there are at least one hundred major languages representing diverse ethnic and cultural communities around the globe. You must keep in mind two crucial points:

1. You need to be aware of cultural differences between you and your reader.
2. The conventions of writing—the words, sentences, even the type of information you offer—can and do change from one culture to another.

The following eight guidelines will help you communicate more successfully with an international audience and significantly reduce the chances of their misunderstanding you.

1. Use common, easily understood vocabulary. Write basic, simplified English. Choose words that are widely understood as opposed to those that are not used or understood by many speakers. Avoid low-frequency words by substituting simpler synonyms; for example, use *stop*, not *refrain; prevent*, not *forestall; discharge*, not *exude; happy*, not *exultant.*

2. Avoid ambiguity. Words that have double meanings force non-native readers to wonder which one you mean. For example, "We fired the engine" would baffle your readers if they were not aware of the multiple meanings of *fire.* Unfamiliar with the context in which *fire* means "start up," a non-native speaker of English might think you're referring to "setting on fire or inflaming," which is not what you intend. Such misinterpretation is likely because most bilingual dictionaries would probably list only those two meanings.

3. Be careful about technical vocabulary. While a reader who is a non-native speaker may be more familiar with technical terms than with other English words, make sure the technical word or phrase you include is widely known and not a word or meaning used only at your plant or office. Double-check by consulting the most up-to-date manuals and guides in your field, but steer clear of technical terms in fields other than the one with which your reader is familiar. Be especially careful about using business words and phrases an international reader may not know, such as "lean manufacturing," "revolving credit," "prime rate," "amortization," and so forth.

4. Avoid idiomatic expressions. The following colorful idiomatic expressions will confuse and may even startle a non-native reader:

I'm all ears	check it out
throw cold water on it	sleep on it
hit the nail on the head	give a heads up to
get the dope on	land in hot water
easy come, easy go	touch and go
get a handle on it	pushed the envelope
right under your nose	it was a rough go

The meanings of those and similar phrases are not literal but figurative—a reflection of our culture, not necessarily your reader's. A non-native speaker of English will approach such phrases as combinations of the separate meanings of the individual words, not as a collective unit of meaning.

A non-native speaker of English—a potential customer in Asia or Africa, for example—might be shocked if you wrote about a sale concluded at a branch office this way: "Last week we made a killing in our office." Substitute a clear, unambiguous translation easily understood in international English: "We made a big sale last week." For "Sleep on it," you might say, "Please take a week or two to make your decision."

5. Delete sports and gambling metaphors. These metaphors, which are often rooted in American popular culture, do not translate word for word for non-native speakers and so again can interfere with communication with your readers. Here are a few examples to avoid:

out in left field	a ballpark figure
struck out	fumbled the ball
drop the ball	out of bounds
down for the count	made a pass
long shot	beat the odds

Use a basic English dictionary and your common sense to find nonfigurative translations for the preceding and similar expressions.

6. Watch units of measure. Do not fall into the cultural trap of assuming that your reader measures distances in miles and feet (instead of kilometers and meters as most of the world does), buys gallons of gasoline (instead of liters), and spends dollars (rather than euros, pesos, marks, rupees, or yen). Just as not everyone in the world uses 110/220 wiring, keep in mind that not everyone sees the world marketplace solely in terms of the U.S. economy. Adapt your message to the readers' practices.

7. Avoid culture-bound descriptions of place and space. For example, when you tell a reader in Hong Kong about the "Sunbelt" or a potential client in Africa about the "Big Easy," will he or she know what you mean? When you write from California to a non-native English speaker in India about the eastern seaboard, meaning the East Coast of the United States, the directional reference may not mean the same thing to your audience as it does to you. Be respectful of your readers' cultural (and physical) environment as well. Thanksgiving is celebrated in the United States in November, but in Canada the holiday is the second Monday in October; elsewhere around the world it may not be a holiday at all. Calling February a winter month does not make sense to someone in New Zealand, for whom it is a summer one.

8. Keep your sentences simple and easy to understand. Short, direct sentences will cause a reader whose native language is not English the least amount of trouble. A good rule of thumb is that the shorter and less complicated your sentences, the easier they will be for a reader to process. Long (more than fifteen words) and complex (multiclause) sentences can be so difficult for readers to unravel that they may skip over them or guess at your message. Do not, however, be insultingly childish as if you were writing for someone in kindergarten. Always try to avoid the passive voice; it is one of the most difficult sentence patterns for a non-native speaker to comprehend. Stick to the common subject-verb-object pattern as often as possible (see Chapter 2, p. 38).

Respecting International Readers' Cultural Traditions

Using simple words and concise sentences certainly will help you to write more effectively and clearly to an international audience. But to avoid even greater troubles, you also must be concerned with respecting the cultural traditions, customs, and preferences of your readers—how they dress, walk, eat, and interact at formal and informal meetings. Cultures differ widely in the way they send and receive information and how they prefer to be addressed, greeted, and informed in a letter. What is acceptable in one culture may be offensive in another. Be aware of physical dimensions of cultural appropriateness as well as verbal ones.

Let's assume that you have to write a sales letter to an Asian business executive. You will have to employ a very different strategy when writing to an Asian executive as opposed to an American one. For the American reader, the best strategy would be to take a direct approach—fast, hard-hitting, to the point—stressing your product's strengths versus the opposition's weaknesses. But such a direct strategy would be counterproductive in a letter to an Asian reader.

The Asian way of doing business, including writing and receiving letters, is far more subtle, indirect, and complimentary than in the United States. The American style of directness and forcefulness would be perceived as rude or unfair in, say, Japan, China, Malaysia, or Korea. A hard sell letter to an Asian reader would be a sign of arrogance, and arrogance suggests inequality for the reader.

Courtesy for an Asian reader is more persuasive than an aggressive description of a product or service. A letter to an Asian reader should convey a friendship in which trust is established first and business details are dealt with later. Rather than starting off with business talk, the letter to Korean readers might begin with a compliment to readers and their company praising them for trustworthiness and wishing them prosperity. A letter to the American executive would undermine the competition by stating how much better the product is, while for most Asian readers, it would be considered impolite to claim that your product is better than another company's. An Asian audience would prefer to avoid anything that hints at impoliteness or assertiveness.

American:	Our Imaging 500 delivers much more extensive internal imaging than any of our competitors' equipment.
Asian:	One of the ways we may be able to serve you is by informing you about our new Imaging 500 MRI (Magnetic Resonance Imaging) equipment.

Respecting Readers' Nationality and Ethnic/Racial Heritage

Do not risk offending any of your readers, whether they are native speakers of English or not, with language that demeans or stereotypes their nationality or ethnic and racial background. Here are some precautions to take.

1. Respect your reader's nationality. Always spell your reader's name and country properly, which may mean adding diacritical marks (e.g., accent marks) not used in

English. If your reader has a hyphenated last name (e.g., Arana-Sanchez), it would be rude to address him or her by only part of the name (e.g., only Arana or only Sanchez).

2. Honor your reader's place in the world economy. Phrases such as "third-world country," "emerging nation," and "undeveloped/underprivileged area" are derogatory. Using such phrases signals that you regard your reader's country as inferior. Use the name of your reader's country instead. Saying that someone lives in the Far East implies that the United States, Canada, or Europe is the center of culture, the hub of the business community. Never use the word "Oriental," which is insulting. Simply say "East Asia."

3. Avoid insulting stereotypes. Expressions such as "oil-rich Arabs," "time-relaxed Latinos," and "aggressive foreigners" unfairly characterize particular groups. Similarly, prune from your communications any stereotypical phrase that insults one group or singles it out for praise at the expense of another—"Mexican standoff," "Russian roulette," "Chinaman's change," "Irish wake," "Dutch treat," "Indian giver." The word *Indian* refers to someone from India; use *Native American* to refer to the indigenous people of North America, who want to be known by their tribal affiliations (e.g., the Sioux).

4. Be visually sensitive to your reader's culture. Colors, for example, carry much cultural symbolism. Do not offend your audience by using colors in a context that would be offensive. Green and orange have a strong political context in Ireland. In China, white does not symbolize purity and weddings but mourning and funerals. Similarly, in India if a married woman wears all white, she is inviting widowhood. A signature or a note written in red would signify anger to an Indonesian reader. And a Saudi audience would be highly offended to see individuals in short-sleeve shirts or bathing suits in any sales literature sent to them.

Here are some culturally conditioned elements of interpersonal communications that you need to be aware of when writing to readers whose culture is different from yours:

- what your status is in relationship to the reader
- how you address the reader in your salutation
- the beginning and the conclusion of your letter
- the type and amount of information you give
- the overall tone you use

Figures 4.20 and 4.21 illustrate the effective principles of writing to an audience of international readers. In Figure 4.20, Emma Corson writes a letter denying credit to a non-native speaker—a letter that requires double tact. She has to consider the cultural expectations of such an audience and needs to use easily understood international English. At the same time, she wants to encourage Mendson to have future business dealings with Consolidated Plastics even though her company must deny the request. Her letter succeeds in doing both; it is diplomatic and acceptably worded.

Patrice St. Jacques, in Figure 4.21 (pp. 114–115), writes an effective sales letter by zeroing in on Etienne Abernathy's ethnic pride and heritage. Although Abernathy's company is located in the United States, as many international businesses are, St. Jacques persuasively sees Abernathy from a much broader cultural perspective.

FIGURE 4.20   A diplomatic letter refusing credit to a non-native speaker of English.

CONSOLIDATED PLASTICS

May 25, 2006

Mr. Jan Buwalda
Mendson SA
Hoofdstraat 23
Dokkum, The Netherlands 1324 XK

Dear Mr. Buwalda:

Thank you very much for your letter inquiring about opening a credit account with our firm. It is always a pleasure to hear from potential customers in Holland. I was most interested to learn about Mendson's diverse activities.

We understand and share your company's wish to have an American supplier to work with you. Having Mendson as a customer would be beneficial for Consolidated Plastics, too. Working with you would allow us to enter a new market.

However, I am sorry that we cannot open any new account on credit. If you would kindly send us your check for the first month's supplies you need, we would rush your shipment to you. This will establish an account with us, and you can charge your second month's supplies on that account.

Please write or e-mail me if you have any questions. I look forward to serving you and Mendson in the future.

Cordially,

Emma Corson

Emma Corson
Accounts Executive

900 Technology Blvd., Bambrake, NH 03243
Phone (603) 555-7000 ▪ FAX (603) 555-4321 ▪ conplastics@compuserv.com
www.conplastics.com

FIGURE 4.21   A sales letter that appeals to a specific international audience.

ISLAND JACQUES

4700 Cyprus Avenue
Philadelphia, PA 19172

7 April 2006

Mr. Etienne Abernathy, President
Seagrove Enterprises
1800 S. Port Haven
Philadelphia, PA 19103-1800

Dear Mr. Abernathy:

Congratulations on winning the Hanover Award for community service.
We in the Port Haven area are proud that a business with Caribbean roots
has received such a distinguished honor.

To celebrate your and Seagrove's success, as well as all your business
entertaining needs (annual banquet, monthly meetings, etc.), I invite you
to Island Jacques. We are a family-owned business that for 30 years has
offered Philadelphia residents the finest Caribbean atmosphere and food
west of the Islands. Our black pepper shrimp, reggae or mango chicken,
and steak St. Lucie—plus our irresistible beef and pork jerk—are the talk
from here to Kingston. You and your guests can also savor our original
Caribbean art and steel drum music.

Island Jacques can offer Seagrove a variety of dining options; with
separate rooms, we are small enough for an intimate party of 4 yet large
enough to accommodate a group of 250. We can do early lunches or late
dinners, depending on your schedule. And we even cater, if that's your
style. Our chefs—Diana Maurier and Emile Danticat—will prepare a
special calypso menu just for you. Also a benefit, our prices are
generously competitive for the Philadelphia area.

www.islandjacques.netdoor.com
856-555-3295

Continued

FIGURE 4.21   (Continued)

Page 2

Please call me soon so you can see Island Jacques's unique hospitality.
For your convenience, I am enclosing a copy of this week's menu
delights. Check out our Web site, too, for a taste of Caribbean sound. We
would love to feature Seagrove as Island Jacques's "Guest of the Week!"

Stay Cool, Mon

Patrice St. Jacques

Patrice St. Jacques
Manager

✓ Revision Checklist

- ❑ Planned what I am going to say to my readers. Did necessary home-work and double-checking to answer any questions. Proved to my readers that I am knowledgeable about my topic.
- ❑ Used an appropriate (and consistent) format for my letters.
- ❑ Signed and proofread my letter.
- ❑ Followed one letter format (full-block or modified) consistently.
- ❑ Organized information in letters in the most effective way for my message and for my readers.
- ❑ Emphasized the "you attitude" with my readers, whether employer, customer/client, or co-worker.
- ❑ Conveyed impression of being courteous, professional, and easy to work with.
- ❑ Used clear and concise language appropriate for my reader.
- ❑ Cut out anything that sounded pompous or bureaucratic.
- ❑ Began my correspondence with reader-effective strategies. If reporting good news, told the reader right away. If reporting bad news, was diplomatically indirect and considerate of my reader's reactions.

- ❑ Followed the four A's of effective sales letters; identified and convinced my target audience.
- ❑ Wrote complaint letters in a calm and courteous tone. Informed the reader what is wrong, why it is wrong, and how the problem should be solved.
- ❑ Wrote adjustment letters that say "Yes" sincerely and to the point. Made those that say "No" fair. Acknowledged reader's point of view and provided clear explanation for my refusal.
- ❑ Sent appropriate collection letters based on audience and time overdue.
- ❑ Took special care to meet the needs of non-native speakers of English in both tone and message.

Exercises

1. Write appropriate inside addresses and salutations to (a) a woman who has not specified her marital status, (b) an officer in the armed forces, (c) a professor at your school, (d) an assistant manager at your local bank, (e) a member of the clergy, (f) your congressional representative.

2. Rewrite the following sentences to make them more personal.
    a. It becomes incumbent on this office to cancel order #2394.
    b. Management has suggested the curtailment of parking privileges.
    c. ALL USERS OF HYDROPLEX: Desist from ordering replacement valves during the period of Dec. 20–30.
    d. The request for a new catalog has been honored; it will be shipped to same address soon.
    e. Perseverance and attention to detail have made this writer important to company in-house work.
    f. The Director of Nurses hereby notifies staff that a general meeting will be held Monday afternoon at 3:00 p.m. sharp. Attendance is mandatory.
    g. Reports will be filed by appropriate personnel no later than the scheduled plans allow.

3. The following sentences from letters are discourteous, boastful, excessively humble, vague, or lacking the "you attitude." Rewrite them to correct those mistakes.
    a. Something is obviously wrong in your head office. They have once more sent me the wrong model number. Can they ever get things straight?
    b. My instructor wants me to do a term paper on safety regulations at a small factory. Since you are the manager of a small factory, send me all the information I need at once. My grade depends heavily on all this.
    c. It is apparent that you are in business to rip off the public.
    d. I have waited for my confirmation for two weeks now. Do you expect me to wait forever or can I get some action?
    e. It goes without saying that we cannot honor your request.

    f. Your application has been received and will be kept on file for six months. If we are interested in you, we will notify you. If you do not hear from us, please do not write us again. The soaring costs of correspondence and the large number of applicants make the burden of answering pointless letters extremely heavy.

    g. My past performance as a medical technologist has left nothing to be desired.

    h. Credit means a lot to some people. But obviously you do not care about yours. If you did, you would have sent us the $249.95 you rightfully owe us three months ago. What's wrong with you?

4. Write a business letter to one of the following individuals.

    a. your mayor, asking for an appointment and explaining why you need one

    b. your college president, stressing the need for more parking spaces or for additional computer terminals in a library

    c. the local water department, asking for information about fluoride supplements

    d. an editor of a weekly magazine, asking permission to reprint an article in a company newspaper

    e. a disc jockey at a local radio station, asking for more songs by a certain group

    f. a computer vendor, asking about costs and availability of software packages; explain your company's special needs

5. Write a letter of inquiry to a utility company, a safety or health care agency, or a company in your town and ask for a brochure describing its services to the community. Be specific about your reasons for requesting the information.

6. Choose one of the following and write a sales letter addressed to an appropriate audience on why they should

    a. work for the same company you do

    b. live in your neighborhood

    c. be happy taking a vacation where you did last year

    d. dine at a particular restaurant

    e. use a particular software program

    f. have their cars repaired at a specific garage

    g. give their real estate business to a particular agency

    h. visit your Web site

7. Find at least two sales letters you, your family, or your firm has received, and in an e-mail or a memo to your instructor or employer evaluate how well they follow the four parts of a sales letter discussed in this chapter. Attach a copy of the sales letters to your evaluation. If your e-mail or memo is addressed to your boss, indicate how you would improve your competition's sales letters.

8. Rewrite the following sales letter to make it more effective. Add any details you think are relevant.

```
Dear Pizza Lovers:

Allow me to introduce myself. My name is Rudy Moore and I am
the new manager of Tasty Pizza Parlor in town. The Parlor is
located at the intersection of North Miller Parkway and 95th
```

Street. We are open from 10 a.m. to 11 p.m., except on the weekends, when we are open later.

I think you will be as happy as I am to learn that Tasty's will now offer free delivery to an extended service area. As a result, you can get your Tasty Pizza hot when you want it.

Please see your weekly newspapers for our ad. We also are offering customers a coupon. It is a real deal for you.

I know you will enjoy Tasty's pizza and I hope to see you. I am always interested in hearing from you about our service and our fine product. We want to take your order soon. Please come in.

9. Send a follow-up letter to one of the following individuals:
   a. a customer who informs you that she will no longer do business with your firm because your prices are too high
   b. a family of four who stayed at your motel for two weeks last summer
   c. a wedding party that used your catering services last month
   d. a customer who exchanged a coat for the purchase price
   e. a customer who purchased a used car from you and who has not been happy with warranty service
   f. a company that bought software from you nine months ago, alerting them to improvements in the software

10. Write a complaint letter about one of the following:
   a. an error in your utility, telephone, or credit card bill
   b. discourteous service you received on an airplane or bus
   c. a frozen food product of poor quality
   d. a shipment that arrived late and damaged
   e. an insurance payment to you that is $100 less than it should be
   f. a television station's policy of not showing a particular series
   g. junk mail or spam that you are receiving
   h. equipment that arrives with missing parts
   i. misleading representation by a salesperson
   j. incorrect information given at a Web site

11. The following story appeared recently in a local newspaper. Based on information in this story, which you may want to supplement, write the following complaint/adjustment letters:
   a. a complaint letter to the city from resident Jo Souers
   b. a complaint letter to Finicky Pet Food from city officials warning about dangers of odors to the residential area
   c. a letter from plant manager Dean Niemann to the residents of Bienville Place subdivision
   d. a letter from city officials to the residents of Bienville Place subdivision

Residents concerned about relocation of pet food plant

OCEAN SPRINGS (AP) – Finicky Pet Food is moving its processing plant from Pascagoula to Ocean Springs, a decision that has some residents concerned of possible odor and other problems.

The plant is moving to an industrial area bordering a subdivision of expensive homes.

"The wind doesn't discriminate," said Jo Souers, who lives in the Bienville Place subdivision. "I don't want this in our neighborhood."

City officials said the plant is moving to an area zoned to accommodate it.

"We don't have a lot of control over it," said city planner Donovan Scruggs. "It is a permitted use for this property."

Scruggs said the property was zoned industrial before the subdivision was built. A body shop, cabinet shop, and boat business are located nearby.

The plant will be built in the small industrial area on U.S. 90, directly across the highway from the Super Wal-Mart.

It is moving into a vacant building, the interior of which has been renovated for its new purpose, city officials said.

The plant will process frozen fish and fish parts for bait and pet food. It will employ 10 workers, with that number doubling during fishing season.

Plant manager Dean Niemann said in a statement that the company no longer needed its Pascagoula location near deep water, which was rented from the county.

Scruggs said the city has investigated the possibility that the plant will emit odors.

"We've told Dean (Niemann) from day one, 'You're locating next to a residential area. If you start stinking, action will be taken,'" Scruggs said.

He said the city has a nuisance ordinance that should handle anything that might arise.

Reprinted with permission of The Associated Press.

---

12. Rewrite the following ineffective adjustment letter saying "No."

```
Dear Customer:

Our company is unwilling to give you a new toaster or to
refund your purchase price. After examining the toaster you
sent to us, we found that the fault was not ours, as you
insist, but yours.

Let me explain. Our toaster is made to take a lot of pun-
ishment. But being dropped on the floor or poked inside with
a knife, as you probably did, exceeds all decent treatment.
You must be careful if you expect your appliances to last.
Your negligence in this case is so bad that the toaster
could not be repaired.

In the future, consider using your appliances according to
the guidelines set down in warranty books. That's why they
are written.
```

Since you are now in the market for a new toaster, let me suggest that you purchase our new heavy-duty model, number 67342, called the Counter-Whiz. I am taking the liberty of sending you some information about this model. I do hope you at least go to see one at your local appliance center.

Sincerely,

13. You are the manager of a computer software company, and one of your salespeople has just sold a large order to a new customer whose business you have tried to obtain for years. Unfortunately, the salesperson made a mistake writing out the invoice, undercharging the customer by $229. At that price, your company would not break even, so you must write a letter explaining the problem so that the customer will not assume all future business dealings with your firm will be offered at such "below market" rates. Decide whether you should ask for the $229 or just "write it off" in the interest of keeping a valuable new customer.
   a. Write a letter to the new customer, asking for the $229 and explaining the problem while still projecting an image of your company as accurate, professional, and very competitive.
   b. Write a letter to the new customer, not asking for the $229 but explaining the mistake and emphasizing that your company is both competitive and professional.
   c. Write a letter to your boss explaining why you wrote letter **a**.
   d. Write a letter to your boss explaining why you wrote letter **b**.
   e. Write a letter to the salesperson who made the mistake, asking him or her to take appropriate action with regard to the new customer.

14. Write a sales letter similar to the one in Figure 4.21 from a manager of one of the following ethnic restaurants or one of your choice. Make sure you include relevant details for the particular audience:
   a. Mexican
   b. Indian
   c. Cuban
   d. Soul food
   e. Czech
   f. Turkish
   g. Vietnamese
   h. Thai
   i. Greek
   j. German
   k. Irish
   l. Chinese
   m. Pakistani
   n. Italian
   o. Australian
   p. French
   q. Portuguese
   r. Hindi

15. Rewrite one of the following letters, making it appropriate for a reader whose native language is not English. As you revise the letter, pay attention to the words you use as well as the sentence constructions you employ. Be sure to consider the reader's cultural traditions.

   a. Dear Mr. Wong,

       It's not every day that you have the chance to get in on the ground floor of a deal so good you can actually taste it.

But Off-Wall Street Mutual can make the difference in your financial future. Give me a moment to convince you.

By becoming a member of our international investing group, you can just about ensure your success. We know all the ins and outs of long-term investing and can save you a bundle. Our analysts are the hotshots of the business and always look long and hard for the most propitious business deals. The stocks we select with your interests in mind are as safe as a bank and not nearly so costly for you. We can save you money by investing your money. We are penny pinchers with our clients' initial investments, but we are King Midas when it comes to transforming those investments into pure gold.

I am enclosing a brochure for you to study, and I really hope you will examine it carefully. You would be foolish to let a deal like Off-Wall Street Mutual pass you by. Go for it.

Hurriedly,

b. Dear Mr. Uko,

My firm is taking a survey of businesses in your part of the world to see if there is any likelihood of getting you on board our international computer network and so I thought I would drop you a line to see if you might like to take the chance. In today's uncertain world, business events can change overnight and without the proper scoop you could be left out in the cold. We can alleviate that mess.

Not only do we interface with major exchanges all around the globe but we also make sure that we get the facts to you pronto. We do not sit on our hands here at Intertel. Check out the enclosed data sheet on who and how we serve and I have no doubts that you will e-mail or ring us up to find out about joining up.

One last point: Can you really risk going out on a limb without first knowing that you have all the facts at your fingertips about worldwide business events? Intertel is there to save you.

Fondly,

5

How to Get a Job: Résumés, Letters, Applications, and Interviews

Obtaining a job today involves a lot of hard work. Before your name is added to a company's payroll, you will have to do more than simply walk into the human resources office and fill out an application form. Finding the *right* job takes time. And finding the right person to fill that job also takes time for the employer.

Steps the Employer Takes to Hire

From the employer's viewpoint, the stages in the search for a valuable employee include the following:

1. deciding what duties and responsibilities go with the job and determining the qualifications the future employee should possess
2. advertising the job on the company Web site, in newspapers, and in professional publications
3. reading and evaluating résumés and letters of application
4. having candidates complete application forms
5. requesting further proof of candidates' skills (letters of recommendation, transcripts)
6. interviewing selected candidates
7. offering the job to the best-qualified individual

Sometimes the steps are interchangeable, especially steps 4 and 5, but generally speaking, employers go through a long and detailed process to select employees. Step 3, for example, is among the most important for employers (and the most crucial for job candidates). At that stage employers often classify job seekers into one of three groups: those they definitely want to interview, those they may want to interview, and those in whom they have no interest.

Steps to Follow to Get Hired

As a job seeker you will have to know how and when to give the employer the kinds of information the preceding seven steps require. You will also have to follow a certain schedule in your search for a job. The following six procedures will be required of you:

1. analyzing your strengths and restricting your job search
2. looking in the right places for a job
3. preparing a résumé
4. writing a letter of application
5. filling out a job application
6. going to an interview

Your timetable should match that of your prospective employer. This chapter shows you how to begin your job search and how to prepare an appropriate résumé and letter that are a part of your job search.

Analyzing Your Strengths

Before you apply for jobs, analyze your job skills, career goals, and interests. Here are some points to consider.

1. Make an inventory of your most significant accomplishments in your major and/or on the job. What are your greatest strengths—writing and speaking, working with people in small groups, organizing and problem solving, speaking a second language, developing software, performing accounting audits, and so on?
2. Decide which speciality within your chosen career appeals to you the most. If you are in a nursing program, do you want to work in a large teaching hospital, for a home health or hospice agency, or in a physician's office? What kinds of patients do you prefer to care for—pediatric, geriatric, psychiatric?
3. What are the most rewarding prospects of a job in your profession? What most interests you about a position—travel, international contacts, on-the-job training, helping people, being creative?
4. What are some of the greatest challenges you face in your career today—or will in five years?
5. Which specific companies or organizations have the best track record in hiring and promoting individuals in your field? What qualifications will such firms insist on from prospective employees?

The *Occupational Outlook Handbook* (*http://www.bls.gov/oco/*) can give you valuable career information on job prospects, requirements, and salary ranges.

Once you answer the previous questions you can avoid applying for positions for which you are either overqualified or underqualified. If a position requires ten years of related work experience and you are just starting out, you will only waste the employer's time and your own by applying. However, if a job requires a certificate or license and you are in the process of obtaining one, go ahead and apply.

Looking in the Right Places for a Job

One way to search for a job is simply to send out a batch of letters to companies you want to work for. But how do you know what jobs, if any, those companies have available, what qualifications they are looking for, and what deadlines they might want you to follow? You can avoid these uncertainties by knowing where to look for a job and knowing what a specific job entails. Consult the following resources for a wealth of job-related information.

   1. **Networking.** Networking pays. It is regarded as the most important strategy to follow. John D. Erdlen and Donald H. Sweet, experts on job searching, cite the following as a primary rule of job hunting: "Don't do anything yourself you can get someone with influence to do for you." Let your professors, friends, classmates, neighbors, relatives, and even your clergy know you are looking for a job. They may hear of something and can notify you. Better yet, they may recommend you for the position—with a phone call, a visit to their own company's human resource department. See how the job seekers in Figures 5.8 (p. 144) and 5.9 (p. 145) have successfully networked with people they know. You can also network with people you don't know personally through Web sites such as:

> *http://network.monster.com*
>
> *http://www.fastcompany.com/cof/*
>
> *http://www.guru.com*
>
> *http://www.groups.yahoo.com*

Career counselors also recommend that you attend job fairs, professional and organization meetings, community and civic functions—places where you can meet the right contact people whom you can ask for advice and also for possible follow-up help and recommendations.

   2. **The Internet.** Prospective employers rely on the Internet to find employees. Companies post job openings and describe precisely what they are looking for in far more detail than in a classified ad. You can learn about jobs by visiting a company's Web site to see if it has vacancies and what the qualifications are for them. You can also consult the many on-line job services that list positions and sometimes give advice, including:

- Findajob.com—*http://www.findajob.com*
- College Grad Job Hunter—*http://www.collegegrad.com*
- CareerBuilder—*http://www.careerbuilder.com*
- JobOptions—*http://www.joboptions.com*
- Monster.com—*http://www.monster.com*
- Yahoo! Careers—*http://www.my.hotjobs.yahoo.com*

The following are some specialized sites:

- For health care professionals—*http://www.medhunters.com*
- For tech jobs—*http://computerjobs.com/homepage.aspx*

- For jobs in business: BizWeb—*www.bizweb.com*
- For jobs in criminal justice—*www.corrections.com*

Make sure you always sign up for job alerts.

3. Newspapers. Look at local newspapers as well as the Sunday editions of large city papers with a wide circulation, such as the *New York Times Job Market* (*http://www.nytimes.com/pages/jobs/*). The *National Business Employment Weekly* (*www.careerjournal.com*), published by the *Wall Street Journal,* also lists jobs in different areas, including technical and managerial positions. You can access job listings found in many large newspapers through CareerPath.com (*http://www.careerpath.com*). Make sure you check every possibly relevant category (for example, jobs for "Computer Programmers" might be listed under "Programmers").

4. Your campus placement office. Counselors keep an up-to-date file of available positions and can also tell you when a firm's recruiter will be on campus to conduct interviews. They can also help you locate summer and part-time work, both on and off campus, positions that might lead to full-time jobs. Most important, they will give you sound advice on your job search, including strategies for finding the right job, salary ranges, and interview tips. Many placement offices also sponsor career fairs to bring job seekers and employers together in specific professional, technical fields.

5. Federal and state employment offices. The U.S. government is one of the biggest employers in the country. During 2004 and 2005, for instance, the most active career site on the Web was operated by the federal government, with 1.4 million new hires. Counselors at federal and state employment centers also help job seekers find career opportunities. Figure 5.1 (p. 126) shows the home page of the Web site for USAJOBS, which helps job seekers find employment opportunities with the U.S. government. Consult the following Web sites for listings of government jobs:

- America's Job Bank—*http://www.ajb.dni.us*
- Federal Jobs.Net—*http://www.federaljobs.net*
- Studentjobs.gov—*http://www.studentjobs.gov*
- U.S. Office of Personnel Management—*http://www.usajobs.opm.gov*

6. Professional and trade journals and associations in your major. Identify the most respected periodicals in your field and search their ads. The *American Journal of Nursing*, for example, carries notices of openings arranged by geographic location in each of its monthly issues; and each issue of *Food Technology* features a section called "Professional Placement," a listing of jobs all over the country. Similarly, *CIO Magazine—IT Professional Research Center* (*http://www.cio.com/research/itcareer/*) can help you find jobs in the computer industry, engineering, and technology. Consult the *Encyclopedia of Associations* (*http://library.dialog.com/bluesheets/html/bl0114.html*) for a list of journals and newsletters for your profession. Many of the journals are also available on-line.

7. The human resources department of a company or agency you would like to work for. Often you will be able to fill out an application even if there is not a current opening. But, do not call employers asking about openings; a visit shows a more serious interest.

FIGURE 5.1   USAJOBS Web site.

8. A résumé database service. A number of on-line services will put your résumé in a database and make it available to prospective employers, who scan the database regularly to find suitable job candidates. Figure 5.2 describes a résumé database service offered by one professional organization—the Association for Computing Machinery (ACM)—for its members. Check to see if a professional society to which you belong (or might join) offers a similar service.

9. Professional employment agencies. Some agencies list two kinds of jobs—those that you can apply for free of charge (because the employer pays the fee) and others that charge a stiff fee, usually a percentage of your first year's salary. If you do use an agency, be sure to ask who pays the fee for the service. Because employment agencies often find out about jobs through channels already available to you, speak to your campus career center first.

Preparing a Résumé

The résumé, sometimes called a **data sheet** or **curriculum vitae,** may be the most important document you prepare for your job search. It deserves your utmost attention. It is a factual and concise summary of your qualifications. A résumé is not your life history or your emotional autobiography, nor is it a transcript of your college work. It is a record of results, showing a prospective employer that you have what it takes (in education and experience) to do the job you are applying for.

FIGURE 5.2   A description of one résumé database service.

Employers Benefit from ACM Résumé Database

The ACM Résumé Database is composed of résumés of ACM members—high-caliber, information-technology professionals who can bring expertise to your company. All résumés are up-to-date and can be searched according to criteria you provide, in a short period of time and at low rates. Single searches as well as annual subscriptions to the database can be requested from the database administrator, Resume-Link, at 614-529-0429. ACM institutional members get a 10% discount off the cost of the search.

And for ACM members! Our database also is now searchable for internships and co-op positions, as well as for full-time and consultant placements. Use this free career development service and submit your résumé on-line at **http://www.Resume-Link.com/**.

The résumé is a short (preferably one-page, never longer than two) outline to accompany your letter of application. Write your résumé before your job search gets underway and certainly before preparing any application letters. Never send a résumé alone, but do bring one with you to an interview. And you should certainly have copies available for recruiters if you schedule campus interviews.

What Employers Like to See in a Résumé

Prospective employers will judge you and your work by your résumé, their first view of you and your qualifications. They want to see the following seven characteristics in an applicant's résumé.

- **Honesty.** Be truthful about your qualifications—your education, experience, and skills. Distorting, exaggerating, or falsifying information about yourself in your résumé is unethical and could cost you the job you get. If you were a clerical assistant to an attorney, don't describe yourself as a paralegal. Employers demand trustworthiness.
- **Attractive.** The document should be pleasing to the eye with appropriate spacing, typeface, and use of boldface; it shows you have a sense of proportion and document design and that you are neat.
- **Carefully organized.** The orderly arrangement of information is easy-to-follow, logical, and consistent; it shows you have the ability to process information and to summarize. Employers prize analytical thinking.
- **Concise.** Generally, keep your résumé to one page, as in Figure 5.3 (p. 130). However, depending on your education or job experience, you may want to

include a second page. Résumés are written in short sentences that omit "I" and that use action-packed verbs, such as those listed in Table 5.1.

- **Accurate.** Grammar, spelling, dates, names, titles, and programs are correct; your résumé shows you can communicate effectively.
- **Current information.** All information is up-to-date and documented, with no gaps or sketchy areas, and demonstrates your computer literacy and ethics.
- **Relevance.** The information is appropriate for the job level, shows that you have the necessary education and experience, and confirms that you can be an effective team player.

TABLE 5.1   Action Verbs to Use in Your Résumé

accommodated	created	informed	reduced
accomplished	customized	initiated	reported
achieved	dealt in	installed	researched
administered	designed	instituted	scheduled
analyzed	determined	instructed	searched
arranged	developed	interacted with	selected
assembled	directed	maintained	served
assisted	drafted	managed	settled
attended	earned	monitored	sold
awarded	elected	motivated	solved
built	established	navigated	supervised
calculated	estimated	negotiated	taught
coached	evaluated	operated	tracked
collected	expedited	organized	trained
communicated	figured	oversaw	tutored
compiled	guided	performed	updated
completed	handled	planned	verified
composed	headed	prepared	weighed
computed	implemented	programmed	won
conducted	improved	reappraised	worked
coordinated	increased	reconciled	wrote

Your goal is to prepare a résumé that shows the employer you possess the sought-after job skills. One that is unattractive, difficult to follow, poorly written, filled with typos and other errors, and not relevant for the prospective employer's needs will not make the first cut.

It might be to your advantage to prepare several versions of your résumé and then adapt each one you send out to the specific job skills a prospective employer is looking for. It pays to customize your résumé. Following the process in the next section will help you prepare any résumé.

The Process of Writing Your Résumé

To write an effective résumé, ask the following important questions:

1. What classes did you excel in?
2. What papers or reports earned you your highest grades?

3. What computer skills have you mastered—languages, software knowledge, navigating and developing Net resources? Knowledge of e-commerce? Ability to design a Web site?
4. What jobs have you had? For how long and where? What were your primary duties?
5. What technical skills have you acquired?
6. Do you work well with people? What skills do you possess as a member of a team?
7. Can you organize complicated tasks or solve problems quickly?
8. Have you won any awards or scholarships or received a raise, bonus, commendation, and/or promotion at work?

Pay *special attention* to your four or five most significant, job-worthy strengths and work especially hard on listing them concisely.

Although not everything you have done relates directly to a particular job, indicate how your achievements are relevant to the employer's overall needs. For example, handling money responsibly or supervising staff in a grocery store points to your ability to perform the same duties in another business context.

Balancing Education and Experience

If you have years of experience, don't flood your prospective employer with too many details. You cannot possibly include every detail of your job(s) for the last ten or twenty years.

- Emphasize only those skills and positions most likely to earn you the job.
- Eliminate your earliest jobs that do not relate to your present employment search.
- Combine and condense skills acquired over many years and through many jobs.

Figure 5.5 (p. 135) shows the résumé of Dora Cooper Bolger who has a great deal of experience to offer prospective employers.

Many job candidates who have spent most of their lives in school are faced with the other extreme: not having much job experience to put down. The worst thing to do is to write "None" for experience. Any part-time, summer, or other seasonal jobs, as well as work done for a library or science laboratory, show an employer that you are responsible and knowledgeable about the obligations of being an employee. Figure 5.3 shows a résumé from Anthony Jones, a student with very little job experience; Figure 5.4 (pp. 131–132) shows the one of María Lopez, a student with a few years of experience.

What to Exclude from a Résumé

Knowing what to exclude from a résumé is as important as knowing what to include. Since federal employment laws prohibit discrimination on the basis of age, sex, race, national origin, religion, marital status, or disability, do not include such information on your résumé. Here are some other details best left out of your résumé:

- salary demands, expectations, or ranges
- preferences for work schedules, days off, or overtime
- comments about fringe benefits

FIGURE 5.3   Résumé from a student with little job experience.

Anthony H. Jones

73 Allenwood Boulevard • Santa Rosa, California 95401-1074 • (707) 555.6390
ajones@plat.com   www.plat.com/users/ajones/resume.html

Web Site Developer • Designer • Graphic Artist

Career Objective

Full-time position as a layout artist with a commercial publishing house using my knowledge of state-of-the-art design technology.

Education

Santa Rosa Junior College, 2004–2006, A.S. degree to be awarded in 2006
Dean's List in 2005; GPA 3.45
Major: Commercial Graphics Illustration, with specialty in design layout
Related courses included:
  • Digital Photography
  • Graphics Programs: Illustrator, Photoshop
  • Desktop Publishing: QuarkXPress, WordPerfect Suite 8

Apprenticeship, 2005–2006, McAdam Publishers
Major projects included:
  • Assisting layout editors with page composition and importing images.
  • Writing detailed reports on digital photography, designs, and artwork used in *Living in Sonoma County* (www.sonomacounty.com) and *Real Estate in Sonoma County* (www.resc.net) magazines.

Experience

Salesperson (part-time), **2001–2003**, Buchman's Department Store
Duties included assisting customers in sporting goods and appliance departments and coordinating sport shop by displaying merchandise.

Computer Skills

Know Quark XPress, WordPerfect Suite 8.

Related Activities

Volunteer; designed Web site and 3-fold brochure for the Santa Rosa Humane Society's 2005 fund drive.

References

References, college transcripts, and a portfolio of Web designs and photographs available on request.

FIGURE 5.4   Résumé from a student with some job experience.

MARÍA H. LOPEZ
1725 Brooke Street
Miami, Florida 32701-2121
(305) 555-3429   **mlopez@eagle.com**

Career Objective Full-time position assisting dentist in providing dental health care and counseling and performing preventive dental treatments, especially in applying my clinical skills in the practice of pedodontics.

Education
August 2004–
May 2006

Miami-Dade Community College, Miami, Florida
Will receive A.S. degree in dental hygiene in May. Have completed nine courses in oral pathology, dental materials and specialties, periodontics, and community dental health.

Currently enrolled in clinical dental hygiene program. Experienced with procedures and instruments used with oral prophylaxis techniques. Subject of major project was proper nutrition and dental health for preschoolers.

Minor area of interest is psychology (twelve hours completed). Received excellent evaluations in business writing course. GPA is 3.3. Bilingual: Spanish/English.

Plan to take American Dental Assistants' Examination on June 2.

1997–2001

Miami North High School, Miami, Florida
Took electives in computers, electronics, and public relations

Experience
April 2002–
July 2004

St. Francis Hospital, Miami Beach, Florida
Full-time unit clerk on the pediatric floor. Duties included ordering supplies, maintaining records, transcribing orders, and greeting and assisting visitors.

June 2001–
April 2002

Murphy Construction Company, Miami, Florida
Secretary-receptionist. Did keyboarding, billing, and mailing in small office (three employees).

Summers
1999–2000

City of Hialeah, Florida
Water meter reader

Computer Skills Proficient in Microsoft Office, Excel

Continued

FIGURE 5.4   (Continued)

Lopez 2

References   The following individuals have written letters of recommendation for my placement file, available from the Placement Center, Miami-Dade Community College, Medical Center Campus, Miami, FL 33127-2225.

Sister Mary James
Pediatric Unit
St. Francis Hospital
10003 Collins Avenue
Miami Beach, FL 33141
(305) 555-5113

Professor Mitchell Pelbourne
Department of Dental Hygiene
Miami-Dade Community College
Medical Center Campus
Miami, FL 33127
(305) 555-3872

Tia Gutierrez, D.D.S.
9800 Exchange Avenue
Miami, FL 33167
(305) 555-1039

Mr. Jack Murphy
1203 Francis Street
Miami, FL 33157
(305) 555-6767

- travel restrictions
- reasons for leaving your previous job
- your photograph (unless you are applying for a modeling or acting job)
- social security number
- comments about your family, spouse, or children
- height, weight, hair or eye color
- personal information, hobbies, interests (unless relevant to the job you are seeking, in which case put under Related Skills)

Save comments about salary and schedules for your interview. The résumé should be written appropriately to get you that interview.

Parts of a Résumé

Name, Address, Phone

At the top of the page center your name (do not use a nickname); address, including your ZIP code; telephone number; and e-mail address. Also, include your Web site and fax number if you have these for an employer to contact you.

Career Objective

One of the first things a prospective employer reads is your career objective statement that tells the employer the specific type of job you are looking for and in what ways you are qualified to hold it. Such a statement should be the result of your focused self-evaluation and will influence everything else you include. Depending on your background and the types of jobs you are qualified for, you might formulate two or three different career or employment objectives to use with different versions of your résumé.

To write an effective career objective statement, ask yourself four basic questions:

1. What kind of job do I want?
2. What kind of job am I qualified for?
3. What capabilities do I possess?
4. What kinds of skills do I want to learn?

Avoid trite or vague goals such as "looking for professional advancement" or "want to join a progressive company." Compare the vague objectives on the left with the more precise ones on the right.

Unfocused	Focused
Job in sales to use my aggressive skills in expanding markets.	Regional sales representative using my proven skills in marketing and communication to develop and expand a customer base.
Full-time position as staff nurse.	Full-time position as staff nurse on cardiac step-down unit to offer excellent primary care nursing and patient/family teaching.

Credentials

The order of the next two categories—**education** and **experience**—can vary. Generally, if you have lots of work experience, list it first as Dora Cooper Bolger did (see Figure 5.5). However, if you are a recent graduate short on job experience, list education first, as Anthony Jones did (see Figure 5.3). María Lopez (Figure 5.4) also decided to place her education before her job experience because the job she was applying for required the formal training she received at Miami-Dade Community College.

Education

Begin with your most recent education first, then list everything **significant since high school.** Give the name(s) of the school(s); dates attended; and degree, diploma, or certificate earned. Don't overlook military schools or major training programs (EMT, court reporter), institutes, internships, or workshops you have completed.

Remember, however, that a résumé is not a transcript. Simply listing a series of courses will not set you apart from hundreds of other applicants taking similar courses across the country. Avoid vague titles such as Science 203 or Nursing IV. Instead, concentrate on describing the kinds of skills you learned.

30 hours in planning and development courses specializing in transportation, land use, and community facilities; 12 hours in field methods of gathering, interpreting, and describing survey data in reports.

Completed 28 hours in major courses in business marketing, management, and materials in addition to 12 hours in computer science, including HTML/Web publishing.

List your grade point average (GPA) only if it is 3.0 or above; otherwise, indicate your GPA in just your major or during your last term, again if it is above 3.0.

Experience

Your job history is the key category for many employers. It shows them that you have held jobs before and that you are responsible. Here are some guidelines about listing your experience.

1. Begin with your most recent position and work backward—in reverse chronological order. List the company or agency name, location (city and state), and your title. Do not mention why you left a job.

2. For each job or activity provide short descriptions of your duties and achievements. Rather than saying you were a secretary, indicate that you wrote business letters and contracts, learned various software programs, designed a company Web site, prepared schedules for part-time help in an office of twenty-five people, or assisted the manager in preparing accounts.

3. In describing your position(s), emphasize any responsibilities that involved handling money; managing other employees; working with customer accounts, services, and programs; or writing letters and reports. Prospective employers are interested in your leadership abilities, financial shrewdness (especially if you saved your company money), tact in dealing with the public, and communications skills. They will also be favorably impressed by promotions you may have earned.

4. If you have been a full-time parent for ten years or a caregiver for a family member or friend, indicate the management skills you developed while running a household and any community or civic service, as Dora Cooper Bolger does in her résumé in Figure 5.5. She skillfully relates her family and community accomplishments to the specific job she seeks.

Related Skills and Achievements

Not every résumé will have this section but the following are all employer-friendly things to include:

- second or third languages you speak or write
- extensive travel
- certificates or licenses you hold
- memberships in professional associations (e.g., American Society of Safety Engineers, Black Student Association, National Hispanic Business Association, Child Development Organization)
- memberships in community groups (e.g., Lions, Red Cross, Elks); list any offices you hold—recorder, secretary, fund drive chairperson

Computer Skills

Knowledge of computer hardware, software, word processing programs, and Web design and search engines is extremely valuable in today's job market. Note how

FIGURE 5.5   Dora Cooper Bolger's résumé organized by skill areas.

DORA COOPER BOLGER
1215 Lakeview Avenue
Westhampton, MI 46532
Voice: 616-555-4772   **Cell:** 616-555-4773   **dbolger@aol.com**

EMPLOYMENT OBJECTIVE   **Seek full-time position as public affairs officer in health care, educational, or charitable facility**

SKILLS, RESPONSIBILITIES, EXPERIENCES

Organizational Communication
- **Delivered** 20 presentations to civic groups on educational issues
- **Recorded** minutes and helped formulate agenda as president of large, local PTA for last 6½ years
- **Possess** excellent software skills in PeopleSoft and Microsoft Word
- **Updated** and **maintained** computerized mailing lists for Teens in Trouble and Foster Parents' Association

Money Management
- **Spearheaded 3 major fund-raising drives** (total of $178,000 collected)
- **Prepared and implemented large family budget** (3 children, 8 foster children) for 15 years
- **Served as financial secretary**, Faith Methodist Church for 4 years

Administration
- **Organized** volunteers for American Kidney Fund (last 5 years)
- **Established** and **oversaw** neighborhood carpool (17 drivers; more than 50 children) for 7 years
- **Coordinated** after-school tutoring program for Teens in Trouble; president since 1995

HONORS   "Volunteer of the Year"(2004), Michigan Child Placement Agency

EDUCATION   A.A., Metropolitan Community College, 1999
B.S., Mid-Michigan College, expected 2006; major: public administration; minor: psychology. GPA 3.45

WORK EXPERIENCE Secretary, 1988–1998 (full and part-time): Merrymount Plastics; Foley and Wasson; Westhampton Health Dept.; G & K Electric

REFERENCES   Available on request

Anthony Jones and Maria Lopez inform perspective employers about their relevant computer competencies in Figures 5.3 and 5.4.

Honors/Awards

List any academic honors you have won (dean's list, department awards, school honors, scholarships, grants, honorable mentions). Memberships in honor societies in your major and professional associations also demonstrate that you are professionally accomplished and active.

References

You can simply say that you will provide references on request or you can list the names, titles, e-mail and street addresses, and telephone numbers of no more than three or four individuals, as María Lopez did. Be sure to obtain their permission first. List your references only when they are well known in the community or belong to the same profession in which you are seeking employment—you profit from your association with a recognizable name or title.

Asking your boss can be tricky. If your current employer knows that your education is preparing you for another profession, ask her or him. However, if you are employed and are looking for professional advancement or a better salary elsewhere, you may not want your current employer to know you are searching for another job until you become a leading candidate.

In this section of your résumé, you may also indicate that a portfolio of your work is available for review, as Anthony Jones did in Figure 5.3.

Organizing Your Résumé

There are two primary ways to organize your résumé: chronologically or by function or skill area.

Chronologically

The résumés in Figures 5.3 and 5.4 are organized chronologically. Information about the job applicants is listed year by year under two main categories—education and experience. This is the traditional way to organize a résumé. It is straightforward and easy-to-read, and employers find it acceptable. The chronological sequence works especially well when you can show a clear continuity toward progress in your career through your job(s) and in schoolwork or when you want to apply for a similar job with another company.

A chronological résumé is appropriate for students who want to emphasize recent educational achievements.

By Function or Skill Area

Depending on your experiences and accomplishments, you might organize your résumé according to function or skill area. According to this plan, you would *not* list your information chronologically in the categories "Experience" and "Education." Instead, you would sort your achievements and abilities—whether from course work, jobs, extracurricular activities, or technical skills—into two to four key skill areas, such as "Sales," "Public Relations," "Training," "Management," "Research,"

"Technical Capabilities," "Counseling," "Group Leadership," "Communications," "Network Operations," "Customer Service," "Working with People," "Multicultural Experiences," "Computer Skills," "Problem-Solving Skills."

Under each area you would list three to five points illustrating your achievements in that area. Skills or functional résumés are often called **bullet résumés** because they itemize the candidate's main strengths in bulleted lists. Some employers prefer the bullet résumé because they can skim the candidate's list of qualifications in a few seconds.

Note Dora Cooper Bolger's profitable use of a functional résumé format in Figure 5.5. She was out of school because of family commitments, yet she uses the experiences she acquired during those years to her advantage in her résumé organized by "Skills, Responsibilities, Experiences." She successfully translates her many accomplishments in managing a home and working on charitable and community projects into marketable skills of great interest to a prospective employer, and no gap of ten years interrupts a work experience list.

Who Should Use a Functional Résumé?

The following individuals would probably benefit from organizing their résumés by function instead of chronologically:

- nontraditional students who have diverse job experiences
- individuals who are changing their profession because of downsizing or seeking new professional opportunities
- individuals who have changed jobs frequently over the last five to ten years
- individuals who are entering the civilian marketplace after retiring from the military

You might want to prepare two different versions of your résumé—one functional and one chronological—to see which sells your talents better. Don't hesitate to seek the advice of your instructor or placement counselor about which one will work best for you.

The On-Line Résumé

Many prospective employers want applications sent to their Web addresses. Consequently, having your résumé on-line will give you the widest possible exposure to attract prospective employers. In addition to sending a hard copy of your résumé by fax or through the mail, you can send it by disk; e-mail; through database services such as the ACM in Figure 5.2; or other Internet channels, including your own Web site.

An on-line résumé contains essentially the same information found in the various types of résumés already discussed. Figure 5.6 (p. 138) is an on-line version of the Anthony Jones résumé in Figure 5.3. While the information is the same, the design is different. An on-line résumé must be scannable so that a prospective employer can read and possibly file it in the company's database. The more matches, or "hits," the employer finds between appropriate keywords on your résumé and the descriptors for the job opening, the greater your chances of being hired. On-line résumés can take many different formats.

FIGURE 5.6   An on-line résumé.

Anthony H. Jones
73 Allenwood Boulevard
Santa Rosa, California 95401-1074
Phone: (707) 555-6390
ajones@plat.com
For additional information: Ahjones1@santarosa.career.edu/~dossier

KEYWORDS

Web designer, computer graphics, Illustrator, Photoshop, QuarkXPress, fund-raiser, budgets, sales, Soapscan, WriteNow, virus protection, team player

OBJECTIVE

A position as layout and Web design editor with commercial publisher

EDUCATION

Santa Rosa Junior College, A.S. degree to be awarded in June 2006. Commercial Graphics Illustration major. Digital photography minor.
GPA 3.45

COMPUTER SKILLS

Excellent working knowledge of computer graphics: Illustrator, Photoshop, QuarkXPress, WordPerfect Suite 8, Soapscan, WriteNow

EXPERIENCE

* Intern in layout and design department. Preparing page composition, importing visuals, manipulating images, McAdam Publishers, 8 Parkway Heights, Santa Rosa, CA 94211
* Salesperson; display merchandise coordinator, Buchman's Department Store, Greenview Mall, Santa Rosa
* Volunteer; designed Web site, brochures, and other artwork for successful fund drive, Santa Rosa Humane Society
* Web designer, graphic artist, proofreader, Thunder: student magazine

REFERENCES

Career Center, Santa Rosa Junior College;
Portfolio available: Ahjones1@santarosa.career.edu/~dossier

Using an On-Line Résumé

To compete successfully for jobs on-line, you will have to adapt the conventional résumé format for transmission as a hypertext document. Use the following seven guidelines to prepare an effective on-line résumé; as you read these guidelines, refer to Figures 5.3 and 5.4.

1. Format your résumé properly and consistently—as an ASCII text file—to be received and read around the globe. That means preparing a document in plain text. Always follow the directions given by the résumé database service or the prospective employer.

2. Do not use italics, bullets, underlining, boldfacing, fancy scripts or hard-to-read fonts, or logos. Such features interfere with the transmission of your résumé, garbling it when a prospective employer clicks on it. To emphasize, use full caps or an asterisk (*) or a plus sign (+) at the beginning of a line.

3. Test your formatting. Send your résumé to a friend's e-mail address to be sure the file is readable.

4. Use hyperlinks at the top of the résumé to connect to key categories. Sample hyperlinks are OBJECTIVE, HIGHLIGHTS, EMPLOYMENT HISTORY, COMPUTER SKILLS, EDUCATION, COMMUNITY SERVICE, and REFERENCES. Highlighting those categories as headers makes it easy for a prospective employer to jump to the résumé section he or she deems most important.

5. Use keywords as hyperlinks. The electronic résumé emphasizes nouns, whereas conventional résumés (see Figures 5.2 and 5.3) use strong verbs. Nouns function as the keywords by which a résumé is scanned by Web search engines and organized in a database; they reflect your specialized skills and experience. Prospective employers search the Web by keywords to find what they want to see in the job seeker's experience, education, or activities. In your résumé, repeat several times the two or three key nouns that most accurately reflect your accomplishments, as Anthony Jones (Figure 5.6) does. In the following list, the on-line keywords on the right should replace the action verbs from conventional résumés on the left.

Conventional Descriptions	On-Line Keywords
edited company newsletter	newsletter editor
wrote technical report	technical writer
performed laboratory tests	laboratory technologist
responsible for managing accounts	accounts manager
won two awards	award winner
solved software problems	software specialist

Don't be afraid of using shop talk (or jargon) for your keywords. An employer searching for a specialist will expect the résumé writer to be aware of current terminology, especially in computer programming or networking.

6. Keep your on-line résumé to two or at the most three screens. Keep in mind a prospective employer may be scrolling through as many as 500 résumés a day to compile a short list of candidates to interview. Consequently, downloading and printing multiple pages makes the employer's job more difficult and does not help your chances.

7. Send a scannable hard copy of your résumé and a cover letter to a prospective employer. Simply posting your résumé on-line is not enough. When you send a hard copy of your résumé, do not fold it. Put it, along with your cover letter, in a large envelope to make it easier for an employer to scan and file.

Posting Résumés On-Line: Some Precautions
When posting your résumé on a database, such as Monster.com or CareerJournal.com, you will have to key information into the on-line forms such services provide for a fee. Be careful that you select only the most relevant and persuasive keywords as embedded links for prospective employers to click on. Make sure, too, that if you use a database service, you make your résumé "cyber-safe" to protect your identity and your current job. Instead of providing personal information (e.g., your name, phone number, or e-mail), as Anthony Jones (Figure 5.3) did for his résumé available on his Web site, use an anonymous e-mail address or account. Also determine who will be able to search your résumé on-line. Most services—for example, Monster.com—allow you to block certain readers, such as your current employer or firms that send out spam, from searching your résumé.

Letters of Application

Along with your résumé, you must send your prospective employer a letter of application, one of the most important pieces of correspondence you may ever write. Its goal is to get you an interview and ultimately the job. Letters you write in applying for jobs should be personable, professional, and persuasive—the three P's. Knowing how the letter of application and résumé work together and how they differ can give you a better idea of how to compose your letter.

How Application Letters and Résumés Differ

The résumé is a compilation of facts—a record of dates, your important achievements, names, places, addresses, and jobs. As noted earlier, you may prepare several different résumés depending on your experience and the job market.

Your letter of application, however, is much more personal. Because you must write a new, original letter to each prospective employer, you may write (or adapt) many different letters. Each letter of application should be tailored to a specific job. It should respond precisely to the kinds of qualifications the employer seeks.

The letter of application is a sales letter that emphasizes and applies the most relevant details (of education, experience, and talents) in your résumé. In short, the résumé contains the raw material that the letter of application transforms into a finished and highly marketable product—you.

Résumé Facts to Exclude from Letters of Application
The letter of application should not simply repeat the details listed in your résumé. In fact, the following details are relevant information you list in your résumé and should *not* be restated in the letter:

- personal data, including license or certificate numbers
- specific names of courses in your major
- names and addresses of all your references

Duplicating those details in your letter gives no new information that might persuade prospective employers that you are the individual they are seeking.

Writing the Letter of Application

The letter of application can make the difference between your getting an interview and being eliminated early from the competition. Keep in mind that employers receive many letters and that you will have to compete for attention. You want your letter to be placed in the "definitely interview" category. Limit your letter to one page. As you prepare your letter, use the following general guidelines.

1. Follow the standard conventions of letter writing (see Chapter 4). Print your letter on good-quality, white 8.5″ × 11″ paper. Proofread meticulously; a spelling error, typo, or grammatical mistake will make you look careless and will ruin your chances of getting the job.

2. Make sure your letter looks attractive. Use wide margins and don't crowd your page. Keep your paragraphs short and readable—four or five sentences (see pp. 160–69 in Chapter 6).

3. Send your letter to a specific person. Never address an application letter "To Whom It May Concern," "Dear Sir or Madam," "Director of Human Resources," or "Dear Employer." Try to get an individual's name by double-checking the company's Web site. If you cannot find the human resources director there, try calling the company's switchboard and be sure to verify the spelling of the person's name and his or her title.

4. Don't forget the "you attitude" (see Chapter 4, pp. 81–85). See yourself as an employer sees you. Focus on how your qualifications meet the employer's needs, not the other way around. Employers are not impressed by vain boasts ("I am the most efficient and effective safety engineer"). One applicant spent so much time on the advantages he would get from the job that he forgot the employer entirely: "I have worked with this kind of equipment before, and this experience will give me the edge in running it." Convince readers that you will be a valuable addition to their organization.

5. Don't be tempted to send out your first draft. Write and rewrite your letter of application until you are convinced it presents you in the best possible light. Getting the job may depend on it. A first or even second draft rarely sells your abilities as well as a third, fourth, or even fifth revision does.

The sections that follow give you some suggestions on how to prepare the various parts of an application letter successfully.

Your Opening Paragraph

The first paragraph of your letter of application is your introduction. It must get your reader's attention by answering three questions:

1. Why are you writing?
2. Where or how did you learn of the vacancy or the company or the job?
3. What is your most important qualification for the job?

Begin your letter by stating directly that you are writing to apply for a job. Don't say that you "want to apply for the job"; such an opening raises the question, "Why don't you, then?"

Avoid an unconventional or arrogant opening: "Are you looking for a dynamic, young, and talented photographer?" Do not begin with a question; be more positive and professional.

If you learned about the job through a newspaper or journal, make sure you italicize or underscore its title.

> I am applying for the food-service manager position you advertised in the May 10 edition of the *Los Angeles Times* on the Internet.

Since many companies announce positions on the Internet, check the Net first to see if their position is listed on-line, as Anthony Jones did (Figure 5.7).

If you learned of the job from a professor, a friend, or an employee at the firm, state so. Take advantage of a personal contact who is confident that you are qualified for the position, as María Lopez (Figure 5.8, p. 144) and Dora Cooper Bolger (Figure 5.9, p. 145) did. But first confirm that your contact gives you permission to use his or her name.

The Body of Your Letter

This section of your letter provides the evidence based on information from your résumé that you are qualified for the job. You might want to spend one paragraph on your educational qualifications and one on your job experience. Highlight your qualifications by citing specific accomplishments; don't simply state what you have done. Tell your reader exactly how your education and job experience qualify you to function and advance in the job advertised. Any homework you do on the company's history, goals, and structure should pay off. Again, note how María Lopez uses her knowledge of Dr. Henrady's specialty in pedodontics to her advantage (see Figure 5.8).

Education

Recent graduates with little work experience will, of course, spend more time on their education. Rather than just claiming you are qualified, give the facts to prove it. For instance, saying that you will graduate with a degree in criminal justice does not explain how, unlike all the other graduates of all the other criminal justice programs, are best qualified for the job. But when you indicate that in 36 hours of course work you have specialized in software security and that you have 12 course hours in business and communications, you say something specific, something persuasive.

Even if you have a lot of experience, don't forget to mention your education, and stress your most important educational accomplishments. Employers want to know how your skills and expertise apply to their particular job. Perhaps your work or civic and community experiences are so rich that you will spend an entire paragraph on them, as Dora Cooper Bolger does (see Figure 5.9). At any rate, do not neglect education for experience or vice versa. Refer to your résumé, and do not forget to say that you are including it with your letter.

Job Experience

After you discuss your educational qualifications, turn to your job experience. But if your experience is your most valuable and extensive qualification for the job, put it before a discussion of your education. If you are switching careers or are returning

FIGURE 5.7   Letter of application from Anthony Jones, a recent graduate with little job experience.

ANTHONY H. JONES
■ ■ ■ ■ ■ ■ ■ ■ ■ ■ ■

73 Allenwood Boulevard
Santa Rosa, California 95401-1074

707.555.6390
ajones@plat.com
www.plat.com/users/ajones/resume/html

May 24, 2006

Ms. Jocelyn Nogasaki
Human Resources Manager
Megalith Publishing Company
1001 Heathcliff Row
San Francisco, CA 94123-7707

Dear Ms. Nogasaki:

I am applying for the layout editor position advertised on your Web site, which I accessed on 14 May. Early next month, I will receive an A.S. degree in commercial graphics illustration from Santa Rosa Junior College.

With a special interest in the publishing industry, I have successfully completed more than forty credit hours in courses directly related to layout design, where I acquired experience using QuarkXPress as well as Illustrator and Photoshop. You might like to know that many of the design patterns of Megalith publications were used as models in my graphic communications and digital photography classes.

My studies have also led to practical experience at McAdam Publishers as part of my Santa Rosa apprenticeship program. While working at McAdam, I was responsible for assisting the design department in page composition and importing images. Other related experience I have had includes creating a Web site for and proofreading the student magazine, *Thunder.* As you will note on the enclosed résumé, I have also had experience in displaying merchandise at Buchman's Department Store.

I would appreciate the opportunity to discuss with you my qualifications in commercial graphics. After June 12, I will be available for an interview at any time that is convenient for you.

Sincerely yours,

Anthony H. Jones

Anthony H. Jones

Encl. Résumé

FIGURE 5.8   Letter of application from María Lopez, a recent graduate with some job experience.

1725 Brooke Street
Miami, FL 32701-2121
mlopez@eagle.com   305-555-3429

May 14, 2006

Dr. Marvin Henrady
839 Causeway Drive
Medical/Dental Plaza
Suite 34
Miami, FL 32706-2468

Dear Dr. Henrady:

Mr. Mitchell Pelbourne, my clinical instructor at Miami-Dade Community College, informs me that you are looking for a dental hygienist to work in your northside office. My education and experience qualify me for that position. This month I will graduate with an A.S. degree from the dental hygienist program at Miami-Dade Community College, and I will take the American Dental Assistants' Examination in early June.

I have successfully completed all course work and clinical programs in oral hygiene, anatomy, and prophylaxis techniques. During my clinical training, I received intensive practical instruction from a number of local dentists, including Dr. Tia Gutierrez. Since your northside office specializes in pedodontal care, you might find the subject of my major project—proper nutrition and dental care for preschoolers—especially relevant.

I have also had some related job experience in working with children in a health care setting. For a year and a half, I was employed as a unit clerk on the pediatric unit at St. Francis Hospital, and my experience in greeting patients, transcribing orders, and assisting the nursing staff would be valuable to you in running your office. You will find more detailed information about me and my experience in the enclosed résumé.

I would welcome the opportunity to talk with you about the position and my interest in pedodontics. I am available for an interview any time after 2:30 until June 11. After that date, I could come to your office any time at your convenience.

Sincerely yours,

María H. Lopez
María H. Lopez

Encl. Résumé

FIGURE 5.9   Letter of application from Dora Cooper Bolger, a recent graduate with community and civic experience.

Dora Cooper Bolger
1215 Lakeview Avenue
Westhampton, MI 46532
Voice: 616-555-4772   **Cell:** 616-555-4773   **dbolger@aol.com**

February 10, 2005

Dr. Lindsay Bafaloukos
Tanselle Mental Health Agency
4400 West Gallagher Drive
Tanselle, MI 46932-3106

Dear Dr. Bafaloukos:

At a recent meeting of the County Services Council, a member of your staff, Homer Strickland, told me that you will be hiring a public affairs coordinator. Because of my extensive experience and commitment to community affairs, I would appreciate your considering me for this opening. I expect to receive my B.S. in Public Administration from Mid-Michigan College next year.

For the last ten years, I have organized community groups with outreach programs similar to Tanselle's. I have held administrative positions in the PTA and the Foster Parents' Association and was president of Teens in Trouble, a volunteer group providing assistance to dysfunctional teens. My responsibilities with Teens have included coordinating our activities with various school programs, scheduling tutorials, and representing the organization before government agencies. I have been commended for my organizational and communication skills. My twenty presentations on foster home care and Teens in Trouble demonstrate that I am an effective speaker, a skill your agency would find valuable.

Because of my work at Mid-Michigan and for Teens and Foster Parents, I have the practical experience in communication and psychology to promote Tanselle's goals. The enclosed résumé provides details about my experience and education.

I would enjoy discussing my work with Teens and the other organizations with you. I am available for an interview any day after 11:00 a.m. Thank you for reaching me at the phone numbers or e-mail address at the top of this letter.

Sincerely yours,

Dora Cooper Bolger

Dora Cooper Bolger

Encl. Résumé

to a career after years away from the work force, start the body of your letter with your experiences or community and civic service as Dora Cooper Bolger does (see Figure 5.9, p. 145). Her volunteer work demonstrates clearly that she has the organizational and communication skills her prospective employer seeks.

Employers like to see continuity between a candidate's school and job experience, as in Figures 5.7 and 5.8. Provide that link by showing how the jobs you have held have something in common with your major—in terms of responsibility, research, customer relations, community service. Show how your course work in computer science helped you to be a more efficient programmer for your previous employer or how your summer jobs for the local park district reinforced your skills in providing client services.

Closing

Make your closing paragraph short—about two or three sentences—but be sure it fulfills the following three important functions:

1. emphasizes once again your major qualifications
2. asks for an interview or a phone call
3. indicates when you are available for an interview

End gracefully and professionally. Don't leave the reader with a single weak, vague sentence: "I would like to have an interview at your convenience." That does nothing to sell you. Say that you would appreciate talking with the employer further to discuss your qualifications. Then mention your chief talent. You might also express your willingness to relocate if the job requires it.

After indicating your interest in the job, give the times you are available for an interview and specifically tell the reader where you can be reached. If you are going to a professional meeting that the employer might also attend, or if you are visiting the employer's city soon, say so.

The following samples show how *not* to close your letter and why not.

Pushy:	I would like to set up an interview with you. Please phone me to arrange a convenient time. (That's the employer's prerogative, not yours.)
Too Informal:	I do not live far from your office. Let's meet for coffee sometime next week. (Say instead that since you live nearby, you will be available for an interview.)
Introduces New Subject:	I would like to discuss other qualifications you have in mind for the job. (How do you know what the interviewer might have in mind?)

Note that the closing paragraphs in Figures 5.8 through 5.10 avoid these errors.

Filling Out a Job Application

At some point during your job search, you will be asked to complete a prospective employer's application form. Application forms can vary tremendously; however, they all ask about your education, any military service, present and previous employment, references, and reasons for wanting to work for the company or agency. Because the topics overlap with those on your résumé, bring the résumé with you to the employer's office. But, *under no circumstances* attach a résumé to a blank form instead of filling the form out.

Some forms ask applicants to give reasons for leaving previous jobs and also require them to write a "personal essay" stating why the company should hire them. Both requirements involve tact. If you were fired from a past job, don't simply state that fact. Provide further relevant information, such as that your company was downsized and you were laid off, or that your company merged and your department was eliminated. More frequently, though, your reasons for leaving a job will be that you received a better offer or decided to return to school or to relocate.

Going to an Interview

There are various ways for a prospective employer to conduct an interview. It might be a one-to-one meeting—you and the interviewer. Or you may visit with a group of individuals who are trying to decide if you would fit in. Or you might have your interview over the telephone or through a videoconference. An interview can last thirty minutes or take all day.

Questions to Expect

The following questions are typical of those you can expect from interviewers, with advice on how to answer them.

- **Why do you want to work for us?** (Recall any job goals you have and apply them specifically to the job under discussion.)
- **What qualifications do you have for the job?** (Mention educational achievements and relevant work experience, especially computer skills.)
- **What could you possibly offer us that other candidates do not have?** (Say "enthusiasm," being a team player, and problem-solving abilities.)
- **Why did you attend this school?** (Be honest—location, costs, programs.)
- **Why did you major in "X"?** (Do not simply say financial benefits; concentrate on both practical and professional benefits. Be able to state career objectives.)
- **Why did you get a grade of "C" in a course?** (Don't say that you could have done better if you'd tried. Explain what the trouble was and mention that you corrected it in a course in which you earned a B or an A.)
- **What extracurricular activities did you participate in while in high school or college?** (Indicate any responsibilities you had—handling money, writing memos, coordinating events. If you were unable to participate in such activities, tell the interviewer that a part-time job, community or church activities, or commuting prevented your participating. Such answers sound better than saying that you did not like sports or clubs in school.)
- **Did you learn as much as you wanted from your course work?** (This is a loaded question. Indicate that you learned a great deal but now look forward to the opportunity to gain more practical skill, to put into practice the principles

FIGURE 5.10   An application for employment.

Application for Employment

COMMUNITY FEDERAL BANK

PLEASE PRINT   DATE _____

POSITION FOR WHICH   **SALARY**
YOU ARE APPLYING _____   **EXPECTATION** _____

PERSONAL INFORMATION
(Please attach a page, if necesssary, to include additional information.)

NAME _____

PRESENT
ADDRESS _____

PERMANENT
ADDRESS _____

SOCIAL   HOME PHONE   WORK PHONE
SECURITY NO. _____   NUMBER _____   NUMBER _____

HOW WERE YOU REFERRED TO US?

SPECIAL SKILLS, ABILITIES, KNOWLEDGE, ETC.
(in addition to paid experience, you may also list skills gained as a volunteer)

PROFESSIONAL REFERENCES (PLEASE INCLUDE TITLE, BUSINESS & PHONE
NUMBER)

_____

_____

_____

_____

_____

_____

**IF HIRED, YOU WILL BE REQUIRED TO PROVIDE PROOF OF AUTHORIZATION
TO WORK IN THE UNITED STATES PRIOR TO BEGINNING EMPLOYMENT**
(The Immigration Reform and Control Act of 1986)

To the best of my knowledge, all of the information in this application and attached résumé
is true and is given voluntarily.

SIGNATURE _____

you have learned; say that you will never be through learning about your major.)

- **What is your greatest strength?** (Say being a team player, cooperation, willingness to learn, ability to grasp difficult concepts easily, managing time or money, taking criticism easily, and profiting from criticism.)
- **What is your greatest shortcoming?** (Be honest here and mention it, but then turn to ways in which you are improving. Don't say something deadly like, "I can never seem to finish what I start" or "I hate being criticized." You should neither dwell on your weaknesses nor keep silent about them. Saying "None" to this kind of question is as inadvisable as rattling off a list of faults.)
- **How do you handle conflict with a co-worker, boss, customer?** (Stress your ability to be courteous and honest and to work toward a productive resolution. State that you avoid language, tone of voice, or gestures that interfere with healthy dialogue.)
- **Why did you leave your last job?** ("I returned to school full-time" or "I moved from Jackson to Springfield." *Never attack your previous employer.* That only makes you look bad.)

What Do I Say About Salary?

Do your homework. Find out what the salary range is for your professional level in your area. (Consult the *Occupational Outlook Handbook, http://www.bls.gov/oco/*.) Ask your instructors or people you know who work for the company, or call a professional organization to which you may belong for information. If the issue of salary comes up, you can then ask your interviewer if the company has established a salary range for the position and better assess where you stand in relationship to that range.

Some Interview Dos and Don'ts

Keep in mind some other interview "dos" and "don'ts."

1. Be on time. In fact, show up about fifteen minutes early in case the interviewer wants you to complete some initial forms.
2. Go to the interview alone.
3. Dress appropriately for the occasion. Never wear blue jeans. Men: Wear a suit and tie. Women: Wear a suit (pants or skirt) or equally businesslike attire.
4. Thank your interviewer(s) for inviting you.
5. Speak slowly and distinctly; do not hurry to finish your sentences or interrupt or finish an interviewer's sentences. Avoid one- or two-word answers, which make you sound unfriendly or unprepared. Do not use slang (e.g., "Right on," "Way to go," "You go, girl") or overly casual language ("Like . . .," "You know?").
6. Refrain from chewing gum, fidgeting, or tapping your foot against the floor, a chair, or a desk.
7. Maintain eye contact with the interviewer; do not sheepishly stare at the floor or the desk. Body language is equally important. For instance, don't fold your arms, which signals that you are closed to the interviewer's suggestions.

FIGURE 5.11   A follow-up letter.

2739 East Street
Latrobe, PA 17042-0312

610-555-6373
mlb@springboard.com

September 20, 2006

Mr. Jack Fukurai
Manager of Human Resources
Transatlantic Piping Company
1334 Ridge Road N.E.
Pittsburgh, PA 17122-3107

Dear Mr. Fukurai:

I enjoyed talking with you last Wednesday and learning more about the security officer position available at Transatlantic Piping. It was especially helpful to take a tour of the plant's north gate section to see the challenges it presents for the security officer stationed there.

As you noted at the interview, my training in surveillance electronics has prepared me to operate the sophisticated equipment Transatlantic has installed at the north gate. I was grateful to Ms. Turner for taking time to demonstrate the equipment.

I am looking forward to receiving the handbook about Transatlantic's employee services. Would it also be possible for you to include a copy of the newsletter from last year that introduced the new security equipment to the employees?

Thank you for considering me for the position and for the hospitality you showed me. I look forward to hearing from you. After my visit last week, I know that Transatlantic Piping would be an excellent place to work.

Sincerely yours,

Marcia Le Borde

Marcia Le Borde

8. Sit up straight; do not slouch.
9. When the interview is over, thank the interviewer for considering you for the job and indicate you look forward to hearing from him or her.

The Follow-Up Letter

Within a week after the interview, it is wise to send a follow-up letter thanking the interviewer for his or her time and interest in you. In your letter, you can reemphasize your qualifications for the job by showing how they apply to conditions described by the interviewer; you might also ask for further information to show your interest in the job and the employer. A sample follow-up letter appears in Figure 5.11.

✓ Revision Checklist

- ❏ Inventoried my strengths carefully to prepare résumé.
- ❏ Restricted the types of job(s) for which I am qualified.
- ❏ Requested letters from professors, employers, and community officials.
- ❏ Identified places where relevant jobs are advertised.
- ❏ Networked with instructors, friends, relatives, clergy, and individuals who work for the companies I want to join that I am in the job market.
- ❏ Checked with state employment office and relevant government agencies.
- ❏ Wrote a focused and persuasive career objective.
- ❏ Determined the most beneficial format of résumé to use—chronological, functional, or both.
- ❏ Prepared an electronic résumé to send on-line if prospective employer so directs.
- ❏ Investigated creating a Web site for my job search-related documents.
- ❏ Made résumé attractive and easy to read with logical and persuasive headings and hyperlinks.
- ❏ Made sure résumé contains neither too much nor too little information.
- ❏ Proofread résumé to ensure everything is correct, consistent, and accurate.
- ❏ Wrote letter of application that shows how my specific skills and background apply to and meet an employer's exact needs.
- ❏ Prepared for interview.
- ❏ Sent prospective employer a follow-up letter within a few days after interview to show interest in position.

Exercises

1. Using at least four different sources, including the Internet, compile a list of ten employers for whom you would like to work. Get their names, street and e-mail addresses, phone numbers, and the names of the managers or human resources officers. Then select one company and write a profile about it—locations, services, kinds of products or services offered, number of employees, clients served, types of schedules used, and other pertinent facts.

2. Which of the following would belong on your résumé? Which would not belong? Why?
   a. student ID number
   b. social security number
   c. the ZIP codes of your references' addresses
   d. a list of all your English courses in college
   e. section numbers of the courses in your major
   f. statement that you are recently divorced
   g. subscriptions to journals in your field
   h. the titles of any stories or poems you published in a high school literary magazine or newspaper
   i. your GPA
   j. foreign languages you studied
   k. years you attended college
   l. the date you were discharged from the service
   m. names of the neighbors you are using as references
   n. your religion
   o. job titles you held
   p. your summer job washing dishes
   q. your telephone number
   r. the reason you changed schools
   s. your current status with the National Guard
   t. the URL of your Web site
   u. your volunteer work for the Red Cross
   v. hours a week you spend reading science fiction
   w. the title of your last term paper in your major
   x. the name of the agency or business where you worked last

3. Indicate what is wrong with the following career objectives and rewrite them to make them more precise and professional.
   a. Job in a dentist's office.
   b. Position with a safety emphasis.
   c. Desire growth position in a large department store.
   d. Am looking for entry position in health sciences with an emphasis on caring for older people.
   e. Position in sales with fast promotion rate.
   f. Want a job working with semiconductor circuits.
   g. I would like a position in fashion, especially one working with modern fashion.

   h. Desire a good-paying job, hours: 8–4:30, with double pay for overtime. Would like to stay in the Omaha area.

   i. Insurance work.

   j. Working with computers.

   k. Personal secretary.

   l. Job with preschoolers.

   m. Full-time position with hospitality chain.

   n. I want a career in nursing.

   o. Police work, particularly in suburb of large city.

   p. A job that lets me be me.

   q. Desire fun job selling cosmetics.

   r. Any position for a qualified dietitian.

   s. Although I have not made up my mind about which area of forestry I shall go into, I am looking for a job that offers me training and rewards based on my potential.

4. Revise the following poor résumé to make it more precise and persuasive. Include additional details where necessary and exclude any details that would hurt the job seeker's chances. Also correct any inconsistencies.

RÉSUMÉ OF

Powell T. Harrison
8604 So. Kirkpatrick St.
Ardville, Ohio
345 37 8760
614 234 4587
harrison@gem.com

PERSONAL	Confidential
CAREER OBJECTIVE	Seek good paying position with progressive Sunbelt company.
EDUCATION	
2003–2005	Will receive degree from Central Tech. Institute in Arch. St. Earned high average last semester. Took necessary courses for major; interested in systems, plans, and design development.
2000–2004	Attended Ardville High School, Ardville, OH; took all courses required. Served on several student committees.
EXPERIENCE	None, except for numerous part-time jobs and student apprenticeship in the Ardville area. As part of student app. worked with local firm for two months.

<u>HOBBIES</u>	Surfing the Net, playing Final Fantasy. Member of Junior Achievement.
<u>REFERENCES</u>	Please write for names and addresses.

---

5. Explain why the following letter of application is ineffective. Rewrite it to make it more precise and appropriate.

Apartment 32
Jeggler Drive
Talcott, Arizona

Monday

Grandt Corporation
Production Supervisor
Capital City, Arizona

Dear Sir:

I am writing to ask you if your company will consider me for the position you announced in the newspaper yesterday. I believe that with my education (I have an associate degree) and experience (I have worked four years as a freight supervisor), I could fill your job.

My schoolwork was done at two junior colleges, and I took more than enough courses in business management and modern technology. In fact, here is a list of some of my courses: Supervision, Materials Management, Work Experience in Management, Business Machines, Safety Tactics, Introduction to Packaging, Art Design, Modern Business Principles, and Small Business Management. In addition, I have worked as a loading dock supervisor for the last two years, and before that I worked in the military in the Quartermaster Corps.

Please let me know if you are interested in me. I would like to have an interview with you at the earliest possible date, since there are some other firms also interested in me, too.

Eagerly yours,

George D. Milhous

---

6. From the Sunday edition of your local newspaper or from one of the other sources discussed in the "Looking in the Right Places for a Job" section (pp. 124–26), find notices for two or three jobs you believe you are qualified to fill and then write a letter of application for one of them.

7. Write a chronologically organized résumé to accompany the letter you wrote for Exercise 6.

8. Write a functional résumé for your application letter in Exercise 6.

9. Write a letter to a local business inquiring about summer employment. Indicate that you can work for only one summer and that you will be returning to school by September 1.

Preparing Documents and Visuals

Designing Successful Documents, Visuals, and Web Sites

As we have seen, to be effective in the world of work you have to write clearly and concisely, but the success of your document depends as much on how it looks as on what it says. You will be expected to design professional looking memos, letters, instructions, and reports as well as to create appropriate visuals to support these documents. This chapter gives you practical advice for making your work more reader-friendly and visually appealing. It also surveys the kinds of visuals you will encounter most frequently and shows you how to read, construct, and write about them. The chapter also includes information about creating Web sites.

In designing documents, you need to project a positive, professional image of yourself, your company, your product. A report filled with nothing but thick unbroken, long paragraphs, with no visual clues to break them up or to make information stand out, is sure to intimidate readers and turn them away. They will conclude that your work is too complex and not worth their effort or time. Your company, too, will win or lose points because of your design choices. A visually appealing Web site or document will enhance a company's reputation and improve its sales. A poorly designed one will not. Consumers will think your firm is inflexible, difficult to do business with, and uncaring about specific problems customers may have over a policy or a set of instructions.

Make your documents look user-friendly by signaling to your audience that your message is

- easy to read
- easy to follow and understand
- easy to recall

You can do all this by breaking material into smaller units that are visually appealing. You can help readers find key points at a glance through **chunking** (using smaller paragraphs) and using lists, boldface type, and bullets. That way they can find your ideas easily the first time through or on a second reading if they have to double back to check or verify a point.

Organizing Information Visually

Take a quick look at Figures 6.1 and 6.2 (pp. 161–164). The same information is contained in each figure. Which appeals to you more? Which do you think would be easier to read? Which is better designed? As the two figures show, design or layout plays a crucial role in an audience's overall acceptance of your work.

Figure 6.2 has this list's positive design characteristics (on the left) while Figure 6.1 has the unfavorable ones (on the right).

- visual appeal
- logical organization
- clarity
- accessibility
- variety
- relevance

- crowded
- disorganized
- hard to follow
- difficult to read
- uneven
- confusing

By incorporating the characteristics of Figure 6.2 into your documents, you can guarantee that your message will be well received.

The ABCs of Print Document Design

The basic elements of effective document design are

- page layout
- typography, or type design, including using color
- graphics, or visuals

The proper arrangement and balance of type, white space, and graphics involve the same level of preparation that you would spend on your research, drafting, revising, and editing. Just as you research your information, you have to research and experiment in order to adopt the most effective design for your document.

Page Layout

Each of your pages needs to coordinate space and text pleasingly. Too much or too little of one or the other can jeopardize the reader's acceptance of your message. Pay attention to the following elements.

   1. White space. White space, which refers to the page's open areas that are free of text and visuals, can help you increase the impact of your message. Skimping on white space by packing too much print on the page distracts the reader from the message

FIGURE 6.1 A poorly designed document.

The results for the recent cholesterol screening at our company's Health Fair were distributed to each employee last week. Many employees wanted to know more information about cholesterol in general, the different types of cholesterol, what the results mean, and the foods that are high or low in cholesterol.

We hope the information provided below will better answer employees' questions concerning cholesterol and our cholesterol screening program.

High cholesterol, along with high blood pressure and obesity, is one of the primary risk factors that may contribute to the development of coronary heart disease and may eventually lead to a heart attack or stroke. Cholesterol is a fatty, sticky substance found in the bloodstream. Excessive amounts of the bad type of cholesterol can deposit on the walls of the heart arteries. This deposit is called plaque and over a long period of time plaque can narrow or even block the blood flow through the arteries.

Total cholesterol is divided into three parts—LDL (low-density lipoprotein), or bad cholesterol; HDL (high-density lipoprotein), or good cholesterol; and VLDL (very low-density lipoprotein), a much smaller component of cholesterol you don't have to worry about. Bad (LDL) cholesterol forms on the walls of your arteries and can cause a lot of damage. Good cholesterol, on the other hand, functions like a sponge, mopping up cholesterol and carrying it out of the bloodstream.

You should have received three cholesterol numbers. One is for your HDL, or good cholesterol, and the other is for your LDL, or bad cholesterol, reading. These two numbers are added to give you the third, or composite, level of your total cholesterol. You are doing fine.

As you can see, a total cholesterol reading of 200 or below is considered safe. Continue what you have been doing. If your reading falls in the moderate risk range of 200–239, you need to modify your diet, get more exercise, and have your cholesterol checked again in six months. If your reading is above 240, see your doctor. You may need to take cholesterol-lowering medication, if your doctor prescribes it. Reducing your total cholesterol by even as little as 25% can decrease your risk of a heart attack by 50%.

The Surgeon General recommends that your LDL, or bad, cholesterol should be below 130. And your HDL, or good, cholesterol needs to be at least above 36. Ideally, the ratio between the two numbers should not be greater than 5 to 1. That is, your HDL should be at least 20% of your LDL. The higher your HDL is, the better, of course. So even if you have a high LDL reading, if your HDL is correspondingly high you will be at less risk.

One of the easiest ways to decrease your cholesterol is to modify your diet. Cholesterol is found in foods that are high in saturated fat. Saturated fat comes from animal sources and also from certain vegetable sources. Foods high in bad cholesterol that you should restrict, or avoid, include whole milk, red meat, eggs, cheese, butter, shrimp, oils such as palm and coconut, and avocados. Generally, food groups low in cholesterol include fruits, vegetables, and whole grains (wheat breads, oatmeal, and certain cereals), lean meats (fish, chicken), and beans.

<u>The goal of our cholesterol screening is to help each employee lower his or her cholesterol level and eventually reduce the risk of heart disease. Besides the advice given above, you can do the following</u>: get regular aerobic exercise—bicycling, brisk walking, swimming, rowing—for at least 30 minutes 3–4 times a week. But get your doctor's approval first. Eat foods low in cholesterol but high in dietary fiber (beans, oatmeal, brown rice). Maintain a healthy weight for your frame to lower your body fat. Minimize stress, which can increase cholesterol. Learn relaxation techniques.

FIGURE 6.2   An effectively designed document with the same text as Figure 6.1.

Cholesterol Screening

The results for the recent cholesterol screening at our company's Health Fair were distributed to each employee last week. Many employees wanted to know more information about cholesterol in general, the different types of cholesterol, what the results mean, and the foods that are high or low in cholesterol. We hope the information provided below will better answer employees' questions concerning cholesterol and our cholesterol screening program.

Determining Risk Factors

High cholesterol, along with high blood pressure and obesity, is one of the primary risk factors that may contribute to the development of coronary heart disease and may eventually lead to a heart attack or stroke. Cholesterol is a fatty, sticky substance found in the bloodstream. Excessive amounts of the bad type of cholesterol can deposit on the walls of the heart arteries. This deposit is called **plaque** and over a long period of time plaque can narrow or even block the blood flow through the arteries.

Separating Types of Cholesterol

Total cholesterol is divided into three parts: (1) **LDL** (low-density lipoprotein), or bad cholesterol; (2) **HDL** (high-density lipoprotein), or good cholesterol; and (3) **VLDL** (very low-density lipoprotein), a much smaller component of cholesterol you don't have to worry about. Bad (LDL) cholesterol forms on the walls of your arteries and can cause a lot of damage. Good cholesterol, on the other hand, functions like a sponge, mopping up cholesterol and carrying it out of the bloodstream.

Continued

FIGURE 6.2   (Continued)

Understanding Your Cholesterol Results

You should have received three cholesterol numbers. One is for your **HDL** (or good cholesterol) and the other is for your **LDL** (or bad cholesterol) reading. These two numbers are added to give you the third, or composite, level of your total cholesterol.

Cholesterol levels can be classified as follows:

Minimal Risk	Moderate Risk	High Risk
below 200	200–239	above 240

As you can see, a total cholesterol reading of 200 or below is considered safe. You are doing fine. Continue what you have been doing. If your reading falls in the moderate risk range of 200–239, you need to modify your diet, get more exercise, and have your cholesterol checked again in six months. If your reading is above 240, see your doctor. You may need to take cholesterol-lowering medication, if your doctor prescribes it. Reducing your total cholesterol by even as little as 25% can decrease your risk of a heart attack by 50%.

Relationship Between Bad and Good Cholesterol

The Surgeon General recommends that your **LDL**, or bad, cholesterol should be below 130. And your **HDL**, or good, cholesterol needs to be at least above 36. Ideally, the ratio between the two numbers should not be greater than 5 to 1. That is, your **HDL** should be at least 20% of your **LDL**. The higher your **HDL** is, the better, of course. So even if you have a high **LDL** reading, if your **HDL** is correspondingly high you will be at less risk.

Recognizing Food Sources of Cholesterol

One of the easiest ways to decrease your cholesterol is to modify your diet. Cholesterol is found in foods that are high in saturated fat. Saturated fat comes

Continued

FIGURE 6.2   (Continued)

from animal sources and also from certain vegetable sources. Foods high in bad cholesterol that you should restrict include:

1. whole milk
2. red meat
3. eggs
4. cheese
5. butter
6. shrimp
7. oils such as palm and coconut
8. avocados

Generally, food groups low in cholesterol include fruits, vegetables, and whole grains (wheat breads, oatmeal, and certain cereals), lean meats (fish, chicken), and beans.

Realizing It Is Up to You

The goals of our cholesterol screening program are to help each employee lower his or her cholesterol level and eventually reduce the risk of heart disease. Besides the advice given above, you can do the following:

- Get regular aerobic exercise—bicycling, brisk walking, swimming, rowing—for at least 30 minutes 3–4 times a week. But get your doctor's approval first.
- Eat foods low in cholesterol but high in dietary fiber (beans, oatmeal, and brown rice).
- Maintain a healthy weight for your frame to lower your body fat.
- Minimize stress, which can increase cholesterol. Learn relaxation techniques.

The author is indebted to Sgt. Mannie E. Hall of the U.S. Army for creating this document.

you really want to convey. White space can entice, comfort, and appeal to the reader's "psychology of space" by

- attracting the reader's attention
- assuring the reader that information is presented logically
- announcing that information is easy to follow
- assisting the reader to organize information visually

Again, compare Figures 6.1 and 6.2. Which document was designed by someone who understands the importance of white space?

2. Margins. Use wide margins, usually 1 to 1½ inches, to "frame" your document with white space surrounding text and visuals. Margins prevent your document from looking cluttered or overcrowded. If your document requires binding, you may have to leave a wider left margin (2 inches).

3. Line length. Most readers find a text line of 10 to 14 words, or 50 to 70 characters (depending on the type size you choose), comfortable and enjoyable to read. Excessively long lines that bump into the margins signal that your work is difficult to read. In the example here, note how the extra-long lines unsettle your reading and tax your eye movement; they signal rough going.

In order to succeed in the world of business, workers must learn to brush up on their networking skills. The network process has many benefits that you need to be aware of. These benefits range from finding a better job to accomplishing your job more easily and efficiently. Through networking you are able to expand the number of contacts who can help you. Networking means sharing news and opportunities. The Internet is the key to successful networking.

On the other hand, do not print a document with too short or extremely uneven lines.

> In order to succeed in the world of
> business, workers must learn
> to brush up on their networking skills. The
> network process has many
> benefits you need to be
> aware of.

Readers will suspect your ideas are incomplete, superficial, or even simple-minded.

4. Columns. Document text usually is organized in either single-column or multi-column formats. Memos, letters, and reports are usually formatted without columns, whereas documents that intersperse text and visuals (such as newsletters and magazines) work better in multicolumn formats.

Typography

Typeface
Readability of your text is crucial. Select a typeface, therefore, that ensures your text is

- legible
- attractive

- functional
- appropriate for your message
- complementary with accompanying graphics

The most familiar typefaces are the following four. Avoid using a typeface that looks like script, and don't mix and switch typefaces. The result makes your work look amateurish and disorganized (see Figure 6.1).

Times Roman   **Frutiger**

Helvetica   Palatino

Type Size

Type size options are almost unlimited, depending on your software package and printer capabilities. Type size is measured in units called **points,** 72 points to the inch. The bigger the point size, the larger the type. Never print your letter or report in 6- or 8-point newspaper ad type or in a size larger than 12-point type. Here are some suggestions.

Times 8 point = footnotes/endnotes

Helvetica 12 point = letters, reports

Palatino 14 point = headings

Frutiger 22 point = title of your report

Type Styles
Type styles include boldface, italics, shadow, underlining, small caps, and shading.

Boldface
Italics
Shadow
Underlining
Small Caps
Shading

Avoid overusing boldface and italics. Use them only when necessary and not for decoration. Do *not* underline the text unless absolutely necessary. Not only will too many special effects make your work harder to read, but you will lose the dramatic impact these features have to distinguish and emphasize key points that do deserve boldface or italic type.

Justification
Sometimes referred to as alignment, justification consists of left, right, full, and center options. Left-justified (also called **unjustified** or **ragged right**) is the preferred method because it allows space between words in lines of text to remain constant and is easier to read.

Our new Web site offers consumers a mall on the Internet. It gives shoppers access to our products and services and makes buying easy and fun. Our new Web site offers consumers a mall on the Internet. It gives shoppers access to our	Our new Web site offers consumers a mall on the Internet. It gives shoppers access to our products and services and makes buying easy and fun. Our new Web site offers consumers a mall on the Internet. It gives shoppers access to our

Left-justified text	Right-justified text

Heads and Subheads
Heads and subheads are brief descriptive words or phrases to introduce or summarize a document or a section or subsection within a document. They are typographical markers that signal starting points and major divisions in your document. They provide helpful landmarks for readers charting their course through a document, as in Figure 6.2. Without heads and subheads your work will look unorganized. They

should be grammatically parallel and not wordy. Note how these headings from a poorly organized proposal from the Acme Company are not parallel.

- What Is the Problem?
- Describing What Acme Can Do to Solve the Problem
- It's a Matter of Time . . .
- Fees Acme Will Charge
- When You Need to Pay
- Finding Out Who's Who

Revised, the heads are parallel and easier for a reader to understand and follow.

- A Brief History of the Problem
- A Description of Acme Solutions
- A Timetable Acme Will Follow
- A Breakdown of Acme's Fees
- A Payment Plan
- A Listing of Acme's Staff

Heads and subheads immediately attract attention and quickly inform readers about the function, scope, purpose, or contents of the document or section. The space around a heading is like an oasis for the reader, signaling both a rest and a new beginning. In designing a document with heads and subheads, follow these guidelines.

- Use a larger type size for heads than for text; major heads should be larger than subheads. If your text is in 10-point type, your heads can be in 16-point type and your subheads in 12- or 14-point type.
- Modify type to differentiate sections. For example, for heads and subheads use uppercase, bold type, underlining, and changes in font style or type.
- Establish a horizontal position for a head, such as centered or aligned left, and keep it consistent throughout the document.

Fourteen-Point Head
Subhead in 12 Point
Use larger type for heads than you do for text; major headings should be larger than subheads. If your text is in 10-point type, your heads may be in 14-point type and your subheads in 12.

Lists
Placing items in a list helps readers by dividing, organizing, and ranking information. Lists emphasize important points and contribute to an easy-to-read page design. Lists can be (a) numbered, (b) lettered, or (c) bulleted. Take a look at the memos, reports, and proposals in Chapters 3, 8, and 9 that effectively use lists.

Using Color

Color can be used in many ways to organize written information and therefore enhance readability. Color visually breaks up long segments of text and can tie important ideas together. For example, using colored boxes to identify special notes in the text helps readers locate important information quickly. Don't overdo it. Use color for functional reasons, *not* just to decorate. Color can be effectively employed for borders and graphic accents, headings, titles, keywords, Internet addresses, sidebars, rules, and boxes that link related facts, figures, or information.

Some Guidelines on Using Color

- Evaluate how the color will look on the page—colors look different on the screen than they do on a sheet of paper. Light colors make objects look larger; dark colors make objects appear smaller. Print a sample page.
- Make sure text colors contrast sharply with background colors.
- Use no more than two or three colors on a page unless there are photographs, illustrations, or graphics.
- Too many bright colors overwhelm the eye, so use them sparingly to call attention to important elements.
- Select "cool" colors, such as blue, turquoise, purple, and magenta, for backgrounds. However, avoid light blue text, which is difficult to read against a dark background.

The Purpose of Visuals

Now that you can design professional looking documents, learn how to integrate visuals for additional support. Here are several reasons why visuals can improve your work; each point is graphically reinforced in Figure 6.3 (p. 170).

1. **Visuals arouse readers' immediate interest.** They catch the reader's eye quickly by setting important information apart and by giving relief from sentences and paragraphs. Note the eye-catching quality of the visual in Figure 6.3.

2. **Visuals increase readers' understanding by simplifying concepts.** A visual *shows* ideas whereas a verbal description only *tells* about them in the abstract. Visuals are especially important and helpful if you must explain a technical process to a non-specialist audience. Visuals help readers see percentages, trends, comparisons, and contrasts. Figure 6.3, for example, shows at a glance the growth of e-commerce.

3. **Visuals are especially important for non-native speakers of English and multicultural audiences.** Given the international audience for many business documents, visuals will make your communication with them easier and clearer. (See Terri Smith Ruckel's report in Figure 9.2, pp. 272–290.)

4. **Visuals emphasize key relationships.** Through their arrangement and form, visuals quickly show contrasts, similarities, growth rates, and downward and upward movements, as well as fluctuations in time, money, and space.

FIGURE 6.3   A line-and-bar chart depicting the growth of e-commerce compared to traditional businesses.

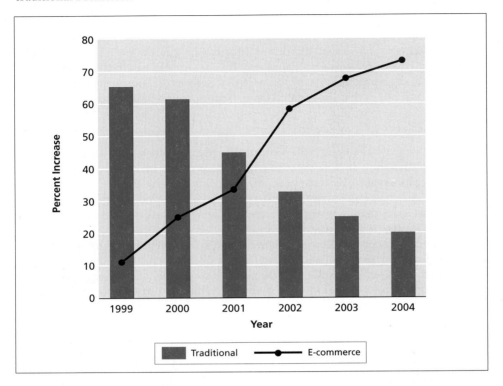

5. Visuals condense and summarize a large quantity of information into a relatively small space. A visual also allows you to streamline your message by saving words. It can record data in far less space than it would take to describe those facts in words alone. Note how in Figure 6.3 the growth rates of two different types of businesses are expressed and documented.

6. Visuals are highly persuasive. Visuals have sales appeal. They can convince readers to buy your product or service or to accept your point of view.

Choosing Effective Visuals: Some Precautions

Select your visuals carefully. Special computer software programs allow you to select, create, and introduce visuals. The following suggestions will help you to choose effective visuals.

1. Use visuals only when they are relevant for your purpose and audience. Never include a visual simply as a decoration. A short report on fire drills, for example, does not need a picture of a fire station. Avoid any visual that is too technical for your readers or that includes more detail than you need to show.

2. Use visuals in conjunction with—not as a substitute for—written work. Visuals do not always take the place of words. In fact, you may need to explain information contained in a visual. A set of illustrations or a group of tables alone may not satisfy readers looking for summaries, evaluations, or conclusions. Note how the visual in conjunction with the description of a magnetic resonance imager (MRI) in Figure 6.4 makes the procedure easier to understand than if the writer had used only words or only a visual. This visual and verbal description is appropriately included in a brochure teaching patients about MRI procedures.

3. Experiment with several visuals. Evaluate a variety of options before you select a particular visual. For instance, a graphics software package such as PowerPoint (see Chapter 10, pp. 305–307) will allow you to represent statistical data in a number of

FIGURE 6.4   A visual used in conjunction with written work.

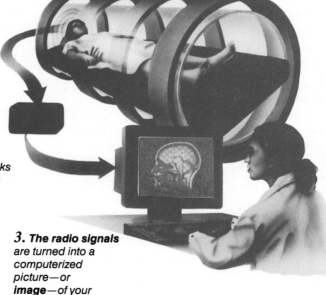

A PICTURE FROM THE INSIDE OUT
At the heart of the magnetic resonance imager is a large magnet that is big enough for you to lie inside. Look at the picture below. The **magnet** directs radio signals to surround sections of your body. When the signals pass through your body, they **resonate** (release a signal). Then your body's response is picked up by a receiver and sent to a computer. The computer analyzes the signal and converts it into a visual **image** of your tissues on a video screen.

1. **The MR Imager** surrounds your body with a harmless **magnetic** field and radio signals that safely pass through your body.

2. **A receiver** picks up and measures the radio signals that leave, or **resonate** from, your body.

3. **The radio signals** are turned into a computerized picture—or **image**—of your body's tissues.

ways. Preview a few different versions of a visual or even different types of visuals to determine which one would be best. Test your visual first to identify parts and find the proper scale.

4. Be prepared to revise and edit your visuals. Just as you draft, revise, and edit your written work to meet your audience's needs, create several versions of your visual to get it right. Expect to change shapes or proportions; experiment with different colors, shadings, labels, and sizes. Avoid any visuals that may distract the reader or contradict your message. Make sure each visual is accurate and ethical, not unclear, distorted, or exaggerated. (Review Chapter 1 on the ethics of using visuals.)

5. Always use high-quality visuals. Your visuals should be clear, easy-to-read, attractive, and relevant. If you photocopy, download, or scan a visual, make sure the copy is clear and readable and does not cut off any part of the original.

6. Consider how your visuals will look on the page. Don't cram visuals onto a page or allow them to spill over your text or margins.

Writing About Visuals: Some Guidelines

Using a visual requires more of you as a writer than simply inserting it into your written work. You need to *use visuals in conjunction with what you write.* The following guidelines will help you (1) identify, (2) insert, (3) introduce, and (4) interpret visuals for your readers. By observing these guidelines, you can use visuals more effectively and efficiently.

Reference Visuals

Always mention in the text of your paper or report that you are including a visual. If you don't alert readers to a specific visual, they may skip it or wonder why it is there.

Identify Visuals

Give each visual a number and a caption (title) that indicates the subject or explains what the visual illustrates. The following are some examples of figure numbers and titles.

- Figure 2. A photo of a cherrypicker.
- Figure 4.1 The proper way to apply for a small business loan.

Cite the Source for Visuals

If you use a visual that is not your own work, give credit to your source (newspaper, magazine, textbook, company, federal agency, individual, or Web site).

Insert Visuals Appropriately

Here are some rules to keep in mind.

- Place visuals as close as possible to the first mention of them in text. By inserting an appropriate visual near the beginning of your discussion, you help readers understand the discussion better than if you placed the visual near the end.

- Never introduce a visual *before* a discussion of it; readers will wonder why it is there. Be sure to tell readers where the visual can be found—"below," "on the following page," "to the right," "at the bottom of page 3."
- Center your visual and, if necessary, box it. Squeezing visuals toward the left or right margins looks unprofessional.
- Never collect all of your visuals and put them in an appendix. Readers need to see them at those points in your discussion where they are most pertinent.

Introduce Your Visuals

Refer to each visual by its number and, if necessary, mention the title as well. In introducing the visual, though, do not just insert a reference to it, such as "See Figure 3.4" or "Look at Table 1." Help readers to understand the relationships in your visual. Here is a lead-in sentence for a visual.

As Figure 3 shows, our store saw a dramatic rise in the shipment of electric ranges over the five-year period as opposed to the less impressive increase in washing machine purchases.

Interpret Your Visuals

Give readers help in understanding your visual and in knowing what to look for. Let them know what is most significant about the visual. Do not expect the visual to explain itself. In a study on the benefits of vanpooling, one writer supplied the following visual, a table.

TABLE 1   Travel Time (in minutes): Automobile versus Vanpool

Private Automobile	Vanpool
25	32.5
30	39.0
35	45.5
40	52.0
45	58.5
50	65.0
55	71.5
60	78.0

Source: U.S. Department of Transportation. *Increased Transportation Efficiency Through Ridesharing: The Brokerage Approach* (Washington, D.C., DOT-OS—40096): 45.

Explaining the table, the writer called attention to it in the context of the report on transportation efficiency.

Although, as Table 1 above suggests, the travel time in a vanpool may be as much as 30 percent longer than in a private automobile (to allow for pickups), the total trip time for the vanpool user can be about the same as with a private automobile because vanpools eliminate the need to search for parking spaces and to walk to the employment site entrance.[1]

What *Not* to Do with a Visual

Here are a few things to remember as you prepare to use visuals.

- Avoid using a visual that distracts from your work (for example, one that is too small, too large, does not use the right type of shading).
- Never use a visual that presents information that contradicts your work.
- Never distort a visual for emphasis.
- Be careful that you don't omit anything when you reproduce an existing visual.
- Never use visuals that discriminate or stereotype (for example, avoid pictures of a work force that excludes female employees).
- Avoid visuals that would be misunderstood or regarded as offensive in another culture.
- Don't offend non-native speakers of English by using a culturally biased color (for example, reconsider using red for warning signals or danger; red in China signals happiness and good fortune and is used at weddings).

Two Categories of Visuals

Visuals can be divided into two categories—**tables** and **figures.** A *table* arranges information—numbers and/or words—in parallel columns or rows for easy comparison of data. Anything that is not a table is considered a figure. *Figures* include graphs, circle charts, bar charts, organizational charts, flow charts, pictographs, maps, photographs, and drawings.

Tables

Tables are parallel columns or rows of information organized and arranged into categories to show changes in time, distance, cost, employment, or some other distinguishable or quantifiable variable. Tables allow readers to compare a great deal of information in a compact space. Tables also summarize material for easy recall—causes of wars; provisions of a law; or differences between a common cold, the flu, and pneumonia.

Parts of a Table

To use a table properly, you need to know the parts that constitute it. Refer to Table 6.1, which labels these parts, as you read the following:

- The main **column** is "Amount Needed to Satisfy Minimum Daily Requirement," and the **subcolumns** are the protein sources for which the table gives data.

---

[1]James A. Devine, "Vanpooling: A New Economic Tool," *AIDC Journal.*

- The **stub** refers to the first vertical column on the left side. The stub column heading is "Source." The stub lists the foods for which information is broken down in the subcolumns.
- A **rule** (or line) across the top of the table separates the headings from the body of the table.

Guidelines for Using Tables

When you include a table in your work, follow these guidelines.

- Number the tables according to the order in which they are discussed in the text (Table 1, Table 2, Table 3).
- Include the table on the same page, where it is most appropriate, whenever possible.
- Keep your table on one page; it is difficult for readers to follow a table spread across different pages.
- Give each table a concise and descriptive title to show exactly what is being represented or compared.
- Use words in the **stub** (a list of items about which information is given), but put numbers under column headings. The "Source" column in Table 6.1 is the stub.
- Supply footnotes (often indicated by small raised letters: [a], [b]) if something in the table needs to be qualified—for example, the number of cups of milk in Table 6.1. Then put that information below the table.

TABLE 6.1   Parts of a Table

Table number

TABLE 1   Efficiency of Some Protein Sources in Meeting an Adult's Minimum Daily Requirements — *Title* — *Rule*

Source	Percent of Protein	Percent of Amino Acids	Amount Needed to Satisfy Minimum Daily Requirement	
			(grams)	(ounces)
Cheese[a]	27	70	227	7.2
Corn	10	50	860	30.0
Eggs	11	97	403	14.1
Fish[a]	22	80	244	8.5
Kidney beans	23	40	468	16.4
Meat[a]	25	68	253	8.8
Milk	4	82	1,311	45.9[b]
Soybeans	34	60	210	7.3

Column headings — *Subheadings*

Stub

Source: From *Biology: The Unity and Diversity of Life,* 4th edition by C. Starr and R. Taggart. Copyright © 1987. Reprinted with permission of Brooks/Cole, a division of Thomson Learning: www.thomsonrights.com. Fax 800-730-2215. — *Origin of data*

[a] = Average value
[b] = Equivalent of 6 cups } *Footnotes*

- Arrange the data you want to compare vertically; it is easier to read down than across a series of rows.
- Place tables at the top (preferable) or bottom of the page and center them on the page rather than placing them up against the right or left margin.
- Don't use more than five or six columns; tables wider than that are more difficult for readers to use.
- Round off numbers in your columns to the nearest whole number to assist readers in following and retaining information.
- Always give credit to the source (the supplier of the statistical information) on which your table is based.

Figures

As mentioned before, any visual that is not a table is classified as a **figure.** The types of figures we examine here are

- line graphs
- circle, or pie, charts
- bar charts
- organizational charts
- flow charts
- pictographs
- photographs
- drawings

Line Graphs

Graphs transform numbers into pictures. They take statistical data presented in tables and put them into rising and falling lines, steep or gentle curves.

Functions of Line Graphs   Graphs vividly portray information that changes, such as

- costs
- sales
- fluctuations
- profits
- distributions
- increases and decreases in (e.g., jobs, houses, etc.)
- employment
- energy levels
- temperatures

Simple Line Graphs   Basically, a simple graph consists of two sides—a **vertical axis** and a **horizontal axis**—that intersect to form a right angle, as in Figure 6.5. The space between the two axes contains the picture made by the graph—the amount of snowfall in Springfield between November 2005 and April 2006. The vertical line represents the **dependent variable** (the snowfall in inches), the horizontal line, the **independent variable** (time in months). The dependent variable is influenced most

FIGURE 6.5   A simple line graph showing the amount of snowfall in Springfield from November 2005 to April 2006.

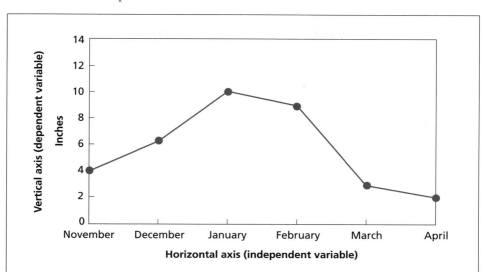

directly by the independent variable, which almost always is expressed in terms of time or distance. The vertical axis is read from bottom to top; the horizontal axis from left to right.

Multiple-Line Graphs   The graph in Figure 6.5 contains only one line per category. But a graph can have multiple lines to show how a number of dependent variables (conditions, products) compare with each other.

The six-month sales figures for three salespeople can be seen in the graph in Figure 6.6 (p. 178). The graph contains a separate line for each of the three salespersons. At a glance readers can see how the three compare and how many dollars each generated per month. Note how the line representing each salesperson is clearly differentiated from the others by symbols and colors. Each line is clearly tied to a **legend** (an explanatory key below the graph) specifying the three salespersons.

Guidelines for Creating a Graph

1. Use no more than three lines in a multiple-line graph so that readers can interpret the graph more easily. If the lines run close together, use a legend to identify individual lines.
2. Label each line to identify what it represents.
3. Keep each line distinct in a multiple-line graph by using different colors, dots or dashes, or symbols. Note the different symbols in Figure 6.6.

FIGURE 6.6   A multiple-line graph showing sales figures for the first six months of 2006 for three salespeople.

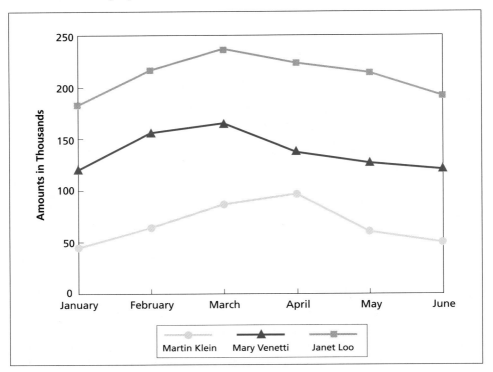

4. Make your graph data points large enough to show a reasonable and ethical number of plotted points (using only three or four data points may distort the evidence).

5. Keep the scale consistent and realistic. If you start with hours, do not switch to days or vice versa. If you are recording annual rates or accounts, do not skip a year or two in the hope that you will save time or be more concise. Do not use, for example, 1997, 1999, 2001, 2002, 2003, 2006. Include all the years you are surveying or equal multiples of them (such as 1998, 2000, 2002, 2004, 2006).

Charts

Among the most frequently used are (1) circle, or pie, charts, (2) bar charts, (3) organizational charts, and (4) flow charts.

Circle Charts   Circle charts are also known as **pie charts,** a name that descriptively points to their construction and interpretation. Tables are more technical and detailed than circle charts. Figure 6.7 shows an example of a pie chart used in a government document. A table or graph with a much more detailed breakdown of, say,

FIGURE 6.7   A three-dimensional circle chart showing the breakdown by department of the proposed Midtown city budget for 2006.

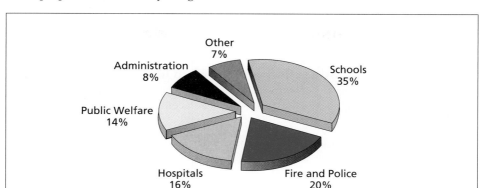

a city's budget would be more appropriate for a technical audience (auditors, budget planners).

The full circle, or pie, represents the whole amount (100 percent or 360 degrees) of something: the entire budget of a company or a family, a population group, an area of land, the resources of an organization or institution. Each slice or wedge represents a percentage or portion of the whole.

A circle chart effectively allows readers to see two things at once: the relationship of the parts to one another and the relationship of the parts to the whole. Follow these seven rules to create and present a circle chart.

1. Keep your circle chart simple. Don't try to illustrate technical statistical data in a pie chart. Pie charts are primarily used for general audiences.

2. Do not divide a circle, or pie, into too few or too many slices. If you have only three wedges, use a bar chart, as discussed later. If you have more than seven or eight wedges, your divisions of the pie will be too narrow. Instead, combine several slices of small percentages (2 percent, 3 percent, 4 percent) into one slice labeled "Other," "Miscellaneous," or "Related Items."

3. Make sure the individual slices total 100 percent, or 360 degrees. The breakdown of percentages to represent a family's budget might be as follows:

Category	Percentage	Angle of slice
Housing	25%	90.0°
Food	22%	79.2°
Energy	20%	72.0°
Clothes	13%	46.8°
Health care	12%	43.2°
Miscellaneous	8%	28.8°
Total	100%	360°

4. Put the largest slice first, at the 12 o'clock position, then move clockwise with proportionately smaller slices. Schools occupy the largest slice in Figure 6.7 because they receive the biggest share of taxes.

5. Label each slice of the pie horizontally. Do not put in a label upside down or slide it in vertically.

6. Shade, color, or cross-hatch slices of the pie to further separate and distinguish the parts. Figure 6.7 effectively uses color. But be careful not to obscure labels and percentages; also make certain that adjacent slices can be distinguished readily from each other.

7. Give percentages for each slice to further assist readers, as in Figure 6.7.

Bar Charts   A bar chart consists of a series of vertical or horizontal bars that indicate comparisons of statistical data. For instance, in Figure 6.8 vertical bars depict increases in number of working mothers. Figure 6.9 uses horizontal bars to depict the nation's top 20 metropolitan areas, based on building permits. The length of the bars is determined according to a scale that your computer software can easily calculate.

FIGURE 6.8   Vertical bar chart.

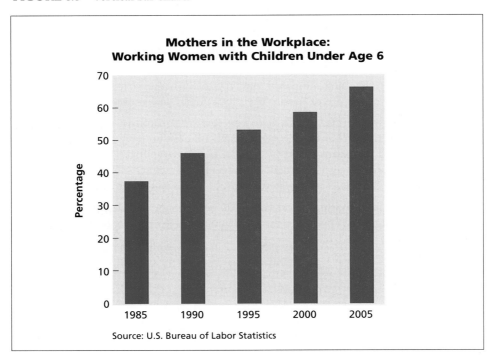

FIGURE 6.9   Horizontal bar chart.

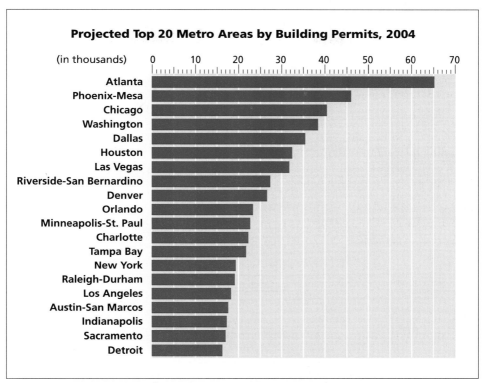

Projected Top 20 Metro Areas by Building Permits, 2004

Source: From *U.S. Housing Markets,*® a publication of the Meyers Group.

Organizational Charts   An organizational chart pictures the chain of command in a company or agency, with the lines of authority stretching down from the chief executive, manager, or administrator to assistant manager, department heads, or supervisors to the work force of employees. Figure 6.10 (p. 182) shows a hospital's organizational chart for its nursing services.

Organizational charts have many advantages in the world of work; they can

- inform employees and customers about the makeup of a company
- show the various offices, departments, and units
- show where people work in relationship to each other in a business
- coordinate employee efforts in routing information to appropriate departments

Flow Charts   A **flow chart** displays the stages in which something is manufactured, or is accomplished, develops, or operates. Flow charts are highly effective in showing the steps of a procedure. They can also be used to plan the day's or week's activities.

A flow chart tells a story with arrows, boxes, and sometimes pictures. Boxes are connected by arrows to show the stages of a process. Flow charts often proceed from left to right and back again, as in the one at the top of the next page, showing the steps to be taken before graduation.

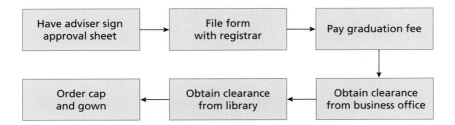

Flow charts can also be constructed to read from top to bottom. Computer programming instructions frequently are written that way. See, for example, Figure 6.11, which uses a computer program's flow chart feature to show the steps a student must follow in writing a research paper.

FIGURE 6.10   An organizational chart representing critical care nursing services at Union General Hospital.

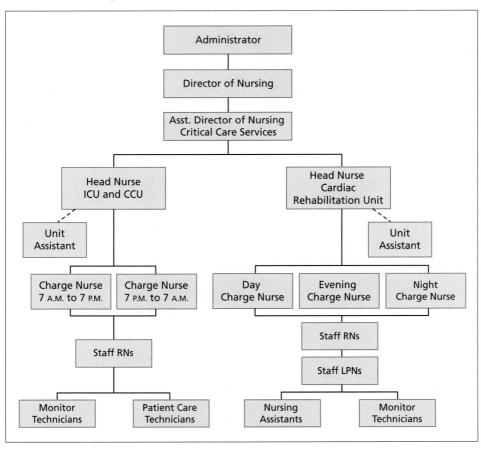

FIGURE 6.11   A computer programming flow chart showing steps in writing a research paper.

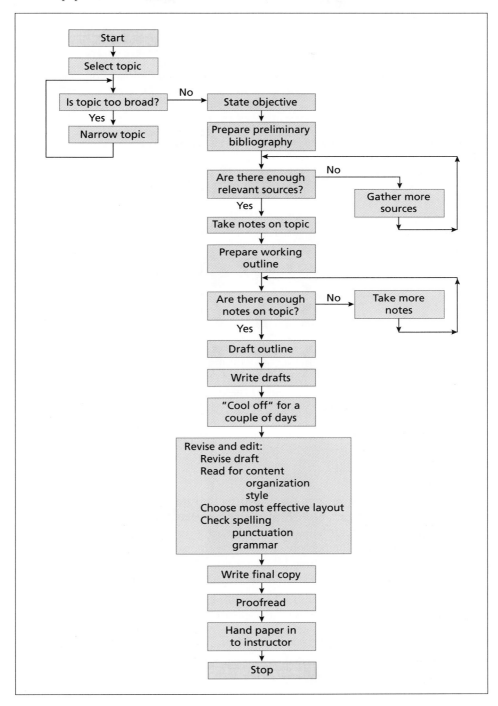

FIGURE 6.12   A pictograph showing the growth of one state's retirement assets.

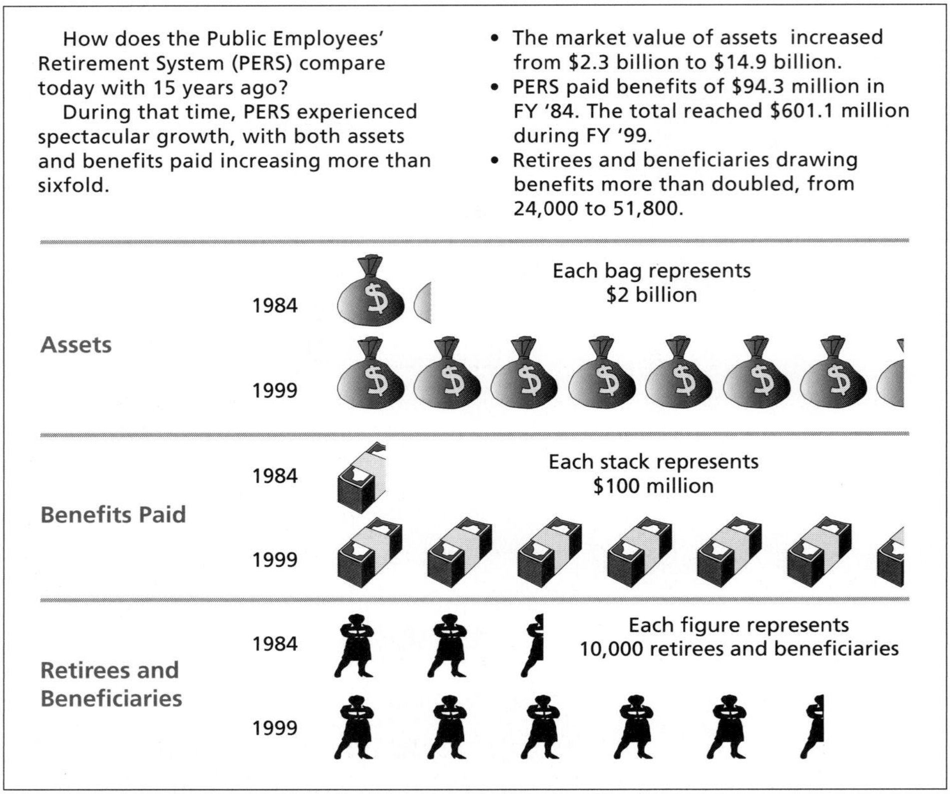

Source: *PERS Member Newsletter,* August 1999. Official Publication of the Public Employees' Retirement System of Mississippi. By permission of Public Employees' Retirement System.

Pictographs

A **pictograph** uses picture symbols (called **pictograms**) to represent differences in statistical data, as in Figure 6.12. A pictograph repeats the same symbol or icon to depict the quantity of items being measured. Each symbol stands for a specific number, quantity, or value. Pictographs are visually appealing and dramatic and are far more appropriate for a nontechnical than a technical audience.

When you create a pictograph, follow these three guidelines:

1. Choose an appropriate symbol for the topic—such as handheld PCs to represent the increase in the number of sales or tractors for the number of farms.
2. Always indicate what unit of measurement or value each icon or symbol equals. Also, indicate the precise quantities involved by placing numbers after the pictures or at the top of the visual so that the reader knows exactly how much the total number of pictograms represents.

3. Increase the number of symbols rather than their sizes because differences in size are often difficult to construct accurately and harder for readers to interpret.

Photographs

Correctly taken or scanned, photographs are an extremely helpful addition to job-related writing. A photograph's chief virtues are realism and clarity. A photo can

- show what an object looks like
- demonstrate how to perform a certain procedure
- compare relative sizes and shapes of objects
- compare and contrast scenes or procedures

Note how the photograph in Figure 6.13 does the first three.

Digital cameras have revolutionized photography, allowing you to supply professional looking, customized photos with your written work. As with other cameras, you point and shoot with a digital camera. But unlike a traditional camera, the digital camera lets you review every photo you take before you print it. You can shoot a photo, take it in slow motion, and play it back, which allows you to scroll, zoom in, blow it up, adjust darkness or light, even change exposures.

Use special care when you take a photograph with either a traditional or a digital camera. The most important point to remember is that what you see and what the camera records might be two different sights. Before you take a photo, decide

FIGURE 6.13   A photo showing how to perform a procedure.

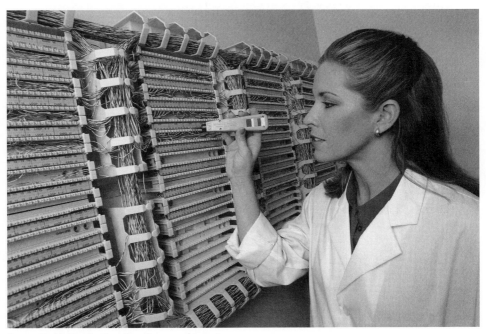

Source: Corbis Royalty Free *(http://www.corbis.com)*

how much foreground and background image you need. Include only the details that are *necessary* and *relevant* for your purpose. Observe the following guidelines:

1. Focus your camera on the most important part of the image.
2. Select the correct angle.
3. Give the right amount of detail. Pictures that include clutter compete for the reader's attention and detract from the subject.
4. Take the picture from the right distance. If you need a shot of a three-story office building, your picture may show only one or two stories if you are standing too close to the building when you photograph it. Standing too far away from an object, however, means that the photograph will reduce the object's importance and record unnecessary details.

Drawings

Drawings can show where an object is located, how a tool or machine is put together, or what signals are given or steps taken in a particular situation. A drawing can be simple, like the one in Figure 6.14, which shows readers exactly where to place smoke detectors in a house.

A more detailed drawing can reveal the interior of an object. Such sketches are called **cutaway drawings** because they show internal parts normally concealed from view. Figure 6.15 (p. 188) is a cutaway drawing of an antilock brake system.

Another kind of sketch is an **exploded drawing,** which blows the entire object up and apart to show how the individual parts are arranged. An exploded drawing comes with most computers and uses **callouts,** or labels, to identify the components. The labels are often attached to the drawing with arrows or lines. As the name suggests, the labels "call out" the parts so that readers can identify them quickly.

Guidelines for Using a Drawing

1. Keep your drawing simple. Include only as much detail as your reader will need to understand what to do, be it to assemble or to operate a mechanism. Do not include any extra details.
2. Clearly label all parts so that your reader can identify and separate them.
3. Decide on the most appropriate view of the object you want to illustrate—aerial, frontal, lateral, reverse, exterior, interior—and indicate in your title which view it is.
4. Keep the parts of the drawing proportionate unless you are purposely enlarging one section.

Designing a Web Site

You may be asked to write the content for a company Web site, update it, or create your own Web site as you apply for a job. A Web site has much in common with the print documents and visuals discussed in this chapter. It has to be clear, reader-friendly, and appropriate for your audience's purpose. But on-line readers expect different things from a Web page than they do from a printed document.

FIGURE 6.14   A drawing showing where to place smoke detectors in a house.

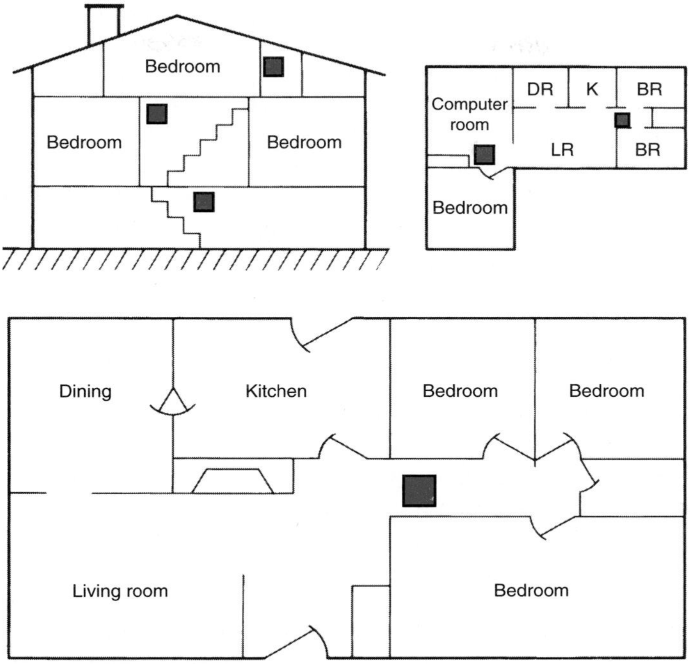

Where to place smoke detectors . . .
In a single-level home (*bottom*), a smoke detector (*square*) should be located outside the sleeping area. A smoke detector should be provided to protect each sleeping area in multi-level homes (*top*) or homes where the sleeping areas are separated. In addition, a detector should be placed at the head of the basement stairs.

Reprinted by permission of *Southern Building.*

Web versus Paper Pages

Clearly, a Web page differs from a memo, letter, or report. Web pages include images, are more colorful, and their content is usually organized into briefer "chunks" or layers of information. Depending on the size of a reader's monitor, too, the amount of text per line and the margins surrounding that text can vary. Text displayed on a computer screen is more difficult to read than on a piece of paper. You need to take this into account as you write, edit, and maintain a Web site. Text squeezed onto a monitor can interfere with the reader's comprehension. Moreover, people usually don't read Web sites from start to finish; they "navigate" through the pages to find the information they want. Readers often start with a home page, then quickly link to another page on the site. The organization of each page—and that of the site overall—is crucial.

FIGURE 6.15   Cutaway drawing of an antilock brake system.

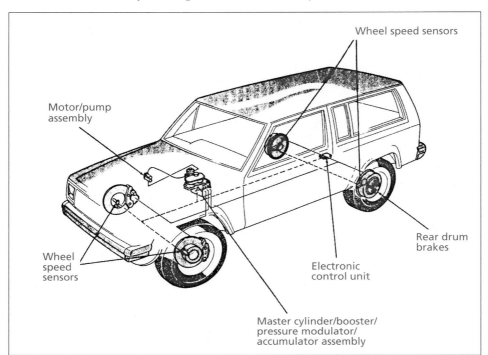

Source: Chilton Automotive Books. *Jeep Wagoneer/Comanche 1984–1996 Repair Manual.* Chilton is a registered trademark of Cahners Business Information, a Division of Reed Elsevier Inc. and has been licensed to W. G. Nichols Inc. Reprinted with permission.

Four Web Design Elements

You do not need to be concerned with technical matters of Web site construction but rather only with the design of a Web page. The following four Web site elements play a crucial role in any design decisions:

- hyperlinks (for menus and other links)
- text paragraphs
- color
- images

Refer to Figure 6.16 as you read the following sections.

Links

Links are the street signs of the Web. They make your site easy for readers to navigate. Usually, they are a one- or two-word description or an icon. By clicking, readers can navigate through the content of your site or jump to completely different Web sites. Links can be found on menus on the side of a home page, as in Figure 6.16.

FIGURE 6.16.   Examples of navigational links.

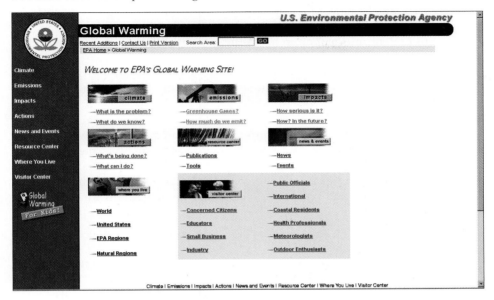

Your links can lead readers to services, news and events, people, maps, FAQs, and other information about your site and your company.

Follow these guidelines to supply helpful links for Web readers.

- Identify links with consistent words or icons.
- Make sure all of your pages are linked and that the links work.
- Make your links easy to find by using underlining to highlight the one- or two-word description or icon in your site. Do not use underlining for other reasons.
- Clearly display all links; do not forget one.
- Don't use too many links by loading a text paragraph with five or six of them.

Text Paragraphs

An on-line audience may not read through your entire Web site. (In fact, they may not have even started at your site.) Because Web readers are unlikely to keep scrolling to find key points, get to your main point quickly. Prepare on-line text so that readers can scan it easily and quickly by doing the following.

- Put the most important part of your message on the top half of the screen so that readers won't miss it or click elsewhere.
- Break up different sections of the text with blank (white) space
- Use headings and subheadings to break information into readable chunks.
- Make paragraphs brief and double-space between each one.
- Keep sentences short.
- Don't make the text too small or difficult to read by disregarding margins.

- Use typefaces and fonts that are easy to read. Avoid fancy script, mixing fonts and sizes, or putting your text in italics or in all capitals; doing so detracts from the attractiveness and functionality of your site.
- Try to present information in lists—the same as this one—to make it highly accessible to readers. Make your message easy to read.
- Make sure the style and tone of your Web site are suitable for the products and services it promotes. Avoid humor, slang, or anything in poor taste.

Color

Color can make any Web document more effective than a black-and-white screen. But a site with a wild array of colors is as unattractive as one in black and white. Use color on a Web site for borders, images, background, and so on. Since color is probably the most difficult design element to control, always discuss it with your company's graphic designer and your boss. Here are some suggestions for using color wisely on a Web site.

- Employ color only for emphasis—to draw attention to a menu, links, or updated content.
- Select colors that suit your audience and support the purpose of your Web site. Avoid dark backgrounds that reduce readability.
- Limit yourself to a few colors, and use those consistently. If you use dark blue for links on one page, they should be dark blue on all pages.
- Choose background colors to establish a sharp contrast between text and background. Readability is your main concern. Dark text on a dark background (purple, green, blue) is almost impossible to read. Similarly, avoid using light text (pastels) on a light screen background.
- Note that the resolution, or sharpness, of a computer screen can drastically affect the way a Web page is displayed. Test your Web page by sending it to a co-worker or supervisor so that he or she can see how it appears on a different screen.

Images

Whether in print or on-line, effective use of images can make your business documents look striking and professional while poor images undermine the communication of your message. The Web depends on images to convey its message. As with color, many factors can affect the way your image appears on a Web site.

- Arrange any images and photos so that they do not mask or bump into text. Proportion is important for achieving a balance between different page elements.
- Choose appropriate icons or images to illustrate menus and page sections.
- Don't overload your page with images, which can increase the time it takes for a visitor to view it. Make sure images are functional and easy-to-see and process.
- Make images consistent with the color palette of your site. Images should complement or contrast with any background colors. If the image and background colors are too similar, the image won't stand out. If the colors are too different, the image may clash with the background.
- Be conservative in using animations or anything that might be viewed as a gimmick, which can distract readers from other content on the page.

✓ Revision Checklist

❑ Arranged information in the most logical, easy-to-grasp order.
❑ Left adequate, eye-pleasing white space in text and margins to frame document.
❑ Maintained pleasing, easy-to-read line length and spacing.
❑ Chose appropriate typeface for message and document.
❑ Did not mix typefaces.
❑ Used effective type size, neither too small (under 10 point) nor too large (over 12 point), for body of text.
❑ Inserted heads and subheads to organize information for reader.
❑ Supplied lists, bullets, numbers to divide information.
❑ Chose most effective visual (table, chart, graph, drawing, photograph) to represent information the audience needs.
❑ Drafted and edited visual until it meets readers' needs.
❑ Selected right amount of technical detail to include in visual.
❑ Made sure every visual is attractive, clear, complete, and relevant.
❑ Gave each visual a number, a title, and, where necessary, a legend and a callout.
❑ Numbered tables and figures consecutively.
❑ Inserted visual near the written description or commentary to which it pertains.
❑ Introduced and interpreted each visual in appropriate place in report or paper.
❑ Acknowledged sources for visuals.
❑ Used plenty of white space on Web site so that visitor is not overloaded with text.
❑ Chose colors carefully so that pages are easy on the eyes and all text is legible.
❑ Gave essential information about product or service.
❑ Selected and designed appropriate hyperlinks (key words) for search engines to find.
❑ Made it easy for visitors to navigate and locate what they need quickly.
❑ Used appropriate visuals that complement and do not compete with text for visitors' attention.

Exercises

1. Find an ineffectively designed document—a form, a set of instructions, a brochure, a section of a manual, a story in a newsletter—and assume that you are a document design consultant. Write a sales letter to the company or agency that prepared and distributed the document, offering to redesign it and any other

documents they have. Stress your qualifications and include a sample of your work. You will have to be convincing and diplomatic—precisely and professionally persuading your readers that they need your services to improve their corporate image, customer relations, and sales or services.

2. Redesign the handwashing document on the next page to make it conform to the guidelines specified in this chapter.

3. One government agency supplied statistics on the world production of oranges (including tangerines) in thousands of metric tons for the following countries during the years 2001–2004: Brazil, 2,005, 2,132, 2,760, 2,872; Israel, 909, 1,076, 1,148, 1,221; Italy, 1,669, 1,599, 1,766, 1,604; Japan, 2,424, 2,994, 2,885, 4,070; Mexico, 937, 1,405, 1,114, 1,270; Spain, 2,135, 2,005, 2,179, 2,642; and the United States, 7,658, 7,875, 7,889, 9,245. Prepare a table with that information and then write a paragraph in which you introduce and refer to the table and draw conclusions from it.

4. Write a paragraph introducing and interpreting the following table.

Year	Soft Drink Companies	Bottling Plants	Per Capita Consumption (Gallons)
1940	750	750	10.3
1945	578	611	12.5
1950	457	466	18.6
1955	380	407	17.2
1960	231	292	15.9
1970	171	229	15.4
1975	118	197	16.0
1980	92	154	18.7
1985	54	102	21.1
1990	43	88	23.1
1995	45	82	25.3
2000	37	78	27.6
2005	34	72	30.1

5. According to a municipal study in 2004 the distribution of all companies classified in each enterprise industry in that city was as follows: minerals, 0.4%; selected services, 33.3%; retail trade, 36.7%; wholesale trade, 6.5%; manufacturing, 5.3%; and construction, 17.8%. Make a circle chart to represent the distribution and write a one- or two-paragraph interpretation to accompany (and explain the significance of) your visual.

6. Make an organizational chart for a business or an agency you worked for recently. Include part-time and full-time employees, but indicate their titles or

WHY SHOULD YOU WASH YOUR HANDS?
Bacteria and viruses (germs) that cause illnesses are spread when you don't wash your hands.
If you don't wash your hands, you risk acquiring:
The common cold or flu
Gastrointestinal illnesses Shigella or hepatitis A
Respiratory illnesses
Should you wash your hands?
You need to wash your hands several times every day. Some important times to wash your hands are:
BEFORE
Preparing or eating food.
Treating a cut wound.
Tending to someone who is sick.
Inserting or removing contacts
After
Using the bathroom.
Changing a diaper or helping a child use the bathroom (don't forget the child's hands)
Handling raw meats/poultry/eggs
Touching pets, especially reptiles
Handling garbage
Sneezing or blowing your nose, or helping a child blow his/her nose
Touching any body fluids like blood or mucus
Being in contact with a sick person
Playing outside or with children and their toys
WHEN SHOULD YOU WASH YOUR HANDS?
There is a right way to wash your hands.
Follow these steps and you will help protect yourself and your family from illness.
Like any good habit, proper hand washing must be taught.
Take the time to teach it to your children and make sure they practice.

functions with different kinds of shapes or lines. Then write a brief letter to your employer explaining why this kind of organizational chart should be distributed to all employees. Focus on the types of problems that could be avoided if employees had access to such a chart.

7. Prepare a flow chart for one of the following activities:
   a. jumping a "dead" car battery
   b. giving an injection
   c. sending an e-mail
   d. painting a set of louvered doors
   e. making an arrest
   f. putting out an electrical fire
   g. joining a chat group on the Internet
   h. preparing a visual using a graphics software package
   i. any job you do

8. Prepare a drawing of one of the following simple tools and include appropriate callouts with your visual.
   a. golf club
   b. hammer
   c. pliers
   d. stethoscope
   e. swivel chair
   f. DVD player
   g. ballpoint pen
   h. table lamp

9. Prepare appropriate visuals to illustrate the data listed in a and b. In a paragraph immediately after the visual, explain why the type of visual you selected is appropriate for the information.
   a. Life expectancy is increasing in America. This growth can be dramatically measured by comparing the number of teenagers with the number of older adults (over age 65) in America during the last few years and then projecting those figures. In 1970 there were approximately 28 million teenagers and 20 million older adults. By 1980 the number of teenagers climbed to 30 million and the number of older adults increased to 25 million. In 1990 there were 27 million teenagers and 31 million older adults. In 2000 the number of teenagers had leveled off to 23 million, but the number of older adults soared to more than 36 million.
   b. Researchers estimate that for every adult in America 3,985 cigarettes were purchased in 1985; 4,100 in 1990; 3,875 in 1995; 3,490 in 2000; and 2,910 in 2005.

10. This visual was prepared to accompany a report on problems pilots have encountered with a particular model of jet engine. Redo the visual to make it easier to read and to organize information. Supply a paragraph to accompany your new visual.

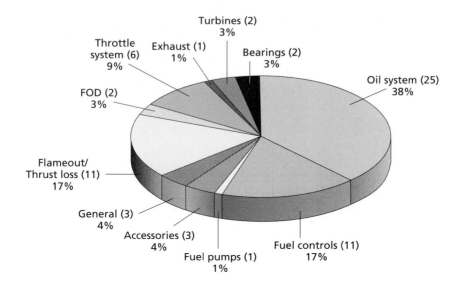

11. Find a Web page that you feel is ineffective. Using the four keys to effective writing, as well as your knowledge of Web page elements, write a one-page assessment of the site, discussing three or four changes that would make it more effective. Attach a printed hard copy of the Web page to your assessment.

12. The home page of the Stanley's Accounting Temps Web site is not designed as effectively as it could be nor was it proofread. Write a one-page memo to your instructor specifying how Stanley's Accounting Temps might better address its on-line customers after reviewing pages 186–190. Group your recommendations under the headings of content, design, and navigation. As a supporting document for your memo, design a new home page for the company by sketching it on a piece of paper or creating it on the computer. (The Stanley's Accounting Temps home page example was created using word processing software.)

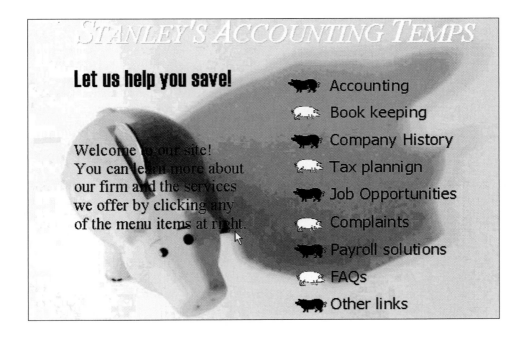

Writing Instructions and Procedures

Clear and accurate instructions are essential to the world of work. Instructions tell—and frequently show—how to do something. They indicate how to perform a procedure (draw blood; change the oil in your car); operate something (a pH meter; a digital camera); construct, install, maintain, adjust, or repair a piece of equipment (an incubator; a scanner). Everyone from the consumer to the specialist uses and relies on carefully written and designed instructions and procedures.

Instructions and Your Job

As part of your job, you may be asked to write instructions, alone or with a group, for your co-workers as well as for the customers who use your company's services or products. Your employer stands to gain or lose much from the quality and the accuracy of the instructions you prepare.

While the purpose of writing instructions is to explain how to perform a task in a step-by-step manner, the purpose of writing procedures is slightly different. Often the two terms are incorrectly used interchangeably. *Procedures* (or policies) describe not a task to be completed, but a set of established rules of conduct to be followed within an organization, such as a business.

This chapter first shows you how to develop, write, illustrate, and design a variety of instructions, and then moves into a discussion of writing procedures (pp. 218–219) about job-related duties.

Why Instructions Are Important

Perhaps no other type of occupational writing demands more from the writer than do instructions because so much is at stake—for both you and your reader. The reader has to understand what you write and perform the procedure, as well. You cannot afford to be unclear, inaccurate, or incomplete. Instructions are significant for many reasons, including safety, efficiency, and convenience.

Safety

Carefully written instructions get a job done without damage or injury. Poorly written instructions can be directly responsible for an injury to the person trying to follow them and may result in costly damage claims or even lawsuits. Notice how the product labels in your medicine cabinet inform users when, how, and why to take a medication safely. Without those instructions, consumers would be endangered by taking too much or too little medicine or by not administering it properly. To make sure your instructions are safe, they must be

- accurate
- consistent
- thorough
- clearly written
- carefully organized

Efficiency

Well-written instructions help a business run smoothly and efficiently. No work would be done if employees did not have clear instructions to follow. Imagine how inefficient it would be for a business if employees had to stop their work each time they did not have or could not understand a set of instructions. Or, equally alarming, what if employees made a number of serious mistakes because of confusing directions, costing a business lost sales and increased expenses? Giving readers helpful tips to make their work easier will also increase their efficiency.

Convenience

Clear, easy-to-follow instructions make a customer's job easier and less frustrating. In the customer's view, instructions reflect a product's quality and convenience. How many times have you heard complaints about a company because the instructions that went with its products were difficult to follow? Poorly written and illustrated instructions will cost you business. Instructions are also a vital part of "service after the sale." Owners' manuals, for example, help buyers to avoid a product breakdown (and the headache and expense of starting over) and to keep it in good working order.

Overview of the Variety of Instructions and Your Audience

Instructions vary in length, complexity, and format. Some instructions are one word long: *stop, lift, rotate, print, erase.* Others are a few sentences long: "Insert blank disk in external disk drive"; "Close tightly after using"; "Store in an upright position."

Instructions can be given in a variety of formats, as Figures 7.1 through 7.3 (pp. 198–200) show. They can be in paragraphs (see Figure 7.5, p. 206), often employ visuals to illustrate each step (Figures 7.1 and 7.3), or use numbered lists (Figures 7.1–7.3). You will have to determine which format is most appropriate for the kinds of instructions you are to write. For writing that affects policies or regulations, as in Figure 7.7 (see pp. 220–221), you will most often use a memo or even e-mail format.

FIGURE 7.1   Instructions that supply a visual with each step.

Proper Brushing

Proper brushing is essential for cleaning teeth and gums effectively. Use a toothbrush with soft, nylon, round-ended bristles that will not scratch and irritate teeth or damage gums.

1

Place bristles along the gumline at a 45-degree angle. Bristles should contact both the tooth surface and the gumline.

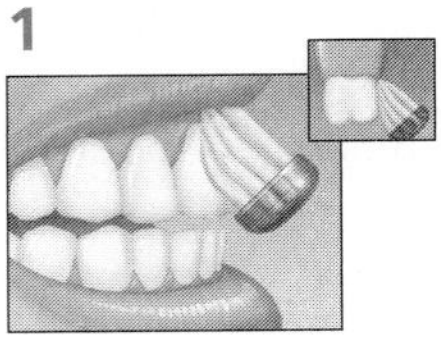

2

Gently brush the outer tooth surfaces of 2–3 teeth using a vibrating back and forth rolling motion. Move brush to the next group of 2–3 teeth and repeat.

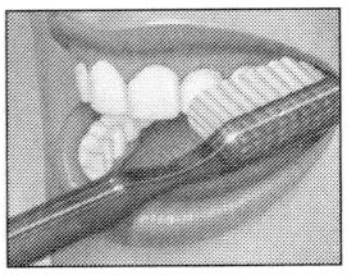

3

Maintain a 45-degree angle with bristles contacting the tooth surface and gumline. Gently brush, using back, forth, and rolling motion along all of the inner tooth surfaces.

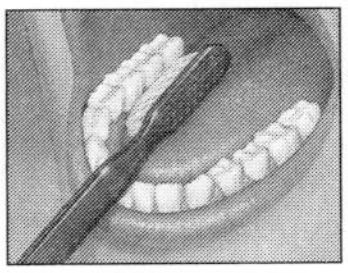

4

Tilt brush vertically behind the front teeth. Make several up and down strokes using the front half of the brush.

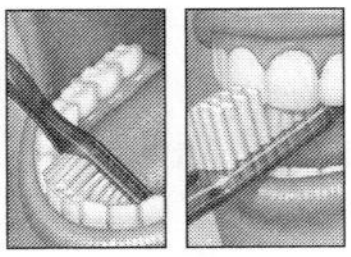

5

Place the brush against the biting surface of the teeth and use a gentle back and forth scrubbing motion. Brush the tongue from back to front to remove odor-producing bacteria.

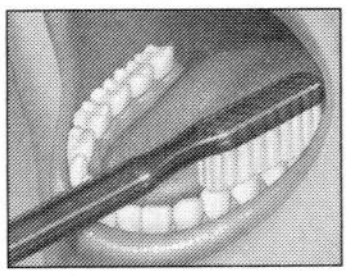

Source: Reprinted by permission of American Dental Hygienists' Association. Illustrations adapted and used courtesy of the John O. Butler Company, makers of *GUM* Healthcare products.

Assessing and Meeting Your Audience's Needs

Put yourself in the readers' position. In most instances you will not be available for readers to ask you questions when they do not understand something. Consequently, they will have to rely only on your written instructions.

FIGURE 7.2   Instructions given in a numbered list describing a sequence of steps.

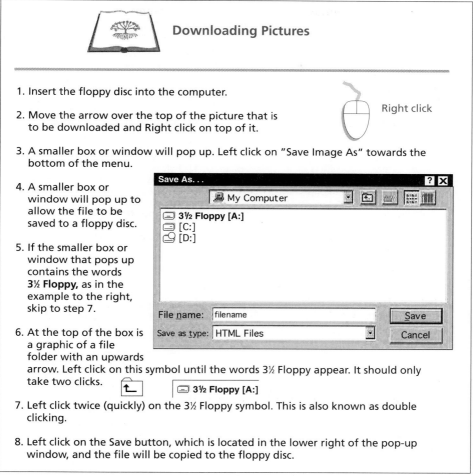

Source: Elkhart (Indiana) Public Library. Reprinted by permission of Brent Ferguson and Diana Gill.

Do not assume that members of your audience have performed the process before or have operated the equipment as many times as you have. (If they had, there would be no need for your instructions.) No writer of instructions ever disappointed readers by making directions too clear or too easy to follow. Keep in mind that your audience will often include non-native speakers of English, a worldwide audience of potential consumers.

Key Questions to Ask About Your Audience

To determine your audience's needs, ask yourself the following questions:

- How and why will my readers use my instructions? (Engineers have different expectations than do office personnel and customers.)

FIGURE 7.3   Instructions in a numbered list on how to assemble an outdoor grill.

ASSEMBLY INSTRUCTIONS

The instructions shown below are for the basic grill with tubular legs. If you have a pedestal grill, or a grill with accessories, check the separate instruction sheet for details not shown here.

NOTE: Make sure you locate all the parts before discarding any of the packaging material.

TOOLS REQUIRED . . . A standard straight blade screwdriver is the only tool you need to assemble your new Meco grill. If you have a pedestal grill, you will need a 7-16 wrench or a small adjustable wrench.

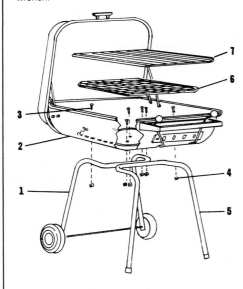

1. Before you start, take time to read through this manual. Inside you will find many helpful hints that will help you get the full potential of enjoyment and service from your new Meco grill.

2. Lay out all the parts.

3. Assemble roller leg (1) to bottom rear of bowl (2) with 1¼" long bolts (3) and nuts (4).

4. Assemble fixed leg (5) to bottom front of bowl (2) with 1¼" long bolts (3) and nuts (4).

5. Place fire grate—ash dump (6) in bottom of bowl (2) between adjusting levers.

6. Place cooking grid (7) on top of adjusting levers. Make sure top grid wires run from front to back of grill.

Source: Meco Assembly Instructions and Owners Manual, Metals Engineering Corp., P.O. Box 3005, Greenville, TN 37743. Reprinted by permission.

- What language skills do they possess—is English their first (native) language?
- How much do my readers already know about the product or procedure?
- How much background information will I have to supply?
- What steps will most likely cause readers trouble?
- Where will my audience most likely be following my instructions—in the workplace, outdoors, in a workshop equipped with tools, or alone in their homes?
- What resources, such as special equipment or power sources, will readers need to perform my instructions successfully?

The Process of Writing Instructions

As we saw in Chapter 2, clear and concise writing evolves when you follow a process. To make sure your instructions are accurate and easy for your audience to perform, follow these steps.

Plan Your Steps

Before writing, do some research to understand completely the job, process, or procedure that you are asking someone else to perform. Make sure you know

- the reason for doing something
- the parts or tools required
- the steps to follow to get the job done
- the results of the job
- the potential risks or dangers

If you are not absolutely sure about the process, ask an expert for a demonstration. Do some background reading and talk to or e-mail colleagues who may have written or followed a similar instruction.

Do a Trial Run

Actually perform the job (assembling, repairing, maintaining, dissecting) yourself or with all your writing team present. Go through a number of trial runs. Take notes as you go along and be sure to divide the job into simple, distinct steps for readers to follow. Don't give readers too much to do in any one step. Each step should be **complete, sequential, reliable, straightforward,** and **easy** for your audience to identify and perform.

Write and Test Your Draft

Transform your notes into a draft (or drafts) of the instructions you want readers to follow. Test your draft(s) by asking someone from the intended audience (consumers, technicians) who may never have performed the job to follow your instructions as you have written them. Observe where the individual runs into difficulty—cannot complete or seems to miss a step, gets a result different from yours.

Revise and Edit

Based on your observations and user feedback, revise your draft(s) and edit the final copy of the instructions that you will give to readers. Always consider whether your instructions would be easier to accomplish if you included visuals.

Analyzing the needs and the background of your audience will help you to choose appropriate words and details. A set of instructions accompanying a chemistry set would use different terminology, abbreviations, and level of detail than would a set of instructions a professor gives a class in organic chemistry.

General Audience: Place 8 drops of vinegar in a test tube with a piece of limestone about the size of a pea.

Specialized Audience: Place 8 gtts of CH_3COOH in a test tube and add 1 mg of CO_3.

The instructions for the general audience avoid the technical abbreviations and symbols the specialized audience requires. If your readers are puzzled by your directions, you defeat your reasons for writing them.

Using the Right Style

To write instructions that readers can understand and turn into effective action, observe the following guidelines.

1. Use verbs in the present tense and imperative mood. Imperatives are commands that have deleted the pronoun *you*. Note how the instructions in Figures 7.1 through 7.4 contain imperatives—"Move the arrow" instead of "You move the arrow." In instructions, deleting the *you* is not discourteous, as it would be in a business letter or report. The command tells readers, "These steps work, so do them exactly as stated." Choose action verbs such as those listed in Table 7.1.

2. Write clear, short sentences in the active voice. Keep sentences short and uncomplicated. Sentences under twenty words (preferably under fifteen) are easy to read. Note that the sentences in Figures 7.1 through 7.4 are, for the most part, under fifteen words.

3. Use precise terms for measurements, distances, and times. Indefinite, vague directions leave users wondering whether they are doing the right thing. The following vague direction is better expressed through precise revision.

Vague: Turn the distributor cap a little. (*How much is a little?*)
Precise: Turn the distributor cap one quarter of a rotation.

TABLE 7.1   Some Helpful Imperative Verbs Used in Instructions

add	determine	increase	pick up	save	tighten
adjust	dig	insert	point	saw	tilt
apply	download	inspect	pour	scan	transect
blow	drag	lift	press	scroll	transfer
boot up	drain	load	prevent	set	trim
call up	drill	loosen	print	send	turn
change	drop	lower	pull	shift	twist
check	ease	lubricate	push	shut off	type
choose	eliminate	measure	raise	slide	unplug
clean	enter	mix	release	slip	use
click	flip	mount	remove	spread	ventilate
clip	flush	move	reply	squeeze	verify
close	forward	notify	review	start	wash
connect	freeze	oil	roll	switch	wear
create	group	open	rotate	tear	wind
cut	hold	paste	rub	thread	wipe
delete	include	peel	run	tie	wire

4. Use connective words as signposts. Connective words specify the exact order in which something is to be done (especially when your instructions are written in paragraphs). Words, such as *first, then, before,* help readers stay on course, reinforcing the sequence of the procedures.

5. Number each step when you present your instructions in a list. You also can use bullets. Plenty of white space between steps also distinctly separates them for the reader.

Using Visuals Effectively

Readers welcome visuals in almost any set of instructions. Visuals are graphic and direct, helping readers to understand what they must do. A visual can

- simplify a process
- identify the location and size of a part
- show the relationships among components
- reinforce or even save words
- illustrate the "right" way and the "wrong" way
- increase readers' confidence
- help get a job done more quickly

The number and kinds of visuals you include will, of course, depend on the procedure or equipment you are explaining and your audience's background and needs. Some instructions may require only one or two visuals. The instructions in Figure 7.2 show users what they can expect to see on a screen as they download a visual. The shot of the screen clarifies the procedure and assists the reader. In Figure 7.1 each step is accompanied by a visual demonstrating a proper technique of brushing teeth.

Another frequently used visual in instructions is an exploded drawing, like the one in Figure 7.3, which helps consumers see how the various parts of the grill fit together, or the one in Figure 7.4 (p. 204), which labels and shows the relationship of the parts of an industrial extension cord.

The Five Parts of Instructions

Except for very short instructions, such as those illustrated in Figures 7.1 through 7.4, or for instructions on policies and regulations (see Figure 7.7, pp. 220–221), a set of instructions generally contains five main parts: (1) an introduction; (2) a list of equipment and materials; (3) the actual steps to perform the process; (4) warnings, cautions, and notes; and (5) a conclusion (when necessary).

Introduction

The function of an introduction is to provide readers with enough *necessary* background information to understand why and how your instructions work. An introduction must make readers feel comfortable and well prepared before they turn to the actual steps.

FIGURE 7.4   Exploded drawing showing how to assemble an industrial extension cord.

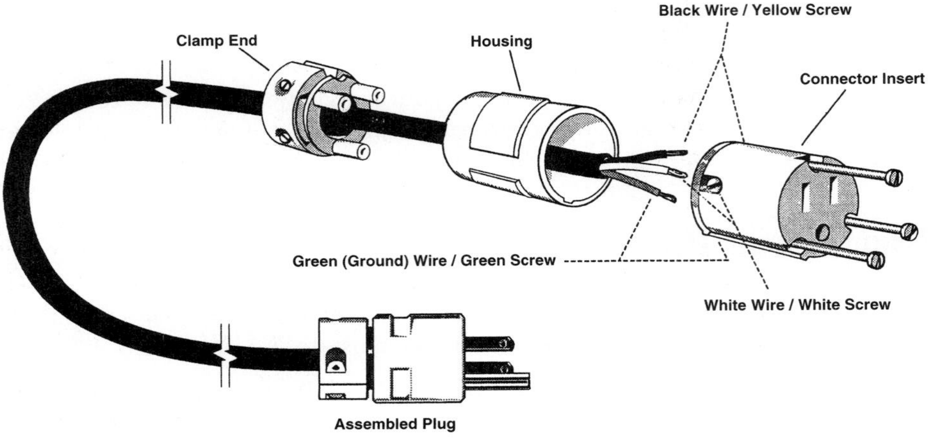

Black Wire / Yellow Screw

Clamp End

Housing

Connector Insert

Green (Ground) Wire / Green Screw

White Wire / White Screw

Assembled Plug

1. Run the end of the cord through the clamp end and then through the center hole of the housing.
2. Pull the cord through until it extends 2 inches beyond the housing.
3. Strip about 1¼ inches of outer insulation from the end of the cord.
4. Twist the exposed ends to prevent stray strands.

Source: Drawing courtesy of Sally Eddy and Georgia-Pacific Company.

What to Include in Introduction

You can do one or all of the following in your introduction. Not every introduction to a set of instructions will contain facts in all four categories of information listed here. Some instructions will require less detail. You will have to judge how much background information to give readers for the specific instructions you write.

1. State why the instructions are useful for a specific audience. Many instructions begin with introductions that stress safety, educational, or occupational benefits. Here is an introduction from a safety procedure describing protective lockout of equipment.

> The purpose of this procedure is to provide plant electrical technicians with a uniform method of locking out machinery or equipment. This will prevent the possibility of setting moving parts in motion, energizing electrical lines; or opening valves while repair, setup, or cleaning work is in progress.

2. Indicate how a particular machine, procedure, or process works. An introduction can briefly discuss the "theory of operation" to help readers understand why something works the way your instructions say it should. Such a discussion sometimes describes a scientific law or principle. An introduction to instructions on how to run an autoclave begins by explaining the function of the machine: "These instructions will teach you how to operate an autoclave, which is used to sterilize surgical instruments through the live additive-free stream."

3. Point out any safety measures or precautions a reader may need to be aware of. By alerting readers early in your instructions, you help them to perform the procedure much more safely and efficiently. Note how Cliff Burgess opens his instructions in Figure 7.5 (pp. 206–207) with a safety warning.

4. Stress any advantages or benefits the reader will gain by performing the instructions. Make the reader feel good about buying or using your product by explaining how it will make a job easier to perform, save the reader time and money, or allow the reader to accomplish a job with fewer mistakes or false starts. Note how the following introduction to a set of instructions on using an auto dial/auto answer modem encourages the reader to want to learn how to operate this system.

Welcome to high-speed telecommunications and congratulations on choosing the Signalman EXPRESSi. You've made an excellent choice. The EXPRESSi is the ideal link between your computer and the ever-expanding world of information utilities, databases, electronic mail, bulletin boards, computer time sharing, and more.

The EXPRESSi can be used in the IBM Personal Computer. And because the EXPRESSi fits inside your PC, it saves valuable desk space and eliminates expensive, bulky cables.[1]

List of Equipment and Materials

Clearly, some instructions, as in Figure 7.1, do not need to inform readers of all equipment or materials they will need. But when you do, make your list complete and clear. Do not wait until the readers are actually performing one of the steps to tell them that a certain type of drill or a specific kind of chemical is required. They may have to stop what they are doing to find the equipment or material; moreover, the procedure may fail or present hazards if users do not have the right equipment at the right time. For example, if a Phillips screwdriver is essential to complete one step, specify that type of screwdriver under the heading "Equipment and Materials"; do not list just "screwdriver."

Steps for Your Instructions

The heart of your instructions will consist of clearly distinguished steps that readers must follow to achieve the desired results. Figure 7.6 (pp. 211–217) contains a model set of steps on how to set up a printer. Note how each step is precisely keyed to the visual, further helping readers perform the procedure. Refer to the figure as

---

[1]Courtesy of Anchor Automation, Inc., Chatsworth, CA.

FIGURE 7.5   An instructional memo listing safety precautions for a general audience.

BURTON WORLDWIDE SYSTEMS

www.burton.com

TO: All Burton Employees
FROM: Cliff Burgess, Environmental Safety   C.B.
RE: Video Display Terminal (VDT) Safety Precautions
DATE: September 12, 2006

Introduction emphasizes reasons for instructions

You may be exposed to some possible health risks in using your computer video display terminal (VDT). These risks include sleep disorders, behavior changes, danger to the reproductive system, and cancer.

Nontechnical explanation offers an analogy

The source of any risks comes from the electromagnetic fields (EMFs) that surround anything that carries an electric current—for example, copiers, circuit breakers, and especially VDTs. Your computer monitor is a major source of EMFs. Magnetic fields can go through walls as easily as light goes through glass.

Although EMFs may affect your health, you can considerably reduce your exposure to these fields by following these three simple steps:

Explains how to use equipment; steps stand out through bullets, bold-face, and spacing

- **Stay at least three feet (an arm's length) away from the front of your VDT.** (The magnetic field is significantly reduced with this amount of distance.)

- **Stay at least four feet away from the sides and back of someone else's VDT.** (The fields are weaker in the front of the VDT but much stronger everywhere else.) Refer to the following sketch, which you may want to post in your office.

Uses visual to clarify instructions

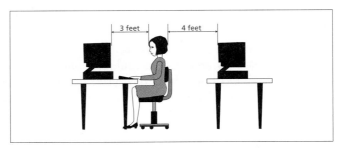

1215 Madison • St. Louis, Missouri 63174
314-555-4300 • FAX 314-555-4311

Continued

FIGURE 7.5   (Continued)

2.

• **Switch your VDT/computer off when you are not using it.** (If the computer has to remain on, be sure to switch off the monitor; screen savers do not affect the exposure to **EMFs**.)

Conclusion reassures readers they are acting safely by following instructions

Our environmental safety team will continue to monitor and investigate any problems. Observing the guidelines above, however, will help you to take all the necessary precautions in order to minimize your exposure to EMFs.

If you have any questions about these procedures or your risk of exposure to EMFs, please e-mail me at cliffb@burton.com.

Source: Reprinted by permission.

you study this section. To make sure that what you write will help your readers understand your steps, observe the following rules.

1. Put the steps in their correct order and number them. If a step is out of order or is missing, the entire set of instructions can be wrong or, worse yet, dangerous. Double-check every step and number each step to indicate its correct place in the sequence of events you are describing.

2. Put only the right amount of information in each step. Giving readers too little information can be as risky as giving them too much. Keep in mind that each step asks readers to perform a single task in the entire process. However, see the next rule for the exception.

3. Group closely related activities into one step. Sometimes closely related actions belong in one step to help the reader coordinate activities and to emphasize their being done at the same time, in the same place, or with the same equipment.

Instructions on how to use a fax machine are clearer when distinct steps are stated separately. The first set of instructions below incorrectly tells users how to transmit a fax by combining steps that must be performed separately. Step 2 asks users to pick up the phone and then dial the number—two separate actions. Step 3 asks users to press the button and hang up the handset, again two actions that cannot be performed simultaneously.

Incorrect: 1. Load the paper into the outgoing document slot, adjusting the paper guides to the appropriate width.
2. Pick up the telephone handset and listen for a dial tone. When you hear the dial tone, dial the number of the receiving fax machine.

       3. When the receiving fax machine answers the ring, press the start button. After the transmission is completed, return the handset to its cradle.

Correct: 1. Load the paper into the outgoing document slot, adjusting the paper guides to the appropriate width.

       2. Pick up the telephone handset and listen for a dial tone.

       3. When you hear a dial tone, dial the number of the receiving fax machine.

       4. When the receiving fax machine answers the ring, press the start button.

       5. After the transmission is completed, return the handset to its cradle.

Don't divide an action into two steps if it has to be done in one. For example, instructions showing how to light a furnace would not list as two steps actions that must be performed simultaneously to avoid a possible explosion.

Incorrect: 1. Depress the lighting valve.

       2. Hold a match to the pilot light.

Correct: 1. Depress the lighting valve while holding a match to the pilot light.

Similarly, do not separate two steps of a computer command that must be performed simultaneously.

Incorrect: 1. Press the CONTROL key.

       2. Press the ALT key.

Correct: 1. While holding down the CONTROL key, press the ALT key.

4. Give the reader hints on how best to accomplish the procedure. Obviously, you cannot do that for every step, but if there is a chance that the reader might run into difficulties you should provide assistance. Particular techniques on how to operate or service equipment also help readers: "If there is blood on the transducer diaphragm, dip the transducer in a blood solvent, such as hydrogen peroxide, Hemosol, etc." If readers have a choice of materials or procedures in a given step, you might want to list those that would give the best performance: "Several thin coats will give a better finish than one heavy coat."

5. State whether one step directly influences (or jeopardizes) the outcome of another. Because all steps in a set of instructions are interrelated, you could not (and should not have to) tell readers how every step affects another. But stating specific relationships is particularly helpful when dangerous or highly intricate operations are involved. You will save the reader time, and you will stress the need for care. Forewarned is forearmed. Here is an example.

Step 2: Tighten fan belt. Failure to tighten the fan belt will cause it to loosen and come off when the lever is turned in step 5.

Do not wait until step 5 to tell readers that you hope they did a good job in tightening the fan belt in step 2. Information that comes after the fact is not helpful.

6. Where necessary, insert graphics to assist readers in carrying out the step. For example, see the drawings of the printer in Figure 7.6 (pp. 211–217).

Warnings, Cautions, and Notes

At appropriate places in your instructions' steps you may have to stop the reader to issue a warning, a caution, or a note. These are found throughout Figure 7.6, especially in Step 4.

Warnings

A warning tells readers that a step, if not prepared for or performed properly, can endanger their safety, as here.

WARNING: UNPLUG MACHINE BEFORE REMOVING PLANTEN GLASS.

ADVERTENCIA: DESENCHUFE LA MANQUINA ANTES DE GUITAR EL VIDRIO.

Cautions

A caution tells a reader how to avoid a mistake that could damage equipment or to take certain precautions—"Wear protective goggles"; "Do not force the plug."

Caution: **Formatting erases all data on the disk**

Notes

A note adds a clarification, provides a helpful hint on how to do the step most efficiently, or lists different options.

At 20 degrees F, a battery uses about 68 percent of its power.

Guidelines on Using Warnings, Cautions, and Notes

1. **Put warnings and cautions in the right place.** Place them immediately next to the step to which they pertain. If you insert a warning or caution statement too early, readers may forget it by the time they come to the step to which it applies. And if you put a warning too late, you almost certainly expose the reader to danger and the equipment to breakdown.

2. **Put warnings and cautions in a distinctive format.** Warnings and cautions should be graphically set apart from the rest of the instructions. There should be no chance that readers will overlook them. Put such statements in capital letters, boldface type, boxes, different colors (red is especially effective for warnings, yellow for cautions).

3. **Include enough explanation to help readers know what to watch out for and what precautions to take.** Do not just insert the word WARNING or CAUTION. Explain what the dangerous condition is and how to avoid it. Look at the examples of warnings and cautions in Step 3 of Figure 7.6 (p. 212).

4. **Do not include a warning or a caution just to emphasize a point.** Putting too many in your instructions will decrease the dramatic impact they should have on readers. Use them sparingly—only when absolutely necessary—so that readers will not be tempted to ignore them.

5. **Use notes only when the procedure calls for them and/or they will help readers.**

Conclusion

Not every set of instructions requires a conclusion. For short instructions containing a few simple steps, such as those in Figures 7.1 through 7.4, no conclusion is necessary. These types of instructions usefully end with the last step the reader must perform. For longer, more involved jobs, a conclusion can help readers finish the process with confidence and accuracy.

When they are necessary, conclusions can provide a succinct wrap-up of what the reader has done; end with a single sentence of congratulations; or can reassure readers, as the conclusion in Cliff Burgess's memo (Figure 7.5, pp. 206–207) does. A conclusion might also tell readers what to expect once a job is finished, describe the results of a test, or explain how a piece of equipment is supposed to operate.

Model of Full Set of Instructions

Study Figure 7.6, which is a set of instructions on setting up an Epson printer, that includes the parts discussed in this chapter: an introduction; a list of materials; numbered steps; and warnings, cautions, and notes. Note how the writer coordinates words with visuals to assist readers.

FIGURE 7.6   Complete set of instructions with steps, visuals, cautions, notes, warnings.

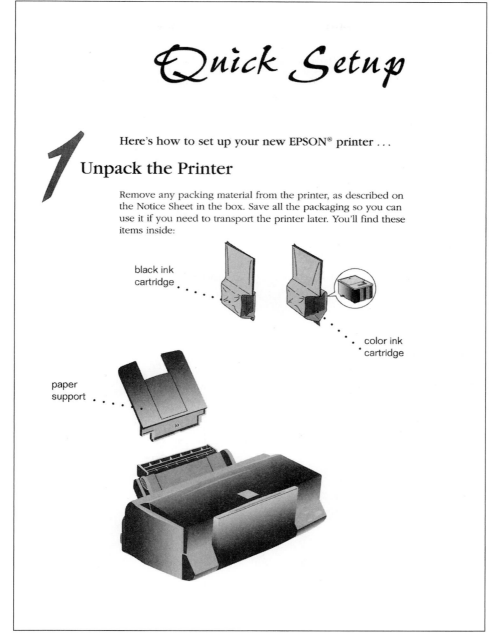

Continued

FIGURE 7.6 (Continued)

Place the printer flat on a stable desk near a grounded outlet. Leave plenty of room in back for the cables and enough room in front for opening the output tray.

Do NOT put the printer:

- In an area with high temperature or humidity
- In direct sunlight or dusty conditions
- Near sources of heat or electromagnetic interference, such as loudspeakers or cordless telephone base units.

Also, be sure to follow the Safety Instructions in the Introduction of your *User's Guide*.

2 Attach the Paper Support

Insert the paper support in the top slot on the back of the printer.

3 Plug In the Printer

First make sure the power is off. Check the ⏻ power button; it's off when its surface is raised above the printer surface.

Caution:
Do not plug the printer into an outlet controlled by a wall switch or timer, or on the same circuit as a large appliance. This may disrupt the power, which can erase memory and damage the power supply.

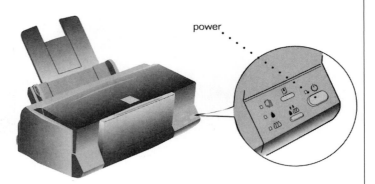

power

Plug the power cord into a properly grounded outlet.

Continued

FIGURE 7.6 (Continued)

 Install the Ink Cartridges

1. Lower the output tray and raise the printer cover.

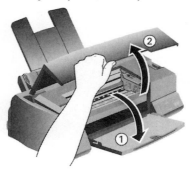

2. Press the ⏻ power button to turn on the printer. The ⏻ power light flashes, the ● and 🞷 ink out lights come on, and the ink cartridge holders move to the installation position.

3. Pull up the ink cartridge clamps.

Caution:
You must remove the tape seal from the top of the cartridge or you will permanently damage it. Don't remove the tape seal from the bottom or ink will leak.

4. Open the ink cartridge packages. Remove the disposable yellow portion of the tape seal on top.

Warning:
If ink gets on your hands, wash them thoroughly with soap and water. If ink gets in your eyes, flush them immediately with water.

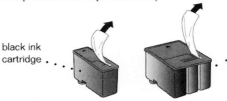

black ink cartridge . . . .

color ink cartridge

Continued

FIGURE 7.6   (Continued)

5. Lower the ink cartridges into their holders with the labels face up and the arrows pointing toward the back of the printer.

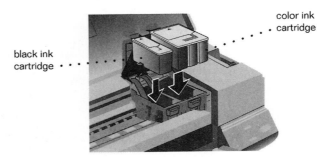

color ink
cartridge

black ink
cartridge

6. Push down the clamps until they lock in place.

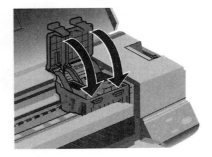

Caution:
Never turn off the printer when the ⏻ power light is flashing.

7. Press the ⬦▥ cleaning button to return the print heads to their home position and charge the ink delivery system. Charging can take up to five minutes, with the ⏻ power light flashing until it's finished.

8. Close the printer cover.

Continued

FIGURE 7.6   (Continued)

5 Load the Paper

1. Slide the left edge guide all the way left and pull out the output tray extension.

2. Fan a stack of plain paper and then even the edges.

3. Load the stack with the printable surface face up. Push the paper against the right edge guide.

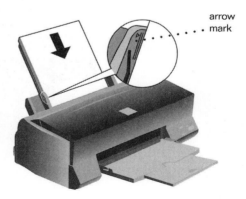

arrow mark

Note:
Don't load paper above the arrow mark inside the left edge guide.

4. Slide the left edge guide back against the stack of paper.

Continued

FIGURE 7.6   (Continued)

 Check the Printer

1. Turn off the printer.

2. While holding down the load/eject button, turn on the printer. Then release the buttons.

3. A page prints out showing the ROM version and a nozzle check pattern. When it's finished, turn off the printer. If you have any problems with the test, see Chapter 6 in your *User's Guide* for more information.

Connect the Printer to Your Computer

You can connect your EPSON Stylus™ COLOR 600 to either an IBM® compatible PC or an Apple® Macintosh® You'll need a shielded, twisted-pair parallel cable to connect to a PC or an Apple System Peripheral-8 cable to connect to a Macintosh. For a complete list of system requirements, see the Introduction of your *User's Guide.*

Connecting to a PC

1. Turn off the printer and your computer.

2. Connect the cable to the printer's parallel interface; then squeeze the wire clips together until they lock in place. (If your cable has a ground wire, connect it now.)

Note:

The printer is assigned to parallel port LPT1; if you want to use a different port, see your Windows documentation for instructions.

ground wire

3. Connect the other end of the cable to your computer's parallel port and secure it as necessary.

Continued

FIGURE 7.6   (Continued)

Connecting to a Macintosh

1. Turn off the printer and your Macintosh.

2. Connect one end of the cable to the serial connector on the back of the printer.

Note:
If you're using a
PowerBook,™ connect your
printer to the modem port.

3. Connect the other end of the cable to either the modem port ✆ or the printer port 🖶 on your Macintosh.

8 Install the Printer Software

Now you need to install the printer software so you can control printing from your computer.

Installing on a PC

You can install the printer software for Windows 95 or Windows 3.1 from the EPSON printer software CD-ROM. If you don't have a CD-ROM drive, you can install the software using the EPSON printer software diskettes.

Installing from the CD-ROM

In addition to the printer driver and utilities, the CD-ROM contains EPSON Answers, a comprehensive online guide that includes:

EPSON ANSWERS
If you have a CD-ROM
drive, you can run EPSON
Answers, the on-screen
guide to your new printer.
It puts you on the right
track quickly and easily.

▶ **How To** for step-by-step printer operating instructions
▶ **Color Guide** with practical color printing information
▶ **Problem Solver** to help you fix printer problems
▶ **Test Print** so you can check your print quality

Follow the instructions inside the CD-ROM case to install the software. To run EPSON Answers, click on its icon in the EPSON program group or folder.

Source: Reprinted by permission of Epson America.

Writing Procedures for Policies and Regulations

Up to this point, we have concentrated primarily on instructions dealing with how to put things together; how to install, repair, or use equipment; and how to alert readers to mechanical or even personal danger(s). But there is another similar type of writing that deals with guidelines for the world of work: procedures. These concern policies and regulations found in employee handbooks and other internal corporate communications, such as Web sites, memos, and e-mails.

Some Examples of Procedures to Write

Procedures deal with a wide range of "how-to" activities within an organization, including the following:

- access a company file or database
- prepare for an audit
- apply for family leave
- dress professionally at work
- route information
- reserve a company vehicle
- take advantage of telecommuting options
- prepare for and respond at a multinational conference
- file a work-related grievance
- request travel expense reimbursement
- operate updated corporate software
- fulfill promotion requirements

Policy procedures have a major impact on a company and its workers; they affect schedules, payrolls, acceptable and unacceptable behaviors at work, and a range of protocols governing the way an organization does business internally and externally.

Meeting the Needs of Your Marketplace

As with instructions, you will have to plan carefully for writing procedures. A mistake in business procedures can be as wide ranging and as costly as an error in a set of assembly instructions—perhaps more so since poorly written procedures can land a company and/or its employees in significant legal trouble.

To avoid such difficulties, spell out precisely what is expected of employees—how, when, where, and why they are to perform or adhere to a certain policy. Use the same strategies as for instructions discussed earlier in this chapter. Leave no chance for misunderstanding or ambiguity; be unqualifyingly straightforward and clear-cut. Determine what information employees need to comply with all the regulations you are specifying.

Many times procedure statements involve a change in the work environment. Help readers by including, whenever necessary, definitions, headings, some prefatory explanations, and an offer to help employees with any questions they may have. Always present a copy of the procedures to management to approve or to revise before sending them to employees.

Figure 7.7 (pp. 220–221)shows a memo from a human resources director notifying employees how they can take advantage of a new flextime arrangement at work, including what they can and cannot do within the framework of flextime. Note how the writer divides her procedures document into an introduction explaining when flextime will go into effect and what choices employees have about it, a section that usefully defines and delineates the concept of flextime, and finally a section containing specific guidelines. These guidelines, while not sequential, function as a series of steps that employees have to follow, and these steps ultimately will affect the entire organization.

The various regulations about what employees cannot do in flextime might be seen as the equivalents of warning and caution statements discussed in this chapter's Warnings, Cautions, and Notes section (pp. 209–210). Note, too, how the writer does not veer off to discuss benefits to the employer or to examine where and how often flextime has been used elsewhere. Finally, this example of procedural writing protects the employer legally by establishing the policies and rules by which an employee's work time is clearly defined and delineated.

Some Final Advice

Perhaps the most important piece of advice to leave you with is this: Do not take *anything* for granted when you have to write a set of instructions. It is wrong and on occasion dangerous to assume that your readers have performed the procedure before, that they will automatically supply missing or "obvious" information, or that they will easily anticipate your next step. No one ever complained that a set of instructions was too clear or too easy to follow.

FIGURE 7.7   Instructions on a new scheduling policy.

WebTech, Inc.   **www.webtech.com**
4300 Ames Boulevard, Gunderson, CO 81230-0999   (303) 555-9721
                                                        FAX (303) 555-9876

TO:	All Employees	DATE:	March 20, 2006
FROM:	Teniqua Bowers T.B.	SUBJECT:	Opting for a Flextime
	Human Resources		Schedule

Effective sixty days from now, on May 10, 2006, employees will have the
opportunity to go to a flextime schedule or to remain on their current 8-hour
fixed schedule. This memo explains the flextime option and establishes the
guidelines and rules you must follow if you choose this new schedule.

Flextime Defined

Flextime is based on a certain number of **core hours** and **flexible hours**. Our
company will be open twelve hours, from 6:00 a.m. to 6:00 p.m. weekdays, to
accommodate both fixed and flextime arrangements. During this 12-hour period,
all employees on flextime will be expected to work eight and one-half consecutive
hours, including a half-hour for lunch. All employees must work a **common core
time from 10:00 a.m. to 4:00 p.m.** but flextime employees will be free to choose
their own starting and quitting times. For instance, they might elect to arrive at
8:00 a.m. and leave at 4:30 p.m., or they may want to start at 9:30 a.m. and leave
at 6:00 p.m.

Flextime Guidelines and Rules

Employees need to understand their individual responsibilities and adjust their
schedules accordingly. All employees must adhere strictly to the following
regulations and realize that flextime schedule privileges can be revoked for
violations.

Continued

FIGURE 7.7   (Continued)

2.

What Flextime Employees Must Do

(1) Be present during core time, arriving and leaving the plant during their flexible work hours.
(2) Observe a minimum unpaid half-hour lunch break each working day.
(3) Cooperate with their supervisors to make sure coverage is provided for their departments from 6:00 a.m. to 6:00 p.m.
(4) Notify supervisors of absences.
(5) Attend monthly corporate meetings even though such meetings may be outside their chosen flextime schedules.
(6) Adhere to dress code during any time they are at work, regardless of their flextimes.
(7) Agree to work on a flextime schedule for a 6-month period.

What Flextime Employees Can't Do

(1) Be tardy during core time.
(2) Switch, bank, borrow, or trade flextime hours with other employees without the approval of an immediate supervisor.
(3) File for overtime without a supervisor's approval.
(4) Self-schedule a vacation by expanding flextime hours.
(5) Switch back and forth between fixed time and flextime.

How Do You Sign Up for Flextime?

If you wish to begin a flextime schedule, first you need to obtain and complete a transfer of hours form from your supervisor. Next, you need to bring that signed form to Human Resources (Admin. 201) to participate officially in this program.

I will be happy to talk to you about this new option and to answer any of your questions. Please call me at ext. 5121, e-mail me at **tbowers@webtech.com**, or come by my office in Admin. 201. Thank you.

✓ Revision Checklist

❑ Analyzed my intended audience's background, especially why and how they will use my instructions.

❑ Tested my instructions to make sure they include all necessary steps in their proper sequence.

❑ Made sure all measurements, distances, times, and relationships are precise and correct.

❑ Avoided technical terms if my audience is not a group of specialists in my field.

❑ Used the imperative mood throughout my instructions.

❑ Wrote clear, short sentences.

❑ Chose effective visuals, labeled them, and placed them next to the step(s) to which they apply.

❑ Made my introduction proportionate to the length and complexity of my instructions and suitable for my readers' needs.

❑ Included necessary background, safety, and operational information in the introduction.

❑ Included a complete list of tools and materials my audience needs to carry out the instructions.

❑ Put instructions in easy-to-follow steps and in the right order.

❑ Used numbers or bullets to label the steps and connective words to indicate order.

❑ Used warnings, cautions, and notes where necessary and in a form that makes them easily seen and read.

❑ Supplied a conclusion that summarizes what readers should have done or reassures them that they have completed the job satisfactorily.

❑ Spelled out clearly responsibilities, benefits, and restrictions of any procedures for readers.

❑ Defined any terms readers may be unfamiliar with in procedures for policies and regulations.

❑ Gave a copy of procedures to administrators for their approval before distributing to employees.

Exercises

1. Find a set of instructions that does not contain any visuals, but that you think should have some graphic material to make it clearer. Design those visuals yourself and indicate where they should appear in the instructions.

2. From a technical manual in your field or an owner's manual, locate a set of instructions that you think is poorly written and illustrated. In a memo to your instructor, explain why the instructions are unclear, confusing, or badly formatted. Then revise the instructions to make them easier for the reader to carry out. Submit the original instructions with your revision.

3. Write a set of instructions in numbered steps (or in paragraph format) on one of the following relatively simple activities.
    a. tying a shoe
    b. using an ATM
    c. unlocking a door with a key
    d. making a call from a cellular phone
    e. planting a tree or a shrub
    f. sewing a button on a shirt
    g. removing a stain from clothing
    h. pumping gas into a car
    i. surfing the Internet
    j. checking a book out of the library
    k. parallel parking a car
    l. shifting gears in a car
    m. photocopying a page from a book

4. Write an appropriate introduction and conclusion for the set of instructions you wrote for Exercise 3.

5. Write a set of full instructions on one of the following more complex topics. Identify your audience. Include an appropriate introduction; a list of equipment and materials; numbered steps with necessary warnings, cautions, and notes; and an effective conclusion. Also include whatever visuals you think will help your audience.
    a. scanning a document
    b. changing a flat tire
    c. testing chlorine in a swimming pool
    d. shaving a patient for surgery
    e. changing the oil and oil filter in a car
    f. surveying a parcel of land
    g. pruning hedges
    h. jumping a dead car battery
    i. using the Heimlich maneuver to help a choking individual
    j. filleting a fish
    k. creating a logo for a letterhead
    l. taking someone's blood pressure
    m. downloading a home page from the Web
    n. painting a car
    o. cooking a roast
    p. flossing a patient's teeth after cleaning
    q. creating a computer file

6. The following set of instructions is confusing, vague, and out of order. Rewrite the instructions to make them clear, easy to follow, and correct. Make sure that each step follows the guidelines outlined in this chapter.

Reupholstering a Piece of Furniture

(1) Although it might be difficult to match the worn material with the new material, you might as well try.
(2) If you cannot, remove the old material.
(3) Take out the padding.
(4) Take out all of the tacks before removing the old covering. You might want to save the old covering.
(5) Measure the new material with the old, if you are able to.
(6) Check the frame, springs, webbing, and padding.
(7) Put the new material over the old.
(8) Check to see if it matches.
(9) You must have the same size as before.
(10) Look at the padding inside. If it is lumpy, smooth it out.
(11) You will need to tack all the sides down. Space your tacks a good distance apart.
(12) When you spot wrinkles, remove the tacks.
(13) Caution: in step 11 directly above, do not drive your tacks all the way through. Leave some room.
(14) Work from the center to the edge in step 11 above.
(15) Put the new material over the old furniture.

P.S. Use strong cords whenever there are tacks. Put the cords under the nails so that they hold.

---

7. Write a set of procedures, similar to Figure 7.7, on one of the following policies or regulations at your school or job site.
   a. offering customer service over the phone or Web
   b. filing a claim for a personal injury on the job
   c. designing an employee's personal space—what is and is not allowed?
   d. using the Internet at work for personal use
   e. ensuring confidentiality at work (to practice professional ethics in the workplace)
   f. enrolling in mandatory courses to maintain a license or certificate
   g. playing music at the workplace
   h. going through an orientation procedure to begin a new job
   i. following an acceptable dress code

8

Writing Effective Short Reports and Proposals

This chapter shows you how to write short reports and proposals, which are among the most important and frequent types of business communications you may be called on to write. Both are crucial to the day-to-day operations of a company or organization. They attract new business or recommend changes (proposals), and then they provide information on progress and/or results (short reports). Short reports and proposals both can use a memo or letter format, and they share many of the same situations. Most important of all, they get crucial information to decision makers who need such information to stay within a budget and remain on schedule, to use personnel in the most efficient ways possible, and to be aware of any problem or delay in order to lessen risk and increase safety and/or production.

Why Short Reports Are Important

A short report can be defined as an organized presentation of relevant data on any topic—money, travel, time, personnel, equipment, management—that a company or agency tracks in its day-to-day operations. Short reports are practical and to the point. They show that work is being done, and they also show your boss that you are alert, professional, and reliable. Short reports are written to co-workers, employers, vendors, and clients. When they are intended for individuals within your organization, short reports are most often sent as memos. But for clients usually you will send your reports out as letters.

Businesses cannot function without short written reports. Reports tell whether

- work is being completed
- schedules are being met
- costs have been contained
- sales projections are being met
- unexpected problems have been solved

You may write an occasional report in response to a specific question, or you may be required to write a daily or weekly report about routine activities.

Short Report Types and Writing Guidelines

To give you a sense of some of the topics you may be required to write about, here is a list of various types of short reports common in the business world.

appraisal report	inventory report	production report
audit report	investigative report	progress/activity report
budget report	justification report	recommendation report
construction report	laboratory report	research report
design report	manager's report	sales report
evaluation report	medicine/treatment	status report
experiment report	error report	survey report
feasibility report	operations report	test report
incident report	periodic report	travel report

This chapter concentrates on five of the most common types of reports you are likely to encounter in your professional work.

1. periodic reports (see Figures 8.1 and 8.2)
2. sales reports
3. progress reports
4. travel reports
5. incident reports

Although there are many kinds of short reports, they all are written for readers who need factual information so that they can get a job accomplished. Never think of the reports you write as a series of casual notes jotted down for *your* convenience.

The following guidelines will help you write any short report successfully.

Do the Necessary Research

An effective short report needs the same careful planning that goes into other on-the-job writing. You may have to test or inspect a product or service or assess the relative merits of a group of competing products or services. Some frequent types of research you can expect to do on the job include the following:

- checking data in reference manuals or code books
- reading background information in professional and trade journals
- reviewing a client's file
- testing equipment
- performing a test or procedure
- conferring with colleagues, managers, vendors, or clients
- describing a site
- attending a conference

Never trust your memory to keep track of all the details that go into making a successful short report. Take notes, either by hand or on your laptop or handheld. A well-kept set of notes will provide you with the basic information you need for your report.

Be Objective and Ethical

Your readers will expect you to report the facts objectively and impartially—costs, sales, weather conditions, eyewitness accounts, observations, statistics, test measurements, and descriptions. Your reports should be truthful, accurate, and complete. Here are some guidelines.

- Avoid *guesswork*. If you don't know or have not yet found out, say so and indicate how you'll try to find out.
- Do not substitute *impressions* or *unsupported personal opinions* for careful research.
- Using *biased, skewed,* or *incomplete data* is unethical. Provide a straightforward and honest account; don't exaggerate or minimize.

Review Chapter 1's section on ethics in business writing (pp. 17–22).

Organize Carefully

Organizing a short report effectively means that you include the right amount of information in the most appropriate places for your audience. Many times a simple chronological or sequential organization will be acceptable for your readers. As you organize your reports, help readers find information easily by using bullets or numbers; headings; and, where appropriate, visuals. Readers will expect your report to contain information on the purpose, findings, recommendations, and a conclusion, as described in the following sections.

Purpose

Always begin by telling readers why you are writing and by alerting them to what you will discuss. Give your readers a summary of key events and details at the beginning to help them follow the remainder of the report quickly. When you establish the scope (or limits) of your report, you help readers zero in on specific times, places, procedures, or problems.

Findings

This should be the longest part of your report and contain the data you have collected—facts about prices, personnel, equipment, events, locations, incidents, or tests. Gather the data from your research; personal observations; interviews; and/or conversations with co-workers, employers, or clients. Give readers the results, but do not overburden your reader.

Conclusion

Your conclusion tells readers what your data means. A conclusion can summarize what has happened; review what actions were taken; or explain the outcome or results of a test, a visit, or a program.

Recommendations

A recommendation informs readers what specific actions you think your company or client should take—market a new product, hire more staff, institute safety measures, select among alternative plans or procedures, and so on. Recommendations must be based on the data you collected and the conclusions you have reached.

Note how the report in Figure 8.1 fails to help readers understand the organization and importance of the information. The revised version of the report, Figure 8.2 (pp. 230–231), clearly illustrates effective report writing; it is an example of a periodic report. The reader is provided with information at regularly scheduled intervals—daily, weekly, bimonthly (twice a month).

The report in Figure 8.2, which was submitted to a police captain, carefully summarizes, organizes, and interprets the data collected over a three-month period from individual activity logs. Because of this report, Captain Alice Martin will be better able to plan future protection for the community and to recommend changes in police services.

Sales Reports

Sales reports provide businesses with a necessary and ongoing record of accounts, on-line and mail purchases, losses, and profits over a specified period of time. They help businesses assess past performance and plan for the future. In doing that, they fulfill two functions: **financial** and **managerial.** As a financial record, sales reports list costs per unit, discounts or special reductions, and subtotals and totals. Like a spreadsheet, sales reports show gains and losses. They may also provide statistics for comparing two quarters' sales.

Sales reports are also a managerial tool because they help businesses make both short- and long-range plans. The restaurant manager's sales report illustrated in Figure 8.3 (p. 232) guides the owners in planning which popular entrées to highlight and which unpopular ones to modify or delete. Note how the recommendations follow logically from the figures Sam Jelinek gives to Gina Smeltzer and Alfonso Zapatta, the owners of The Grill.

Progress Reports

A progress report informs readers about the status of an ongoing project. It lets them know how much and what type of work has been done by a particular date, by whom, how well, and how close the entire job is to being completed. A progress report emphasizes whether you are

- maintaining your schedule
- staying within your budget
- using the proper equipment
- making the right assignments
- identifying an unexpected problem or possible glitch
- providing adjustments in schedules, personnel, and so on
- completing the job efficiently, correctly, and according to codes

FIGURE 8.1   An example of a poorly written, poorly organized, and poorly formatted periodic report.

To Serve and To Protect

Greenfield Police Department

Emergency 555-1000   **Administration** 555-1001   **Traffic** 555-1002

TO: Capt. Alice Martin
FROM: Sergeants Daniel Huxley, Jennifer Chavez,
            and Ivor Paz
Vague   SUBJECT: Crime rate
          DATE: July 12, 2006

Introduction doesn't tell reader anything about overall picture

This report will let you know what happened this quarter as opposed to what happened last quarter as far as crimes are concerned in Greenfield. This report is based on statistics the department has given us over the quarter.

Throws facts at reader without any sense of reader's needs

Irrelevant data

Here we'll let the facts speak for themselves. From Jan.-Mar. we saw 126 robberies while from Apr.-June we had 106. Home burglaries for this period: 43; last period: 36. 33 cars were stolen in the period before this one; now we have 40. Interestingly enough, last year at this time we had only 27 thefts. Four of them involved heirlooms.

No analysis or guided commentary— just undigested numbers

Homicides were 9 this time versus 8 last quarter; assault and battery charges were 92 this time, 77 last time. Carrying a concealed weapon 11 (10 last quarter). We had 47 arrests (55 last quarter) for charges of possession of a controlled substance. Rape charges were 8, 1 less than last quarter. 319 citations this time for moving violations: speeding 158/98, and failing to observe the signals 165/102 last quarter. DUIs were good this quarter—only 45, or 23 fewer than last quarter.

Hard-to-follow comparisons and contrasts

Misdemeanors this time: disturbing peace 53; vagrancy/public drunkenness 8; violating leash laws 32; violating city codes 39, including dumping trash. Last quarter the figures were 48, 59, 21, 43.

Conclusion provides no summary or recommendation

We believe this report is complete and up to date. We further hope that this report has given you all the facts you will need.

FIGURE 8.2   A well-prepared periodic report, revised from Figure 8.1.

To Serve and To Protect

Greenfield Police Department

Emergency 555-1000   **Administration** 555-1001   **Traffic** 555-1002

TO: Captain Alice Martin
FROM: Sergeants Daniel Huxley, Jennifer Chavez, and Ivor Paz
SUBJECT: Crime rate for the second quarter of 2006
DATE: July 12, 2006

From April 1 to June 30, 852 crimes were committed in Greenfield, representing
a 5 percent increase over the 815 crimes recorded during the previous quarter.

TYPES OF CRIME
The following report, based on the table below, discusses the specific types of
crimes, organized into four categories: **robberies and theft, felonies, traffic,
and misdemeanors**.

Table 1. Comparison of the 1st and 2nd Quarter Crime Rates in Greenfield

CATEGORY	1st Quarter	2nd Quarter
ROBBERIES and THEFT		
Commercial	63	75
Domestic	36	43
Auto	33	40
FELONIES		
Homicides	16	13
Assault and battery	77	92
Carrying a concealed weapon	10	11
Poss. of a controlled substance	55	47
Rape	9	8
TRAFFIC		
Speeding	165	158
Failure to observe signals	102	98
DUI	78	45
MISDEMEANORS		
Disturbing the peace	48	53
Vagrancy	40	48
Public drunkenness	19	40
Leash law violations	21	32
Dumping	35	37
Other	8	12

Robberies and Theft
The greatest increase in crime was in robberies, 20 percent more than last
quarter. Downtown merchants reported 75 burglaries, exceeding $985,000.
The biggest theft occurred on May 21 at Weisenfarth's Jewelers when three
armed robbers stole more than $97,000 in merchandise. (Suspects were

Continued

FIGURE 8.2   (Continued)

apprehended two days later.) Home burglaries accounted for 43 crimes, though the thefts were not confined to any one residential area. We also had 40 car thefts reported and investigated.

Felonies
Homicides decreased slightly from last quarter—from 16 to 13. Charges for battery, however, increased—15 more than we had last quarter. Arrests for carrying a concealed weapon were nearly identical this quarter to last quarter's total. But the 47 arrests for possession of a controlled substance were appreciably down from the first quarter. Arrests for rape for this quarter also were less than last quarter's. Three of those rapes happened within one week (May 6–12) and have been attributed to the same suspect, now in custody.

Traffic
Traffic violations for this period were lower than last quarter's figures. This quarter's citations for moving violations (335) represent a 5 percent increase over last quarter's (322). Most of the citations were issued for speeding (158) or for failing to observe signals (98). Officers issued 45 citations to motorists for DUI, an impressive decrease over the 78 DUIs issued last quarter. The new state penalty of withholding a driver's license for six months of anyone convicted of driving while under the influence appears to be an effective deterrent.

Misdemeanors
The largest number of arrests in this category were for disturbing the peace—53. Compared to last quarter, this is an increase of 10 percent. There were 88 charges for vagrancy and public drunkenness, an increase from the 59 charges last quarter. We issued 32 citations for violations of leash laws, which represents a sizable increase over last quarter's 21 citations. Thirty-seven citations were issued for dumping trash at the Mason Reservoir.

CONCLUSION
Overall, while the crime rate has decreased in traffic (especially DUIs) and possession of controlled substances this quarter, we have seen a marked increase in arrests for robberies and battery.

RECOMMENDATIONS
To help deter robberies in the downtown area, we recommend the following:

- increasing surveillance units in the area
- offering merchants our workshop on safety and security precautions, as we did during the first quarter

Historically, battery arrests have risen during the second quarter. Our recommendations to counter that trend include:

- continuing to work closely with the Neighborhood Watch Group
- putting more foot and bicycle patrols in the neighborhoods with the highest incidence of battery reports

FIGURE 8.3   A sales report to a manager.

Thegrill

Dayton, OH 43210 • (813) 555-4000 • (813) 555-4100 fax • www.Thegrill.com

TO: Gina Smeltzer   DATE: June 28, 2006
         Alfonso Zapatta, owners
FROM: Sam Jelinek S J.   SUBJECT: Analysis of entrée sales
         Manager

As we agreed at our monthly meeting on June 4, here is my analysis of entrée sales for two weeks to assist us in our menu planning. Below is a record of entrée sales for the weeks of June 13–19 and June 20–26 that I have compiled into a table for easier comparisons.

	Portion size	June 13–19 Amount	Percentage	June 20–26 Amount	Percentage	2 weeks combined Amount	Percentage
Cornish Hen	6 oz.	238	17	307	17	545	17
Stuffed Young Turkey	8 oz.	112	8	182	10	294	12
Broiled Salmon Steak	8 oz.	154	11	217	12	371	13
Brook Trout	12 oz.	182	13	252	14	434	9
Prime Rib	10 oz.	168	12	198	11	366	11
Lobster Tails	2–4 oz.	147	10	161	9	308	10
Delmonico Steak	10 oz.	56	4	70	4	126	4
Moroccan Chicken	6 oz.	343	25	413	23	756	24
		1,400	100	1,800	100	3,200	100

Recommendations
Based on the figures in the table above, I recommend that we do the following:

1. Order at least 100 more pounds of prime rib for each two-week period to be eligible for further quantity discounts from the Northern Meat Company.
2. Delete the Delmonico steak entrée because of low acceptance.
3. Introduce a new chicken or fish entrée to take the place of the Delmonico steak; I would suggest grilled lemon chicken to accommodate those patrons interested in a tasty, low-fat, lower-cholesterol entrée.

Please give me your reactions within the next week. It shouldn't take more than a few days to implement these changes.

Almost any kind of ongoing work can be described in a progress report—research for a paper, construction of an apartment complex, preparation of a Web site, documentation of a patient's rehabilitation. Progress reports are often prepared at key phases, or milestones, in a project.

Audience for a Progress Report

A progress report is intended for people who generally are not working alongside you but who need a record of your activities to coordinate them with other individuals' efforts and to learn about problems or changes in plans. For example, since supervisors may not be in the field or branch office or at a construction site, they will rely on your progress report for much of their information. Customers, such as a contractor's clients, often expect reports on how carefully their money is being spent. That way they can adjust schedules or alter specifications if there is a risk of going over budget.

The length of the progress report will depend on the complexity of the project. Dale Brandt's assessment of the progress his construction company is making in renovating Dr. Burke's clinic is given in a two-page letter in Figure 8.4 (pp. 234–235); however, a report on organizing a workshop on time management might require only a short e-mail.

Frequency of Progress Reports

Progress reports can be written daily, weekly, monthly, quarterly, or annually. Your specific job and your employer's needs will dictate how often you have to keep others informed of your progress. Contractor Brandt determined that three reports, spaced four to six weeks apart, would be necessary to keep Dr. Burke posted; Figure 8.4 is the second of those reports.

Parts of Progress Reports

Progress reports should contain information on (1) the work you have done, (2) the work you are currently doing, and (3) the work you will do.

How to Begin a Progress Report

In a brief introduction, cover the following:

- indicate why you are writing the report
- provide any necessary project titles or codes
- detail specific dates
- help readers recall the job you are doing for them

If you are writing an initial progress report, supply background information in the opening. But, if you are submitting a subsequent progress report, your introduction should remind the reader about where your previous report left off and where the current one begins. Note how Dale Brandt's first paragraph in Figure 8.4 calls attention to the continuity of his work.

How to Continue a Progress Report

The body of the report should provide significant details about costs, materials, personnel, and times for the major stages of the project.

- Emphasize completed tasks, not false starts. If you report that the carpentry work or painting is finished, readers do not need an explanation of paint viscosity or geometrical patterns.
- Omit routine or well-known details ("I had to use the library when I wanted to read the back issues of *Safety News* that were not on the Web").

FIGURE 8.4   The second of three progress reports from a contractor to a customer.

Brandt Construction Company

Halsted at Roosevelt, Chicago, Illinois 60608-0999 • 312-555-3700 • Fax: 312-555-1731
http://www.brandt.com

April 27, 2006

Dr. Pamela Burke
1439 Grand Avenue
Mount Prospect, IL 60045-1003

Dear Dr. Burke:

Here is my second progress report about the renovation work being done at your
new clinic at Hacienda and Donohue. Work proceeded satisfactorily in April
according to the plans you had approved in March.

Review of Work Completed in March
As I informed you in my first progress report on March 31, we tore down the
walls, pulled the old wiring, and removed existing plumbing lines. All the gutting
work was finished in March.

Work Completed During April
By April 8, we had laid the new pipes and connected them to the main septic line.
We also installed the two commodes, the four standard sinks, and the utility
basin. The heating and air-conditioning ducts were installed by April 13. From
April 19–23, we erected soundproof walls in the four examination rooms, the
reception area, your office, and the laboratory. We had no problems reducing the
size of the reception area by five feet to make the first examination room larger,
as you had requested.

Problems with the Electrical System
We had difficulty with the electrical work, however. The number of outlets and
the generator for the laboratory equipment required extra-duty power lines that
had to be approved by both Con Edison and Cook County inspectors. The
approval slowed us down by three days. Also, the wholesaler, Midtown Electric,
failed to deliver the recessed lighting fixtures by April 26 as promised. Those
fixtures and the generator are now being installed. Moreover, the cost of those
fixtures will increase the materials budget by **$2,888.00**. The cost for labor is as
we had projected—**$89,450**.

Work Remaining
The finishing work is scheduled for May. By May 10, the floors in the examination
rooms, laboratory, washrooms, and hallways should be tiled and the reception area

Continued

FIGURE 8.4   (Continued)

---

page 2

and your office carpeted. By May 12, the reception area and your office should be paneled and the rest of the walls painted. If everything stays on schedule, touch-up work is scheduled for May 17–21. You should be able to move into your new clinic by May 24.

You will receive a third and final progress report by May 11. Thank you again for your business and the confidence you have placed in our company.

Sincerely yours,

Dale Brandt

Dale Brandt

- Describe in the body of your report any snags you encountered that may affect the work in progress (see Dale Brandt's section on electrical problems in Figure 8.4). It is better for the reader to know about trouble early in the project so that appropriate changes or corrections can be made.

How to End a Progress Report

The conclusion should give a timetable for the completion of duties or submission of the next progress report. Give the date by which you expect work to be completed. Be realistic; do not promise to have a job done in less time than you know it will take. Readers will not expect miracles, only informed estimates. Even so, any conclusion must be tentative. Note that the good news Dale Brandt gives Dr. Burke about moving into her new clinic is qualified by the words "If everything stays on schedule." He is also well aware of the "you attitude" by thanking Dr. Burke again for her business.

Travel Reports

Reporting on the trips you take is an important professional responsibility. In documenting what you did and saw, travel reports keep readers informed about your efforts and how they affect ongoing or future business. Travel reports also should be written after you attend a convention or sales meeting or call on customers.

Questions Travel Reports Answer

Specifically, this report should answer the following questions for your readers.

- Where did you go?
- When did you go?
- Why did you go?
- Whom did you see?
- What did they tell you?
- What did you do about it?

For a business trip, you are also likely to have to inform readers how much it cost and to supply them with receipts for all of your expenses.

Common Types of Travel Reports

Travel reports can cover a wide range of activities and are called by different names to characterize those activities. Most likely, you will encounter the following three types of travel reports.

1. Site inspection reports. These reports inform managers about conditions at a branch office or plant, a customer's business, or on the advisability of relocating an office or other facility. After visiting the site, you will determine whether it meets your employer's (or customer's) needs. Site inspection reports provide information about the physical plant, the environment (air, soil, water, vegetation), or computer or financial operations.

Figure 8.5, which begins with a recommendation, is a report written to a district manager interested in acquiring a new site for a fast-food restaurant.

2. Field trip reports. These reports, often assigned in a course, are written after a visit to a plant, military installation, office complex, hospital, detention center, or other facility to show what you have learned about the operation of a place. You will be expected to describe how an institution is organized, the technical procedures and/or equipment it uses, pertinent ecological conditions, or the ratio of one group to another. The emphasis in such reports is on the educational value of the trip. For example, "From my visit to Water Valley, I learned a great deal about the health care delivery system at an extended care facility; this will help me during my internship next term."

3. Home health or social work visits. Nurses, social workers, and probation officers report daily on their visits to patients and clients. Their reports describe clients' lifestyles, assess needs, and make recommendations. They are often divided into Purpose of the Visit, Description of the Visit, and Action Taken as a Result of the Visit.

How to Gather Information for a Travel Report

Regardless of the kind of travel report you have to write, your assignment will be easier and your report better organized if you follow these suggestions.

1. Before you leave on the field trip, site inspection, or visit, be sure you are prepared, including:
   a. Obtain all necessary names; street, e-mail, and Web site addresses; and telephone and fax numbers.
   b. Check previous correspondence, case studies, contracts, or agreements.

FIGURE 8.5   A site inspection report using a map.

VAIL'S

TO: Dale Gandy *BA*   DATE: July 2, 2006
FROM: Beth Armando   SUBJECT: New Site for Vail's #8
         Development Department

Recommendation
The best location for the new Vail's Chicken House is the vacant Dairy World shop at the northeast corner of Smith and Fairfax Avenues—1701 Fairfax. I inspected this property on June 21 and 22 and also talked to Marge Bloom, the broker at Crescent Realty representing the Dairy World Company.

The Location
Please refer to the map below. Located at the intersection of the two busiest streets on the southeast side, the property will allow us to take advantage of the traffic flow to attract customers. Being only one block west of the Cloverleaf Mall should also help business.

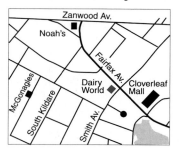

Customers will have easy access to our location. They can enter or exit Dairy World from either Smith or Fairfax. Left turns on Smith are prohibited from 7 a.m. to 9 a.m., but since most of our business is done after 11 a.m., the restriction poses few problems.

Denver, CO 87123   (303) 555-7200   http://www.vails.com

Continued

FIGURE 8.5   (Continued)

Area Competition
Only two other fast-food establishments are in a one-mile vicinity. McGonagles, 1534 South Kildare, specializes in hamburgers; Noah's, 703 Zanwood, serves primarily seafood entrées. Their offerings will not directly compete with ours. The closest fast-food restaurant serving chicken is Johnson's, 1.8 miles away.

Parking Facilities
The parking lot has space for 45 cars, and the area at the south end of the property (38 feet x 37 feet) can accommodate 14 to 15 cars. The driveways and parking lot were paved with asphalt last March and appear to be in excellent condition. We will also be able to make use of the drive-up window on the north side of the building.

The Building
The building has 3,993 square feet of heated and cooled space. The air-conditioning and heating units were installed within the last fifteen months and seem to be in good working order; nine more months of transferable warranty remain on these units.

The only major changes we must make are in the kitchen. To prepare items on the Vail's menu, we would need to add three more exhaust fans (there is only one now) and expand the grill and cooking areas. The kitchen also has three relatively new sinks and ample storage space in the sixteen cabinets.

The restaurant has a seating capacity of up to 54 persons; 10 booths are covered with red vinyl and are comfortably padded. A color-coordinated serving counter could seat 8 to 10 patrons. The floor does not need to be retiled, but the walls will have to be painted to match Vail's color decor.

    c. Download work orders, instructions, or other documents pertinent to your visit—for example, Web sites and ads.

    d. Bring a laptop with you whenever possible.

2. When you return from your trip, keep the following hints in mind as you compile your travel report.

    a. Write your report promptly. If you put it off, you may forget important items.

    b. Do not include everything you saw or did on the trip. Exclude irrelevant details, such as whether it was enjoyable, what you ate, or how delighted you were to meet people.

    c. As you edit the final copy of your report, check to make sure you have listed names and calculated figures correctly.

Incident Reports

The short reports discussed thus far in this chapter have dealt with routine work. They have described events that were anticipated, planned, or supervised. But every business or agency runs into unexpected trouble that delays routine work. More often than not, these circumstances need to be documented in an incident report. Employers, and on some occasions government inspectors, insurance agents, and attorneys, must be informed about those events that interfere with or threaten normal, safe operations. Incident reports can be submitted as a memo, as in Figure 8.6 (pp. 240–241), or on specially prepared forms your employer or a government agency expects you to follow.

When to Submit an Incident Report

An incident report is required when there is, for example:

- an accident—fire, automobile, physical injury
- a law enforcement offense
- an environmental danger, including a computer virus
- a machine breakdown
- a delivery delay
- a cost overrun
- a production slowdown

Figure 8.6 (pp. 240–241) shows an incident report submitted by the engineer on duty about a train accident; it was written as a memo.

Protecting Yourself Legally

An incident report can be used as legal evidence, and it then becomes part of a permanent legal record. It frequently concerns the two topics over which powerful legal battles are waged—health and property.

You have to be very careful about collecting and recording details. Make sure your report is not sketchy or incomplete and not biased. To avoid these errors, you may have to interview employees or bystanders; travel to the accident site; check manuals, code books, or other guides; consult safety experts; and/or research records.

FIGURE 8.6   An incident report in memo format.

THE GREAT HARVESTER RAILROAD
Des Moines, IA 50306-4005
http://www.ghrr.com

TO: Angela O'Brien, District Manager
           James Day, Safety Instructor
FROM: Nick Roane, Engineer *N.R.*
DATE: March 3, 2006
SUBJECT: Derailment of Train 28 on March 3, 2006

DESCRIPTION OF INCIDENT

Give time, location { At 7:20 a.m. on March 3, 2006, I was driving Engine 457 traveling north at a speed of fifty-two miles an hour on the single main-line track four miles east of Ridgeville, Illinois. Weather conditions and visibility were

Describe what happened { excellent. Suddenly the last two grain cars, 3022 and 3053, jumped the track. The train automatically went into emergency braking and stopped immediately. There were no injuries to the crew. But the train did not stop before both grain cars turned at a 45° angle. After checking the cars, I found that half the contents of their loads had spilled. The train was not carrying any hazardous chemical shipments.

Explain what was done { I notified Supervisor Bill Purvis at 7:40 a.m., and within forty-five minutes he and a section crew arrived at the scene with rerailing equipment. The section crew removed the two grain cars from the track, put in new ties, and made the main-line track passable by 9:25 a.m. At 9:45 a.m. a vacuum car arrived with Engine 372 from Hazlehurst, Illinois, and its crew proceeded with the cleanup operation. By 10:25 a.m. all the spilled grain was loaded onto the cars brought by the Hazlehurst train. Bill Purvis notified Barnwell Granary that their shipment would be at least three hours late.

CAUSES OF INCIDENT

Determine likely cause { Supervisor Purvis and I checked the stretch of train track where the cars derailed and found it to be heavily worn. We believe that a fisher joint slipped when the grain cars hit it, and the track broke. You can see the location of the cracked fisher joint in the drawing below.

Continued

FIGURE 8.6   (Continued)

Page 2

Offer recommendations to solve or prevent problem from recurring

RECOMMENDATIONS
We made the following recommendations to the switch yard in Hazlehurst to be carried out immediately.
1. Check the section of track for ten miles on either side of Ridgeville for any signs of defective fisher joints.
2. Repair any defective joints at once.
3. Instruct all engineers to slow down to five to ten mph over this section of the track until the rail check is completed.

To ensure you write an incident report that is legally proper, follow these guidelines.

1. Be accurate, objective, and complete. Recount clearly and reliably what happened in the order it took place. Never omit or distort facts; the information may surface later, and you could be accused of a cover-up. Do not just write "I do not know" for an answer. If you are not sure, state why. Also be careful that there are no discrepancies in your report.

2. Give facts, not opinions. Provide a factual account of what actually happened, not a biased interpretation of events. Indirect words (e.g., "I guess," "I wonder," "apparently," "perhaps," or "possibly") weaken your objectivity. Stick to details you witnessed or that were seen by eyewitnesses. Identify witnesses or victims by giving names, addresses, places of employment, and so on. But, keep in mind that stating what someone else saw is regarded as hearsay and therefore is not admissible in a court of law. State only what *you* saw or heard.

When you describe what happened, avoid drawing uncalled-for conclusions. Do *not* take sides. Consider the following statements of opinion and fact.

Opinion: The patient seemed confused and caught himself in his IV tubing.
  Fact: The patient caught himself in his IV tubing.

Opinion: The equipment was defective.
  Fact: The bolt was loose.

Be careful, too, about blaming someone. Statements such as "Baxter was incompetent" or "The company knew of the problem but did nothing about it" are libelous remarks.

In law enforcement work, further identify suspects by their aliases and by any distinctive characteristics—for example, "jagged 4-inch scar on left forearm."

3. Do not exceed your professional responsibilities. Answer only those questions you are qualified to answer. Do not presume to speak as a detective, an inspector, a physician, or a supervisor. Do not represent yourself as an attorney or a claims adjuster when writing the incident report.

Writing Successful Proposals

A proposal is a detailed plan of action that a writer submits to a reader or group of readers for approval. The readers are usually in a position of authority—supervisors, managers, department heads, company buyers, boards of private foundations, elected officials, military or civic leaders—to endorse or reject the writer's plan.

Proposals are written for many purposes and many different audiences. You can write an internal proposal, for example to your boss, seeking authorization to hire staff, change a procedure, or to purchase a new piece of equipment for the office. Or, you can write a sales proposal to potential customers, offering a product or a service (such as offering to supply a fire chief with special firefighting gear, or offering an office manager a line of ergonomically designed furniture).

Depending on the job, proposals can vary greatly in size and in scope. A proposal to your employer could easily be conveyed in a page or two, the length of a short report. To propose doing a small job for a prospective client—redecorating a waiting room in an accountant's office—a letter with information on costs, materials, and a timetable might suffice. The sales letter in Figure 4.8 (p. 91) illustrates a short proposal in letter format. Proposals can be *unsolicited*—that is, they originate with you—or they can be *solicited*, requested by a company or organization, as in Figure 8.9 (pp. 251–253).

Proposals Are Persuasive Plans

Proposals, whether large or small, must be highly persuasive to succeed. Without your audience's approval, your plan will never go into effect, however accurate and important you think it is. Your enthusiasm is not enough to persuade readers; you have to supply hard evidence. Your proposals must convince readers that your plan will help them improve their businesses, make their jobs easier, save them money, enhance their image, or all of these.

The tone of your proposal should be **"Here is what I can do for you."** Stress the precise benefits and improvements of your plan. Show readers how approving your plan will save them time and money or will improve employee morale or customer satisfaction.

Every proposal you write must exhibit a "can do" attitude, putting the reader and his or her company's needs at the center of your work. Yates Engineering has won millions of dollars of business through its reader-centered proposals. Its slogan is "On time . . . within budget . . . to your satisfaction." Time, budget, and your readers' satisfaction and convenience are among the ingredients of a winning proposal. Notice how the FedEx advertisement in Figure 8.7 succinctly appeals to customers' time, convenience, and costs.

Internal Proposals

The primary purpose of an internal proposal, such as the one shown in Figure 8.8, is to offer a realistic and constructive plan to help your company run its business more efficiently and economically.

On your job you may discover a better way of doing something or a more efficient way to correct a problem. You believe that your proposed change will save your employer time, money, or further trouble. (Note how Tina Escobar and Oliver Jabur identified and researched a more effective and less costly way for Community Federal Bank to conduct business and to satisfy its customers; see Figure 8.8, pp. 245–248.)

Generally speaking, your proposal will be an informal, in-house message, so a brief (usually one- or two-page) memo or e-mail should be appropriate. You decide to notify your department head, manager, or supervisor, or your employer may ask you for specific suggestions to solve a problem that has already been identified.

Typical Topics for Internal Proposals

An internal proposal can be written about a variety of topics, including the following:

- purchasing new or more advanced equipment to replace obsolete or inefficient computers, transducers, robots, and the like or upgrading equipment

FIGURE 8.7   An example of a "can-do" attitude.

- obtaining document security software and offering training sessions to show employees how to use it
- recruiting new employees or retraining current ones on a new technique or process
- eliminating a dangerous condition or reducing an environmental risk to prevent accidents—for employees, customers, or the community at large
- improving communication within or between departments of a company or agency
- expanding work space or making it more efficient, private, ergonomically beneficial to employees, or more inviting to customers

As the list shows, internal proposals cover almost every activity or policy that can affect the day-to-day operation of a company or agency.

Following the Proper Chain of Command

Writing an internal proposal requires you to be aware of and sensitive to office politics. It may be wise first to meet with your boss to see if she or he has already identified the problem or has specific suggestions on how to solve it. Then you might provide your boss with a draft and ask for revisions or feedback.

You cannot assume that your reader(s) will automatically agree with you that there is a problem or that your plan is the only way to tackle it. To be successful, write your internal proposal keeping in mind the needs and likes of your boss and others who may have to sign off on it. Remember that your boss will expect you to be very convincing about both the problem you say exists and the changes you are advocating in the workplace under his or her supervision. Don't step on corporate toes. Similarly, you may need the approval of individuals in other offices, departments, or branches of your organization.

Organization of Internal Proposals

A short internal proposal follows a relatively straightforward plan of organization, from identifying the problem to solving it. Internal proposals usually contain four parts, as shown in Figure 8.8: **purpose, problem, solution,** and **conclusion.** Refer to the figure (pp. 245–248) as you read the following discussion.

The Purpose

Begin your proposal with a brief statement of why you are writing to your supervisor: "I propose that . . ." State why you think a specific change is necessary now. Then succinctly define the problem and emphasize that your plan, if approved by the reader, will solve that problem.

The Problem

Prove that a problem exists. Document its importance for your boss and your company; as a matter of fact, the more you show, with concrete evidence, how the problem affects the boss's work (and area of supervision), the more likely you are to persuade him or her to act. Here are some guidelines for documenting a problem.

- Avoid vague (and unsupported) generalizations such as: "We're losing money each day with this procedure (piece of equipment)"; "Costs continue to escalate";

FIGURE 8.8   An internal proposal.

COMMUNITY FEDERAL BANK

http://www.comfedbank.com

EQUAL HOUSING
LENDER

POWELL
584-5200

MONROE
413-6000

LANGSTON
796-3009

TO: Michael L. Sappington, Executive Vice President
             Dorothy Woo, Langston Regional Manager

FROM: Tina Escobar, Oliver Jabur, ATM Services

DATE: June 11, 2006

RE: A proposal to install an ATM at the Mayfield Park branch

PURPOSE

Clearly states why proposal is being sent

We propose a cost-effective solution to what is a growing problem at the Mayfield Park branch in Langston: inefficient servicing of customer needs and rising personnel costs. We recommend that you approve the purchase and installation, within the next three to four months, of an ATM at Mayfield. Such action is consistent with Community's goals of expanding branch banking services and promoting our image as a self-serve yet customer-oriented institution.

THE PROBLEM WITH CURRENT SERVICES AT MAYFIELD PARK

Identifies problem by giving reader necessary background information

Currently, we employ four tellers at Mayfield. However, too much is being spent on personnel/salary for routine customer transactions. In fact, as determined by teller activity reports, nearly 25 percent of the four tellers' time each week is devoted to routine activities easily accommodated by ATMs. Outlined in the table below is a breakdown of teller activity for the month of May:

Provides easy-to-read table

Teller #	Total Transactions	Routine Transactions
1	6,205	1,551
2	5,989	1,383
3	6,345	1,522
4	6,072	1,518
	24,611	5,974

Divides problem into parts— volume, financial, personnel, customer service

Clearly, we are not fully using our tellers' sales abilities when they are kept busy with routine activities. To compound the problem, we expect business to increase by at least 25 percent at Mayfield in the next few months, as projected by this year's market survey. If we do not install

Continued

FIGURE 8.8   (Continued)

page 2

an ATM, we will need to hire a fifth teller, at an annual cost of $20,800 ($15,500 base pay plus approximately 30 percent for fringes), for the additional 6,000 transactions we project.

Verifies that problem is widespread

Most important, customer needs are not being met efficiently at Mayfield. Recent surveys done for Community Federal by Watson-Perry demonstrate that our customers are inconvenienced by not having an ATM at Mayfield. They are unhappy about long waits in line to do simple banking business, such as deposits, withdrawals, and loan payments, and about having to drive to other branches to do after-hours banking. Conversations we had with manager Rachael Harris-Ignara at Mayfield confirm customers' complaints.

Ultimately, the lack of an ATM at Mayfield Park hurts Community's image. With ATMs available to Mayfield residents at local stores and other banks, our institution risks having customers and potential customers go elsewhere for their banking needs. We not only miss the opportunity of selling them on our other services but also risk losing their business entirely.

A SOLUTION TO THE PROBLEM

Purchasing and installing an ATM at Mayfield Park will result in significant savings in personnel costs and time. We will

Relates solution to individual parts of the problem

- Save money by not having to hire a fifth teller
- Allocate teller duties more efficiently and productively by assisting customers with questions and transactions not handled through an ATM, such as opening a new account; purchasing savings bonds, CDs, traveler's checks, and foreign currency; and Internet banking
- Increase time for tellers to cross-sell our services, including our new line of nontraditional banking products—annuities, mutual funds, debit cards, and global market accounts
- Service customer retirement options by having tellers track IRAs, 401(k)s, 403(b)s, and Simples
- Improve customer satisfaction by giving them the option of meeting their banking needs electronically or through a teller
- Ease the stress on our tellers at Mayfield Park

Shows problem can be solved and stresses how

It is feasible to install an ATM at Mayfield. This location does not pose the difficulties at some older branches. Mayfield offers ample room to install a drive-up ATM in the stubbed-out fourth drive-up lane. It is away from the heavily congested area in front of the bank, yet it is

Continued

FIGURE 8.8   (Continued)

easily accessible from the main driveway and the side drive facing Commonwealth Avenue, as the photograph below shows.

Photo courtesy Taylor Wilson

Judging from the ATM vendor's past work, the ATM could be installed and operational within two to three months. That is the amount of time it took to install ATMs at the first two locations in Powell and for Archer Avenue in Langston. Moreover, by authorizing the expenditure at Mayfield within the next month, you will ensure that ATM service is available long before the Christmas season.

COSTS

The costs of implementing our proposal are as follows:

Itemizes costs

Diebold Drive-up ATM	$28,000.00
Installation fee	2,000.00
Maintenance (1 year)	1,500.00
	$31,500.00

Interprets costs for reader

This $31,500, however, does not truly reflect our annual costs. We would be able to amortize, for tax purposes, the cost of installation of the ATM over five years. Our annual expenses would, therefore, look like this:

$30,000 (28,000 + 2,000) divided by 5 years =
$6,000.00 + 1,500 (maintenance), or <u>$7,500 per year</u>.

Continued

FIGURE 8.8   (Continued)

Compared with the $20,800 a year the bank would have to expend
for a fifth teller at Mayfield, the annual depreciated cost for the ATM
($7,500) reduces by nearly two-thirds the amount of money the bank
will have to spend for much more efficient customer service.

<u>CONCLUSION</u>

*Stresses
benefits for
reader and
bank as
a whole*

Authorizing an ATM for the Mayfield Park branch is both feasible
and cost effective. Adoption of this proposal will save our bank more
than $13,000 in teller services annually, reduce customer complaints,
and increase customer satisfaction and approval. We will be happy
to discuss this proposal with you anytime at your convenience.

"The trouble occurs frequently in a number of places"; "Numerous complaints
have come in"; "If something isn't done soon, more problems will result."

- Provide details about the problem, such as the amount of money or time a company is actually losing per day, week, or month. Emphasize the financial trouble
so that you can show in the next section how your plan offers an efficient and
workable solution.
- Indicate how many employees (or work hours) are involved or how many customers are inconvenienced or endangered by a procedure or condition. Notice
how Escobar and Jabur include such information in a table in their proposal in
Figure 8.8.
- Verify how widespread a problem is or how frequently it occurs by citing
specific occasions. Again, see how Escobar and Jabur cite evidence from the
Watson-Perry survey and the interviews they conducted with the manager of
the Mayfield branch.
- Relate the problem to an organization's image, corporate reputation, or influence (where appropriate). Pinpoint exactly how and where the problem lessens
your company's effectiveness or hurts its standing in the market. Indicate who
is affected and how the problem affects your company's business community,
as the writers do especially well in the first paragraph of Figure 8.8 (p. 245).

The Solution or Plan

In this section describe the change you propose and want approved. Your reader
will again expect to find factual evidence. Be specific. Supply details that answer the
following questions: (1) Is the plan workable—can it be accomplished here in our
office or plant? (2) Is it cost-effective—will it really save us money in the long run and
not lead to even greater expenses?

To get the reader to say "Yes" to both questions, supply the facts you have gathered as a result of your research. For example, if you propose that your firm buy a new piece of equipment, do the necessary homework to locate the most efficient and cost-effective model available, as Tina Escobar and Oliver Jabur did for the proposal in Figure 8.8.

- Supply the dealer's name, the costs, major conditions of service and training contracts, and warranties.
- Describe how your firm could use the equipment to obtain better or quicker results in the future.
- Cite specific tasks the new equipment can perform more efficiently at a lower cost than the equipment now in use.

A **proposal to change a procedure** must address the following questions.

- How does the new (or revised) procedure work?
- How many employees or customers will be affected by it?
- When will it go into operation?
- How much will it cost the employer to change procedures?
- What delays or losses in business might be expected while the company switches from one procedure to another?
- What employees, equipment, or locations are already available to accomplish the change?

The costs, in fact, will be of utmost importance. Make sure you supply a careful and accurate budget. Moreover, make the costs attractive by emphasizing how inexpensive they are compared to the cost of *not* making the change, as Escobar and Jabur do in the section labeled **"Costs."** Be sure to double-check your math.

It is also wise to raise alternative solutions, before the reader does, and to discuss their disadvantages. Notice how Tina Escobar and Oliver Jabur do that in Figure 8.8 by showing why installing an ATM is more feasible than hiring a fifth teller.

The Conclusion

Your conclusion should be short—a paragraph or two at the most. Remind readers that (a) the problem is ongoing and serious, (b) the reason for change is justified and will be beneficial to your organization, and (c) action needs to be taken. Reemphasize the most important benefits. Escobar and Jabur stress the savings that the bank will see by following their plan as well as the increase in customer satisfaction. Also indicate that you are willing to discuss your plan with the reader, a necessity in arguing for a corporate change at any level.

Sales Proposals

A sales proposal is the most common type of proposal. Its purpose is to sell your company's products or services for a set fee. A short sales proposal is a marketing tool that includes a sales pitch as well as a detailed description of the work you propose to do. Figure 8.9 (pp. 251–253) contains a sales proposal in response to a company's request.

The Audience and Its Needs

Your audience will usually be one or more executives who have the power to approve or reject a proposal. Unlike readers of an internal proposal, your audience for a sales proposal may be even more skeptical since they may not know you or your work. You can increase your chances of success by trying to anticipate their possible reasons for rejecting the plan as you propose it, and reasons for accepting a competitor's proposal.

Make sure your proposal has a competitive edge. Readers will compare your plan with those they receive from other proposal writers. Your proposal has to convince readers that the product and the service your company offers are more reliable, economical, efficient, and timely than those of another company. Here is where your homework pays off.

Organizing Sales Proposals

Most sales proposals include the following elements: introduction, description of the proposed product or service, timetable, costs, qualifications of your company, and conclusion.

Introduction

The introduction to your sales proposal can be a single paragraph in a short sales proposal or several pages in a more complex one. Basically, your introduction should prepare readers for everything that follows in your proposal. The introduction itself may contain the following sections, which sometimes may be combined.

1. **Statement of purpose and subject of proposal.** Tell readers why you are writing and identify the specific subject of your work. Briefly define the solution you propose. Tell them exactly what you propose to do for them. Be clear about what your plan covers and, if there could be any doubt, what it does not do.

2. **Background of the problem you propose to solve.** Show readers that you are familiar with their problem and why it is important. In a solicited proposal like the one in Figure 8.9, this section is usually unnecessary because the potential client has already identified the problem and wants to know how you would address it. In that case, just point out how your company would solve the problem, mentioning your superiority over your competitors (see the third paragraph of the figure (pp. 251–252).

In an unsolicited proposal, you need to describe the problem in convincing detail, identifying the specific trouble areas. Depending on the type of proposal you submit, you may want to focus briefly on the dimensions of the problem—when it was first observed, who/what it most acutely affects, and the specific organizational/community context in which the problem is most troubling.

Description of the Proposed Product or Service

This section is the heart of your proposal. Before spending their money, customers will demand hard, factual evidence of what you claim can and should be done. Here are some points that your proposal should cover.

FIGURE 8.9   A proposal in response to a request from a company.

Reynolds Interiors • 250 Commerce Avenue S.W. • Portland, OR 97204-2129

January 21, 2006

Mr. Floyd Tompkins, Manager
General Purpose Appliances
Highway 11 South
Portland, OR 97222

Dear Mr. Tompkins:

Begins with request for bids

In response to your request listed on your Web site for bids for an appropriate floor covering at your new showroom, Reynolds Interiors is pleased to submit the following proposal. We appreciated the opportunity to visit your facility in order to submit this proposal.

Identifies best solution

After carefully reviewing your specifications for a floor covering and inspecting your new facility, we believe that **Armstrong Classic Corlon 900** is the most suitable choice. We are enclosing a sample of the Corlon 900 so you can see how carefully it is constructed.

Corlon's Advantages

Describes product's features that benefit reader

Guaranteed against defects for a full three years, **Corlon** is one of the finest and most durable floor coverings manufactured by Armstrong. It is a heavy-duty commercial floor 0.085-inch thick for protection. Twenty-five percent of the material consists of interface backing; the other 75 percent is an inlaid wear layer that offers exceptionally high resistance to everyday traffic. Traffic tests conducted by the Independent Floor Covering Institute repeatedly proved the superiority of **Corlon's** construction and resistance.

Distinguishes product from competitors'

Another important feature of **Corlon** is the size of its rolls. Unlike other leading brands of similar commercial flooring—Remington or Treadmaster—**Corlon** comes in 12-foot-wide rather than

http://www.reynolds.com • 503-555-8733 • Fax: 503-555-1629

Continued

FIGURE 8.9 (Continued)

2

6-foot-wide rolls. This extra width will significantly reduce the number of seams on your floor, thus increasing its attractiveness and reducing the dangers of the seams splitting.

Installation Procedures

Explains how job is done The **Classic Corlon** requires that we use the inlaid seaming process, a technical procedure requiring the services of a trained floor mechanic. Herman Goshen, our floor mechanic, has more than fifteen years of experience working with the inlaid seam process. His professional work and keen sense of layout and design have been consistently praised by our customers.

Installation Schedule

Gives realistic timetable We can install the **Classic Corlon** on your showroom floor during the first week of March, which fits the timetable specified in your request. The material will take three and one-half days to install and will be ready to walk on immediately. We recommend, though, that you not move equipment onto the floor for 24 hours after installation.

Costs

The following costs include the **Classic Corlon** tile, labor, and tax:

Itemizes all costs	750 sq. yards of **Classic Corlon** at $23.50/sq. yd.	$17,625.00
	Labor (28 hrs @ $18.00/hr.)	$ 504.00
	Sealing fluid (10 gals. @ $15.00/gal.)	$ 150.00
	Total	$18,279.00
	Tax (5 percent)	$ 913.95
	GRAND TOTAL	**$19,192.95**

Our costs are $250.00 under those you specified in your request.

Continued

FIGURE 8.9   (Continued)

3

Reynolds's Qualifications

Establishes
history of
service

Reynolds Interiors has been in business for more than 28 years. In that time, we have installed many commercial floors in Portland and its suburbs. In the last year, we have served more than 60 customers, including the new multipurpose Tech Mart plant in Portland. We would be happy to furnish you with a list of satisfied customers.

Conclusion

Encourages
reader to
accept

Thank you for the opportunity to submit this proposal. We believe you will be pleased with the appearance and durability of an Armstrong **Corlon** floor. If we can provide you with any further information, please call us or visit us at our Web site.

Sincerely yours,

Neelow Singh

Neelow Singh
Sales Manager

Jack Rosen

Jack Rosen
Installation Supervisor

---

1. Carefully show potential customers that your product or service is right for them. Stress particular benefits of your product or service most relevant to your reader. Blend sales talk with descriptions of hardware.

2. Describe your work in suitable detail. Specify what the product looks like; what it does; and how consistently and well it will perform in the readers' office, plant, hospital, or agency. You might include a brochure; picture; diagram; or, as the writer of the proposal in Figure 8.9 does, a sample of your product for customers to study.

3. Stress any special features, maintenance advantages, warranties, or service benefits. Convince readers that your product is the most up-to-date and efficient one they could select. Highlight features that show the quality, consistency, or security of your work. For a service, emphasize the procedures you use, the terms of the service, even the kinds of tools you use, especially any state-of-the-art equipment.

Timetable

A carefully planned timetable shows readers that you know your job and that you can accomplish it in the right amount of time. Your dates should match any listed in a company's proposal request. Provide specific dates to indicate

- when the work will begin
- how the work will be divided into phases or stages
- when you will be finished
- whether any follow-up visits or services are involved

For proposals offering a service, specify how many times—an hour, a week, a month—customers can expect to receive your help; for example, spraying three times a month if your company offers exterminating service.

Costs

Make your budget accurate, complete, and convincing. But, give customers more than merely the bottom-line cost. Show exactly what readers are getting for their money so that they can determine if everything they need is included. Itemize costs for

- specific services
- equipment and materials
- labor (by the hour or by the job)
- transportation
- travel
- training

If something is not included or is considered optional, say so—additional hours of training, replacement of parts, upgrades, and the like. If you anticipate a price increase, let the customer know how long current prices will stay in effect. That information may spur them to act favorably now.

Qualifications of Your Company

Emphasize your company's accomplishments and expertise in providing similar services and/or equipment. Mention the names of a few local firms for whom you have worked that would be able to recommend you. But never misrepresent your qualifications or those of the individuals who work with or for you. Your prospective client can verify whether you have in fact worked on similar jobs during the last five to six years.

Conclusion

This is the "call to action" section of your sales proposal. Encourage your reader to approve your plan by stressing major benefits of your plan. Offer to answer any questions the reader may have. Some proposals end by asking readers to sign and return a copy of the proposal indicating their acceptance, as the proposal in Figure 8.9 does.

✓ Revision Checklist

❑ Had a clear sense of how my readers will use my report.

❑ Provided significant information about costs, materials, personnel, and times so readers will know that my work consists of facts, not impressions.

❑ Double-checked all data—costs, figures, dates, places, and equipment numbers.

❑ Began report with statement of purpose that clearly described the scope and significance of my work.

❑ Incorporated tables and other pertinent visuals to display data whenever appropriate.

❑ Explained clearly what the data means.

❑ Determined that recommendations logically follow from the data and are realistic.

❑ Adhered to all ethical and legal requirements in writing an incident report.

❑ Identified a realistic problem—one that is restricted and relevant to my topic and my audience's needs.

❑ Tried effectively to convince audience that the problem exists and needs to be solved.

❑ Incorporated details demonstrating the scope and importance of the problem.

❑ Persuasively emphasized benefits of solving the problem according to the proposal; incorporated the "you attitude" throughout.

❑ Offered a solution that can be realistically implemented—that is, it is both appropriate and feasible for audience.

❑ Used specific figures and concrete details to show how proposal will save time and money.

❑ *For internal proposals:* Demonstrated how proposal benefits my company and my supervisor; took into account office politics in describing problem and solution; discussed proposal with co-workers and/or supervisors who may be affected.

❑ *For sales proposals:* Related my product or service to prospective customer's needs; showed a clear understanding of those needs.

❑ Prepared a comprehensive and realistic budget; accounted for all expenses; itemized costs of products and services.

❑ Provided a timetable with exact dates for implementing proposal.

Exercises

1. Assume that you are a manager of a large apartment complex (200 units). Write a periodic report based on the following information—26 units are vacant, 38 soon will be vacant, and 27 soon will be leased (by June 1). Also add a section of recommendations to your supervisor (the head of the real-estate management company for which you work) on how vacant apartments might be leased more quickly and perhaps at increased rents. Consider important information such as decorating, advertising, and installing a new security system.

2. Assume you work for a household appliance store. Prepare a sales report based on the information contained in the following table. Include a recommendations section for your manager.

	Number Sold	
Product	*October*	*November*
Kitchen Appliances		
Refrigerators	72	103
Dishwashers	27	14
Freezers	10	36
Electric Ranges	26	26
Gas Ranges	10	3
Microwave Ovens	31	46
Laundry Appliances		
Washers	50	75
Dryers	24	36
Air Treatment		
Room Air Conditioners	41	69
Dehumidifiers	7	2

3. Submit a progress report to your writing teacher on what you have learned in his or her course so far this term, which writing skills you want to develop in greater detail, and how you propose doing so. Mention specific memos, e-mails, letters, instructions, reports, or proposals you have written or will soon write.

4. Compose a site inspection report on any part of the college campus or plant, office, or store in which you work that might need remodeling, expansion, re-wiring for computer use, or new or additional air-conditioning or heating work.

5. Write a report to an instructor in your major about a field trip you have taken recently—to a museum, laboratory, health care agency, correctional facility, radio or television station, agricultural station, or office. Indicate why you took the trip, name the individuals you met on the trip, and stress what you learned and how that information will help you in course work or on your job.

6. Write an incident report about one of the following problems. Assume that it has happened to you. Supply relevant details and visuals in your report. Iden-

tify the audience for whom you are writing and the agency you are representing or trying to reach.

a. After hydroplaning, your company car hits a tree and has a damaged front fender.

b. You have been the victim of an electrical shock because an electrical tool was not grounded.

c. You twist your back lifting a bulky package in the office or plant.

d. Your boat capsizes while you are patrolling the lake.

e. The crane you are operating breaks down and you lose a half-day's work.

f. The vendor shipped the wrong replacement part for your computer, and you cannot complete a job without buying a more expensive software package.

g. An electrical storm knocked out your computer; you lost 1,000 mailing label addresses and will have to hire additional help to complete a mandatory mailing by the end of the week.

7. Write a short internal proposal, similar to the one by Tina Escobar and Oliver Jabur in Figure 8.8 (pp. 245–248), recommending to a company or a college a specific change in procedure, equipment, training, safety, personnel, or policy. Make sure your team provides an appropriate audience (college administrator, department manager, or section chief) with specific evidence about the existence of the problem and your solution for it. Possible topics include

a. providing more and safer parking

b. forming a Usenet or listserv group

c. purchasing new office or laboratory equipment or software

d. hiring more faculty, student workers, or office help

e. reorganizing or redesigning the school yearbook, company annual report, sales catalog, or Web site

f. changing the decor/furniture in a student or company lounge

g. increasing the number of weekend or night classes in your major

h. adding more health-conscious offerings to the school or company cafeteria menu

i. altering the programming on a campus radio station

j. expanding distance learning offerings

8. Write a sales proposal, similar to the one in Figure 8.9 (pp. 251–253), on one of the following services or products you intend to sell or on a topic your instructor approves.

a. providing exterminating service to a store or restaurant

b. supplying a hospital with rental television sets for patients' rooms

c. designing Web sites

d. offering temporary office help or nursing care

e. providing landscaping and lawn care service

f. testing for noise, air, or water pollution in your community or neighborhood

g. furnishing transportation for students, employees, or members of a community group

h. supplying insurance coverage to a small firm (five to ten employees)

i. cleaning the parking lot and outside walkways at a shopping center

j. selling a piece of equipment to a business

k. offering a training program for employees

CHAPTER 9

Writing Careful Long Reports

This chapter introduces you to long reports—and how they are written, organized, and documented. It is appropriate to discuss long reports in one of the last chapters of this book because they require you to use and combine many of the writing skills and research strategies you have already learned. In business, a long report can be the culmination of many weeks or months of hard work on an important company project.

Characteristics of a Long Report

The following sections explain some of a long report's key elements. A model long report (Figure 9.2) appears at the end of the chapter (pp. 272–290).

Scope

A long report is a major study that provides an in-depth view of a key problem or idea. For example, a long report written for a course assignment may be eight to twenty pages long; a report for a business or industry may be that long or, more likely, much longer, depending on the scope of the subject. The implications of a long report are wide-ranging for a business or industry—relocating a plant, adding a new line of equipment, changing a computer programming operation.

The long report examines a problem in detail, while the short report covers just one part of the problem. Unlike a short report, a long report may discuss not just one or two current and routine events, but rather a continuing history of a problem or idea (and the background information necessary to understand it in perspective).

The titles of some typical long reports further suggest their extensive (and in some cases exhaustive) coverage:

- *The Use of Virtual Reality Attractions in Theme Parks in Jersey City*
- *Public Policy Implications of Expanding Health Care Delivery Systems in Tate County*

- *The Transportation Problems in Kingford, Oregon, and the Use of Monorails*
- *The Contributions of Internet Medicine in Providing Health Care in Rural Areas: Ways to Serve Southern Montana*

Research

A long, comprehensive report requires lots of research. Research can be done over time using the Internet and other sources—books, articles, laboratory experiments, on-site visits and tests, interviews with key individuals, and the writer's own observations. Through such research you can track down the relevant background information and discover what experts have said about the subject and what they propose should be done.

Preparing a proposal can lead to writing a long report. You might suggest a change to an employer, who then would ask you to write a long report containing the research necessary to implement that change.

Format

A long report is too detailed and complex to be adequately organized in a memo or letter format. The product of thorough research and analysis, the long report gives readers detailed discussions and interpretations of large quantities of data. To present the information in a logical and orderly fashion, the long report contains various parts, sections, headings, subheadings, documentation, and supplements (appendixes) that would never be included in a short report. The long report, as in Figure 9.2, gives readers a variety of visuals, including charts, a graph, and even a multicultural calendar.

Timetable

A long report is generally commissioned by a company or an agency to explore with extensive documentation a subject involving personnel, locations, costs, safety, or equipment. Many times a long report is required by law—for example, investigating the feasibility of a project that will affect the ecosystem. When you prepare a long report for a class project, select a topic that really interests you because you will spend a good portion of the term working on it. Here is a possible timetable for a long report.

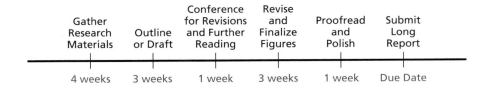

Audience

The audience for a long report is always individuals in the top levels of management—presidents, vice presidents, superintendents, directors—who make executive, financial, and organizational decisions. These individuals are responsible for long-range planning, seeing the big picture so to speak. A long report written about a campus issue or problem may at first be read by your instructor and then sent to an appropriate decision maker, such as a dean of students, a business manager, a director of athletics, or the head of campus security.

Collaborative Effort

The long report in the world of business may not be the work of one employee. Rather, it may be a collaborative effort—the product of a committee or a group. Your instructor may ask you to work in a group (or alone) in preparing your long report.

To be successful, a collaborative writing team should observe the following six guidelines as well as the procedures for collaboration in the writing process (pp. 44–45).

1. **Understand and agree on the important goals, organization, and deadlines for the report.** Everyone needs to be on the "same page" from start to finish.

2. **Establish group rules early on and stick to them.** Decide when and where the group will meet, how and when the group members are to communicate with each other (fax, telephone, e-mail), how information is to be shared and with whom and how often, when various tasks are to be completed, and what "fail-safe" mechanisms are in place if and when problems arise.

3. **Put the good of the group ahead of individual egos.** Group harmony and productivity are essential if the long report is to get done on time. Individual members need to be active participants and keen listeners. Getting one's own way can slow down the overall success of the report. In the business world, sometimes a report bears only the boss's name, not the name of the group that prepared it.

4. **Agree on the group's organization.** The group can appoint a leader who keeps the team on-task by being a cheerleader, a scheduler, a peacemaker who can resolve conflicts quickly, and also a referee who knows when to call time-out.[1] The leader must be skilled in interpersonal interactions. Members must also determine the best methods of cooperating with each other.

5. **Identify each member's responsibilities precisely.** There must be a fair distribution of labor so that each member can use his or her particular and proven skills. One member of the group may be responsible for document design and visuals, another for research and documentation, another for writing drafts, and still another for making an oral presentation. The entire group, however, should share responsibility for the overall preparation, design, writing, and submission of the report.

---

[1] Adapted from Hendrie Wesigner, *Emotional Intelligence at Work* (New York: Jossey-Bass, 1997).

6. Provide clear and positive feedback at each meeting and for each part of the report the group prepares. Members need to come to meetings prepared, raise important questions, and make thoughtful recommendations. Not showing up, arguing, or failing to turn assignments in on time jeopardizes the entire project.

The Process of Writing a Long Report

Because your work will be spread over many weeks, you need to see your report not as a series of static or isolated tasks but as an evolving project. Before you embark on that project, review the information on the writing process in Chapter 2. You may also want to review the flow chart in Figure 6.11 (p. 183), which illustrates the different stages in writing a research paper. The following guidelines will also help you plan and write a long report.

1. Identify a significant topic. You'll have to do some preliminary research—general reading, on-line searching, conferring with and interviewing experts—to get an overview of key ideas and individuals involved, and the implications for your company and/or community. Note the kinds of research Terri Smith Ruckel did for her long report (see Figure 9.2, pp. 272–290). As she did, expect to search a variety of print and Internet sources, to read and evaluate them, and to incorporate them into your work.

2. Expect to confer regularly with your supervisor(s) and/or team members. In these meetings, be prepared to ask pertinent and researched questions to pin down exactly what your boss wants.

3. Revise your work often. Be prepared to work on several outlines and drafts. Your revisions may sometimes be extensive, depending on what your boss, instructor, or collaborative team recommends. You may have to consult new sources and arrive at a new interpretation of those sources.

4. Keep the order flexible at first. Even as you work on your drafts and revisions, keep in mind that a long report is not written in the order in which the parts will finally be assembled. You cannot write in "final" order—abstract to recommendations. Instead, expect to write in "loose" order to reflect the process in which you gathered information and organized it for the final copy of the report. Usually, the body is written first, the introduction later so that the authors can make sure they have not left anything out. The abstract, which appears very early in the report, is always written after all the facts have been recorded and recommendations made or conclusions drawn.

5. Prepare both a day-to-day calendar and a checklist. Keep both posted where you do your work—above your desk or computer, or use your computer's built-in calendar program, if available—so that you can track your progress. The calendar should mark **milestones**—that is, dates by which each stage of your work must be completed. Match the dates on your calendar with the dates your instructor or employer may have given you to submit an outline, progress report(s), and the final copy. Your checklist should list the major parts of the long report. As you complete each section, check it off. Before assembling the final copy of your report, use the checklist to make sure you have not omitted something.

Parts of a Long Report

A long report may include some or all of the following twelve parts, which form three categories: *front matter* (letter of transmittal, title page, table of contents, list of illustrations, abstract), *report text* (introduction, body, conclusion, recommendations), and *back matter* (glossary, references cited, any appendixes).

Front Matter

As the name implies, the front matter of a long report consists of everything that precedes the actual text of the report. Such elements introduce, explain, and summarize to help the reader locate various parts of the report. Use lowercase roman numerals for front matter page numbers, not Arabic numbers.

Letter of Transmittal
This three- or four-paragraph (usually only one-page) letter states the purpose, scope, and major recommendation of the report. It highlights the main points of the report that your readers would be most interested in. If written to an instructor, the letter should additionally note that the report was done as a course assignment. (See Terri Smith Ruckel's letter on p. 272 for a sample letter of transmittal for a business report.)

Title Page
Find out what your boss or instructor prefers. Basically, your title page should contain the full title of your report and how you have restricted it in time, space, or method. Avoid titles that are vague, too short, or too long.

Vague Title:	A Report on the Internet: Some Findings
Too Short:	The Internet
Too Long:	A Report on the Internet: A Study of Dot.com Companies, Their History, Appeal, Scope, Liabilities, and Their Relationship to On-going Work Dealing with Consumer Preferences and Protection Within the Last Five Years in the Midwest

For a report for a class assignment, give your instructor's name and the specific course for which you prepared the report. For most other long reports, the title page needs

- the name(s) of the report writer(s)
- the date of the report
- the name of the firm or individual for whom the report was prepared

U.S. Trade Deficit Mushroomed

The nation's balance of trade dropped from its high point, a $12 billion surplus in 1975, to a deficit of more than $271 billion in 1999. As barriers to global trade have fallen, trade has assumed growing importance to the U.S. economy. Supporters of trade liberalization say that encouraging the flow of goods, services and capital among nations benefits everyone, but labor unions say it encourages manufacturers to transfer operations overseas, costing Americans jobs and increasing the deficit.

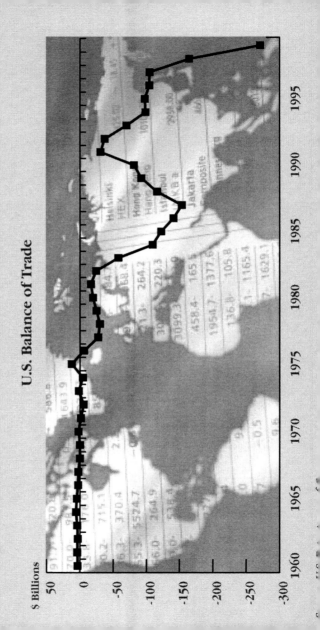

U.S. Balance of Trade

$ Billions

Table of Contents

The table of contents lists the major headings and subheadings of your report and tells readers on which pages they can be found. Essentially, a table of contents shows how you organized your report and emerges from many outlines and drafts. The items on those outlines frequently expand, shrink, and move around until you decide on the formal divisions and subdivisions of your report.

List of Illustrations

This list contains the titles for all of the visuals and indicates where they can be found in your long report.

Abstract

An abstract summarizes the report, including the main problem you investigated, the conclusions you reached, and any recommendations you may make. It is usually one paragraph long.

Abstracts may be placed at various points in long reports—on the title page, on a separate page, or as the first page of the report text.

The abstract may be the most important part of your report. Not every member of your audience will read your entire report, but almost everyone will read the abstract. For example, the president of the corporation or the director of an agency may use the abstract as the basis for approving the report and passing it on for distribution. Look at the abstract Terri Smith Ruckel prepared for her readers (p. 275).

Text of the Report

The text of a long report consists of an introduction, the body, conclusions, and sometimes recommendations.

Introduction

The introduction may constitute as much as 10 or 15 percent of your report, but it should not be any longer. The introduction is essential because it tells readers why your report was written and thus helps them to understand and interpret everything that follows. Do not put your findings, conclusions, or recommendations in your introduction.

Do not regard the introduction as one undivided block of information. It includes related parts, which should be labeled with subheadings. Here are the types of information to include in your introduction.

1. **Background.** To understand why your topic is significant, readers need to know about its history including information on who was originally involved, when, and where; how someone was affected by the issue; what opinions have been expressed on the issue; what the implications of your study are. See how the report on multinational employees (Figure 9.2, pp. 272–290) provides useful background information on when, where, how, and why these employees entered the U.S. work force and the effect of 9/11 on such workers and their employers.

2. Problem. Identify the problem or issue that led you to write the report. Because the problem you investigate will determine everything you write about in the report, you need to state it clearly and concisely. Here is a problem statement from a report on how construction designs have not taken into account the requirements of a growing number of seniors and disabled Americans.

> The construction industry has not satisfactorily met the needs for accessible workplaces and homes for all age and physical ability groups. The industry has relied on expensive and specialized plans to modify existing structures rather than creating universally designed spaces that are accessible to everyone.

3. Purpose statement. The purpose statement tells readers why you wrote the report and what you hope to accomplish or prove. It expresses the goal of all your research. Like the problem statement, the purpose statement does not have to be long or complex. A sentence or two will suffice. You might begin simply by saying, "The purpose of this report is. . . ."

4. Scope. This section informs readers about the specific limits—number and type of issues, time, money, locations, personnel, and so forth—you have placed on your investigation. You inform readers about what they will find in your report, or what they won't, through your statement about the scope of your work. The long report in Figure 9.2 concentrates on adapting the U.S. workplace to meet the communication and cultural needs of a work force of multinational employees, not trends in the international market—two completely different topics.

Body

This section, also called the *discussion,* is the longest, possibly making up as much as 70 percent of your report. The body contains statistical information, details about the environment, and physical descriptions, as well as the various interpretations and comments of the authorities whose work you consulted as part of your research.

The body of your report should

- be carefully organized to reveal a coherent and well-defined plan
- separate material into meaningful parts to identify the major issues
- clearly relate the parts to each other
- use headings to help your reader identify major sections more quickly

Your organization should reflect the different headings (and even subheadings) included in your report; use them throughout to make it easy to follow. The headings, of course, will be included in the table of contents. (Note how Figure 9.2 is carefully organized into four sections.)

In addition to headings at the beginning of each major section of the body, tell readers what they will find in that section and why. The report in Figure 9.2 does an effective job of providing such internal summaries.

Conclusion(s)

The conclusion should tie everything together for readers by presenting the findings of your report. For a research report based on a study of sources located through various reference searches, the conclusion should summarize the main viewpoints of the authorities whose works you have cited. Perhaps your instructor will ask you to assess in your conclusion which resource materials were most thorough and helpful and why. For a marketing report done for a business, you must spell out the implications for your readers in terms of costs, personnel, products, location, and so forth.

Recommendations

The recommendation(s) section tells readers what should be done about the findings recorded in the conclusion. Your recommendation shows readers how you want them to solve the problem your report has focused on. Readers will expect you to advise them on a specific course of action—what equipment to purchase, when to expand a market, how to establish or revise a Web site or even an intranet, whom to hire for which positions or programs, and so on.

Back Matter

Included in the back matter of the report are all of the supporting data that, if included in the text of the report, would bog the reader down in details and cloud the main points the report makes.

Glossary

The glossary is an alphabetical list of the specialized vocabulary used in a long report and the definitions. A glossary might be unnecessary if your report does not use a highly technical vocabulary or if *all* members of your audience are familiar with the specialized terms you do use.

References Cited

Any sources cited in your report—Web sites, books, articles, television programs, interviews, reviews, audiovisuals—are usually listed in this section. Always ask your instructor or employer how he or she wants information to be documented.

Appendix

An appendix contains supporting materials for the report—tables and charts too long to include in the discussion, sample questionnaires, budgets and cost estimates, correspondence about the preparation of the report, case histories, transcripts of telephone conversations.

Documentation

Documentation is important for at least three reasons.

1. It demonstrates you have done your homework by consulting books, journals, newspapers, government documents, and Web publications to support your claims.

2. It gives proper credit to those sources. Citing a work is not a simple act of courtesy; it is a point of law. By documenting your sources, you avoid *plagiarism*—stealing someone else's ideas and listing them as your own. If you are found guilty of plagiarism, you could be expelled from school or fired from your job.

3. It informs readers where they can locate your sources to find additional information or to verify your facts. (Note the range of sources Terri Smith Ruckel cites on pp. 289–290.)

What Must Be Documented?

If you document the following materials, you can avoid plagiarism as well as assist your readers:

- any direct quotation(s), even a single phrase or key word
- any paraphrase or summary of someone's written work, oral report, presentation, or Web site
- any interpretations or conclusions expressed verbally or in writing that are not your own or any views that you could not have reached without the help of another source
- any statistical data that you have not compiled yourself
- any visuals you did not prepare yourself—from the Internet or elsewhere

The cartoon in Figure 9.1 humorously reminds readers that there are no excuses for plagiarism.

Parenthetical Documentation

Two frequently used systems of parenthetical documentation are found in the *MLA Handbook for Writers of Research Papers* and the *Publication Manual of the American Psychological Association*. The Modern Language Association (MLA) system is used primarily in the humanities and other related disciplines; the APA system is used in psychology, nursing and allied health disciplines, the social sciences, and in some business and technological fields. Both MLA and APA use parenthetical, or in-text, documentation. That is, the writer tells readers directly in the text of the paper, at the moment the acknowledgment is necessary, what reference is being cited.

MLA   "Creating an effective Web site was among the top three priorities businesses have had over the last two years" (Morgan 203).

APA   "Creating an effective Web site was among the top three priorities businesses have had over the last two years" (Morgan, 2006, p. 203).

The MLA citation "(Morgan 203)" or the APA "(Morgan, 2006, p. 203)" informs readers that the writer has borrowed information from a work by Morgan, specifically from page 203. APA also includes the year Morgan's work was published. Such a source (author's last name, year, and page number) obviously does not supply complete documentation. Instead, the parenthetical reference points readers to an alphabetical list of works that appears at the end of the report. The list, called "Works Cited" in MLA or "References" in APA, contains full bibliographic data—titles, dates, Web addresses, publishers, page numbers, and so on—about each source cited in your report. Every work that appears in your report must be listed in your references section. To provide accurate parenthetical documentation for your readers, first carefully prepare your Works Cited or References list (see next subsection) so that you know which sources you are going to cite in the right form and at the right place in your text.

FIGURE 9.1   A cartoon reminding readers that there is no excuse for plagiarism.

"Really? Someone told me it's
not plagiarism if they're dead."

© Mark Tyler Nobelman/*www.mtncartoons.com.*

Keep your documentation brief and to the point so that you do not interrupt the reader's train of thought. In most cases, all you will need to include is the author's last name, date, and appropriate page number(s) in parentheses, usually at the end of sentences. When you mention the author's name in your sentence, though, MLA and APA both advise that you do not redundantly cite it again parenthetically; for example:

MLA   Moscovi claims that "Tourism has increased 21 percent this quarter" (76)

APA   Moscovi (2006) claims that "Tourism has increased by 21 percent this quarter" (p. 76)

For unsigned articles or radio and television programs, use a shortened title in place of an author's name parenthetically.

MLA   Shrewd bosses know that "chain-of-command meetings provide the opportunity to pass information up as well as down the administrative ladder" ("Working Smarter, Not Harder" 33).

APA   Shrewd bosses know that "chain-of-command meetings provide the opportunity to pass information up as well as down the administrative ladder" (Working Smarter, Not Harder, 2005, p. 33).

Similarly, if you list the title of a reference work in the text of your paper, do not repeat it in your documentation.

MLA   According to the *Encyclopedia Britannica,* Cecil B. DeMille's *King of Kings* was seen by nearly 800,000,000 individuals (3: 458).

APA   According to the *Encyclopedia Britannica* (2001), Cecil B. DeMille's *King of Kings* was seen by nearly 800,000,000 individuals (3, p. 458).

The first number in parentheses in both versions refers to the volume number of the *Encyclopedia Britannica;* the second is the page number in that volume.

References or Works Cited Pages

Examples of some of the entries you are likely to include in your References or Works Cited lists follow. Note the differences in the placement of information, punctuation, use of italics and quotation marks, and capitalization between MLA and APA. Regardless of which system you follow, arrange entries alphabetically and double-space within and between each entry.

Book by One Author

MLA   Walker, Juliet Kirkpatrick. *The History of Black Business in America: Capitalism, Race, Entrepreneurship.* New York: Macmillan, 1999.

APA   Walker, J. K. (1999). *The history of black business in America: Capitalism, race, entrepreneurship.* New York: Macmillan.

Book by Two Authors

MLA   Sellen, Abigail, and Richard Harper. *The Myth of the Paperless Office.* Cambridge, MA: MIT P, 2001.

APA   Sellen, A., & Harper, R. (2001). *The myth of the paperless office.* Cambridge, MA: MIT.

Book by Three Authors

MLA   Czinkota, Michael, Ilkka Ronkainen, and Michael Moffett. *International Business.* Chicago: Thomson, 2002.

APA   Czinkota, M., Ronkainen, I., & Moffett, M. (2002). *International business.* Chicago: Thomson.

Book by a Corporate Author

MLA   Computer Literacy Foundation. *PC's in the Classroom.*
         2nd ed. New York: Technology P, 2005.

APA   Computer Literacy Foundation. (2005). *PC's in the
         classroom* (2nd ed.). New York: Author.

Edited Collection of Essays

MLA   Leinbach, Thomas, and Stanley Brunn, eds. *The Worlds
         of Electronic Commerce: Economic, Geographical,
         and Social Dimensions.* New York: Wiley, 2001.

APA   Leinbach, T., & Brunn, S. (2001). *The worlds of
         electronic commerce: Economic, geographical,
         and social dimensions.* New York: Wiley.

Works Included in a Collection of Essays

MLA   Curry, James. "Beyond Transaction Costs: E-commerce and
         the Power of the Internet Dataspace." *The Worlds
         of Electronic Commerce: Economic, Geographical,
         and Social Dimensions.* 2 vols. Ed. T. Leinbach and
         S. Brunn. New York: Wiley, 2001. 45-66.

APA   Curry, J. (2001). Beyond transaction costs: E-commerce
         and the power of the internet dataspace. In
         T. Leinbach and S. Brunn (Eds.), *The worlds
         of e-commerce: economic, geographical, and
         social dimensions* (pp. 45-66). New York: Wiley.

Pamphlet or Brochure

MLA   National Institute on Aging. *Bound for Good Health.*
         Bethesda: National Institute on Aging, 2006.

APA   National Institute on Aging. (2006). *Bound for good
         health.* [Brochure]. Bethesda, MD: Author.

Article in a Professional Print Journal

MLA   Reese, Shelly. "The New Wave of Gen X Workers."
         Business & Health 17.6 (2004): 19-24.

APA   Reese, S. (2004). The new wave of Gen X workers.
         Business & Health 17(6), 19-24.

Article in a Print Magazine

MLA   Wang, Penelope. "Building Wealth: How Are You Doing?"
         Money 31.7 (July 2002): 68-79.

APA   Wang, P. (2002, July). Building wealth: How are you
       doing? *Money 31*(7), 68–79.

MLA   Crowley, Geoffrey, and Karen Springer. "Are Body Scans
       a Scam?" *Newsweek* 20 May 2002: 67–68.

APA   Crowley, G., & Springer, K. (2002, May 20). Are body
       scans a scam? *Newsweek,* 67–68.

Signed Encyclopedia Article

MLA   Strock, O. J. "Telemetering." *McGraw-Hill Encyclopedia
       of Science and Technology.* 8th ed., 1997.

APA   Strock, O. (1997). Telemetering. In *McGraw-Hill
       Encyclopedia of Science and Technology* (Vol. 20,
       p. 738). New York: McGraw-Hill.

Unsigned Encyclopedia Article

MLA   "The Internet." *Encyclopedia of Information Science and
       Technology.* 2nd ed. 2004.

APA   The Internet. (2004). *Encyclopedia of information
       science and technology.*

On-line Encyclopedia

MLA   Henderson, David Robert. "Inflation." *The Concise
       Encyclopedia of Economics.* 1993. Retrieved
       December 17, 2005 from <http://www.econlib.org/
       library/CEE.html>.

APA   Henderson, D. (1993). Inflation. The concise encyclopedia
       of economics. Retrieved December 17, 2005, from
       http://www.econlib.org/library/CEE.html

Article in a Newspaper

MLA   Hutcherson, James T. "Corporation Optimizes Advertising
       Online." *Wall Street Journal* 1 Feb. 2002: B3, B5.

APA   Hutcherson, J. (2002, February 1). Corporation optimizes
       advertising online. *The Wall Street Journal,* pp. B3, B5.

Article in an On-line Journal

MLA   Melka, Mary. "Ergonomically Designed Office Eliminates
       Light Fixtures to Use Paper-Thin Diodes."
       Business Online Feb. 2003. 1 March 2004.
       <http://buson./com/search/weekly/>.

APA   Melka, M. (2003). Ergonomically designed office
       eliminates light fixtures to use paper-thin diodes.

Business Online. Retrieved March 1, 2003, from
http://buson.com/search/weekly/

Personal Interview

MLA   Chin, Barbara. Professor of Physics, Northwest College.
E-mail interview. 15 October 2005.

Interviews, conversations, and presentations are not included in APA References, but you still must document them in your paper as follows:

APA   Barbara Chin, Professor of Physics (personal
communication, October 15, 2005), predicted that
"within the next three years voice activated
computers would be found in the business world."

E-mail Correspondence

MLA   Zeke, Cho-Martin. E-mail to the author. 17 Feb. 2005.

APA   Treat as an unpublished interview and cite parenthetically in the text.

Electronic Newsgroup Message

MLA   Abuya, Violet. "Procedures for New Nurses."
On-line posting. 30 Sept. 2005. St. Mary's
Hospital Home Page. 18 June 2002 <http://
www.saintmaryshome.com/>.

APA   Abuya, V. (2002, June 18). Procedures for new nurses.
Message posted to http://www.saintmaryshome.com/

A Model Long Report

The following long report (Figure 9.2, pp. 272–290) was written by a senior training specialist, Terri Smith Ruckel, for her boss, the human resources director who commissioned it. Ruckel's main task was to demonstrate what U.S. businesses should do to meet the needs of multinational workers and thus promote diversity in the workplace. She gathered relevant data primarily through reading print and electronic sources and interviewing experts. Ruckel was also sensitive to current events, most noticeably 9/11, that affect both international workers and their employers.

The report in the figure follows the American Psychological Association (APA) system of documentation. Although APA no longer recommends a table of contents or list of illustrations, we supply these pages as models for students who are asked to use them.

Figure 9.2 contains all of the parts of a long report discussed in this chapter except a glossary and an appendix. (Intended for a general reader interested in learning more about the problems multinational workers face, Ruckel's report does not contain the technical terms and data that would require a glossary and an appendix.) Note how her cover letter introduces her report and its significance for RPM Technologies.

FIGURE 9.2   Transmittal letter and long report.

RPM Technologies

4500 Florissant Drive   St. Louis, MO 63174

314.555.2121   www.rpmtech.com

August 15, 2005

Jesse Butler
Human Resources Director
RPM Technologies
St. Louis, MO 63174

Dear Director Butler:

With this letter I am enclosing my report on effective ways to recruit and retain a multinational work force for RPM Technologies, which you requested six weeks ago. My report argues for the necessity of adapting the workplace to meet the needs of multinational employees, including promoting cultural sensitivity and making business communications more understandable.

Multinational workers undoubtedly play a major role in U.S. business. With their technical skills and homeland contacts, they can help RPM Technologies compete in the global marketplace. Moreover, the global perspective provided by a multinational work force would allow RPM Technologies to be better-informed to cope with issues related to the 9/11 attacks.

RPM needs to recruit qualified multinational workers aggressively and then provide equal opportunities in the workplace. But U.S. firms like RPM must also be sensitive to cultural diversity and communication demands. By including cross-cultural training—for native and non-native English-speaking employees alike—businesses promote cultural sensitivity. In-house language programs and plain-English or translated versions of corporate documents will further improve the workplace environment for multinational employees.

I hope you will find this report useful and relevant in your efforts to attract more multinational employees to RPM Technologies. If you would like to discuss it with me, I can be reached at extension 5406 or by e-mail at the address below.

Sincerely yours,

Terri Smith Ruckel
Senior Training Specialist
truckle@britestar.com

Enclosure

Adapting the U.S. Workplace for Multinational Employees in the New Millennium

Terri Smith Ruckel
Senior Training Specialist
RPM Technologies

August 15, 2005

Prepared for

Jesse Butler
Human Resources Director
RPM Technologies

Table of Contents

List of Illustrations

Abstract

U.S. businesses can gain a competitive advantage in today's global marketplace by attracting and retaining a multinational work force. This new wave of immigrants is in great demand for their technical skills and economic ties to their homelands. These workers are an invaluable resource to companies in a post–9/11 world. U.S. firms must recruit qualified multinational employees and then provide them with opportunities to succeed in the workplace. Yet many companies still adhere to policies designed for native speakers of English. Businesses should offer cultural sensitivity training to employees who are native speakers of English while still encouraging communication among multinational workers. To promote sensitivity, businesses should adapt the workplace environment to meet the cultural, religious, and social needs of their multicultural work force. Finally, businesses need to ensure, either through translations or plain-English versions, that all documents are understandable to multinational workers. Businesses also could offer non-native speakers of English in-house language instruction while providing foreign language training for their employees who are native speakers of English.

Introduction

Background

The U.S. work force is undergoing a remarkable revolution. The Bureau of Labor Statistics predicts that by the year 2010, the U.S. work force will comprise 158 million workers who must fill an estimated 168 million jobs (2003). The most dramatic change in the U.S. work force will be in the growing numbers of multinational employees. By 2025, according to the U.S. Chamber of Commerce, the number of international residents in the United States is projected to rise from 26 million to 42 million (2003). The new wave of immigrants—Indians, Pakistanis, Hispanics, Asians, Caribs, and East Europeans—will increase to an unprecedented 37 percent of the labor force by 2010 and continue to soar thereafter. Even in light of new immigration reforms mandated by the events of 9/11, the Office of the Census Bureau allots immigration figures as 820,000 persons per year, confirming that the United States is becoming the most multiculturally diverse country in the global village (2000).

New York City: Setting the Trend

Immigration figures for New York City exemplify this trend in the national work force. The city today has the largest, most ethnically varied immigrant population in its 400-year history (Martin, 2002). New York has attracted immigrants from more than 200 countries, and the city trades with nearly all those countries. During a New York City symposium on immigration sponsored by the Department of State, Joseph Salvo, Chief of the Population Division of New York's Department of City Planning, reported on the increasing complexity of New York's immigrant population, noting that one-third of the city's black population arrived from the Caribbean or West Africa. And though 900,000 Puerto Ricans live in New York City, more than 700,000 Dominicans and immigrants from all over the Caribbean and Latin America are among the city's newest inhabitants (Appel, 2001). Looking a little further into the future, Carlos Harrison, editor of *Latinos,* the largest Hispanic publication in the United States, believes that by 2025 Hispanics will "comprise more than one-quarter of the U.S. population, with most of them residing in New York City and the Southwest" (LaJoya, 2002).

Immigration: Then and Now

Although the United States has long been called a nation of immigrants, the experiences of the current influx of new arrivals differ radically from those of their predecessors (U.S. Chamber of Commerce, 2003). The first great surge of immigration occurred in the late nineteenth and early twentieth centuries. At the peak of the immigration wave, from 1901 to 1910, nearly 9 million individuals entered the United States, mostly from west and central European countries, as shown in Figure 1(a). Many of those new citizens

2

never went back to their homeland (Brown, 2003). Today's immigrants, however, arrive from India, Pakistan, China, Mexico, Indonesia, the Philippines, and almost every other place across the globe, as Figure 1(b) reveals.

Actively maintaining ties with their native countries, today's new immigrants travel back and forth so regularly they have become what could be called global citizens. In many cases, they use their contacts back in their homeland to start new businesses. For example, as more immigrants from

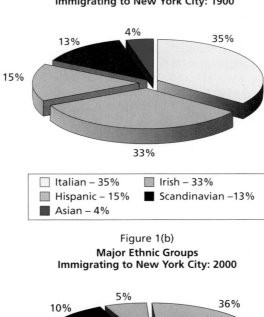

Figure 1(a)
**Major Ethnic Groups
Immigrating to New York City: 1900**

☐ Italian – 35%	▨ Irish – 33%
▨ Hispanic – 15%	■ Scandinavian –13%
■ Asian – 4%	

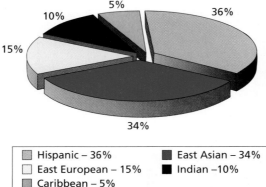

Figure 1(b)
**Major Ethnic Groups
Immigrating to New York City: 2000**

▨ Hispanic – 36%	■ East Asian – 34%
☐ East European – 15%	■ Indian –10%
▨ Caribbean – 5%	

Source: Brown, 2003.

3

Latin America and the Caribbean have settled in New York, the city's exports to those regions have increased (Levanthall, 2000).

Undeniably, many modern-day immigrants possess high levels of technical training. The on-line journal *Asian American Village* reports that California's Silicon Valley has significantly benefited from the immigration of Asians who come with graduate degrees and advanced technical training. Scientists and engineers, who have relocated from a number of Asian countries, now hold more than 33 percent of the Valley's highly technical positions (Shih, 2003). Figure 2 indicates the countries of origin of Silicon Valley's Asian immigrants and lists each country's specific percentage of immigration. Despite the business downturn suffered by the information technology industry following the 9/11 events, from October 1, 2001, to March 30, 2002, IT (information technology) employers applied to the Immigration and Naturalization Service to bring in 105,800 more foreign workers (Francis, 2002). Murali Krishna Devarakonda, president of the Immigrants Support Network established for immigrants in Silicon Valley, observes, "Employers need us. We contribute significantly to the economy" (Stone & Conway, 2001, p. 37).

Furthermore, those multinational workers who do not arrive with technical skills already in hand quickly enroll in training and education programs. Higher education officials in New York City estimate that during the 2002 school year, non-native speakers of English accounted for more than 50 percent of full-time, first-year students in the City University of New York

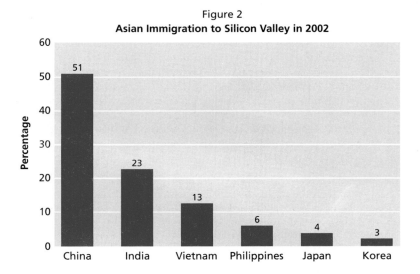

Figure 2
Asian Immigration to Silicon Valley in 2002

4

system, which has been called a "microcosm of the United States as a whole" (Martin, 2003).

The Challenge to U.S. Businesses

As the nation's population becomes more culturally diverse, U.S. firms are being challenged to organize and conduct business in new ways. In the new millennium, companies are striving to adapt their corporate policies and training to fit the communication needs of a growing group of multinational consumers and employees (Adamson, 2003). Enterprising U.S. firms have already begun to adapt to this new multilingual climate. CEO Didier Moretti of Annuncio Software in Los Altos, California, boasts about the high level of cultural diversity of his employees: "The last time we counted, we had 18 languages, ranging from French to Italian to German, several Indian languages, a few Chinese dialects, and Arabic. I think having a diversity of backgrounds is a big help. Both small and large businesses . . . need to think about hiring employees who can relate to customers in foreign markets" (Hamilton, 2002, p. 37). As Murali Devarakonda concluded, "Multinational employees excel in the U.S. business culture, and employers profit from their expertise and contacts" (Johnson, 2003, p. 45).

Problem

U.S. businesses need to consider seriously how they will meet the cultural and communication demands of this important work force. Unfortunately, many corporate policies and programs were created for native-born, English-speaking employees (Adamson, 2003; Martin, 2003). Rather than rewarding multinational workers, such companies unintentionally punish them. Moreover, there seems to be little agreement about how best to address the communication challenges of this new multilingual, highly technical work force.

U.S. businesses must provide effective training strategies and work opportunities to accommodate this new wave of multinational workers effectively. The traditional workplace has to be transformed to understand and to honor the ways in which multinational employees communicate about business and even home-related activities. Native English-speaking employees as well as their international co-workers must be better-prepared to understand and appreciate each other as well as their international customers.

Purpose

The purpose of this report is to argue that because of increasing numbers of multicultural employees in the workplace, U.S. businesses must recognize and provide for the needs of a culturally diverse work force.

5

Scope

This report explores cultural diversity in the U.S. workplace in the new millennium and suggests ways for the United States to compete successfully in the global village by providing equal employment opportunities for multinational workers, fostering cross-cultural literacy, and improving training in intercultural communication.

Discussion

Providing Equal Workplace Opportunities for Multinational Employees

Aggressive Recruitment of People from Diverse Cultures

A multilingual work force makes good business sense for the new millennium. Organizations can hire people who are able to assist them with the day-to-day business of providing services and products for a culturally diverse global market. To accomplish that, firms need to establish or modify hiring policies and procedures to attract the best-qualified multinational workers for the job. Working cooperatively with the Immigration and Naturalization Service, companies gain the assurance of recruiting the most qualified, professional, and trustworthy staff.

To begin with, companies could establish specific goals concerning multinational recruitment and adopt policies such as linking managerial bonuses to fulfilling those goals (Martin, 2003). Routine visits to U.S. campuses by company recruiters provide excellent opportunities to identify the best-qualified multinational job candidates. Some companies even visit foreign universities that have distinguished technical programs to attract qualified multinational employees. These searches combined with Internet screening for applicants can find the best potential multinational employees. Moreover, a company can advertise its eagerness to attract and to sustain a culturally diverse work force in the United States as well as abroad.

Capitalizing on the power of diversity is necessary in a growing global market because, logically, customers buy from the people they can relate to culturally. Union Bank of California, for instance, effectively serves the diverse West Coast population, especially its Asian and Hispanic customers. Accordingly, the bank has a successful recruitment history of hiring employees with language skills in Japanese, Vietnamese, Korean, and Spanish. In fact, Union Bank is regarded as one of the top five companies for Asian employees (Hamilton, 2002; Robinson & Hickman, 1999). Making up 25.6 percent of the bank's work force, Asians lead in the representation of ethnic employees. Seven of the bank's seventeen-member board of directors are also Asian Americans. Figure 3 shows Union Bank's track record in hiring multinational employees.

6

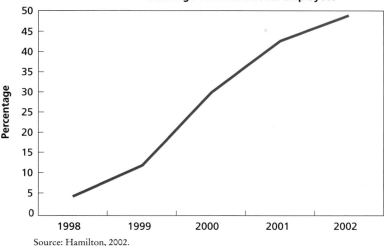

Figure 3
Union Bank of California
Growth in Percentage of Multinational Employees

Source: Hamilton, 2002.

Another successful business, Darden Restaurants of Orlando, Florida, selected Richard Rivera, a Hispanic, to serve as president of Red Lobster—the nation's largest full-service seafood chain. Overseeing 680 restaurants nationwide, Rivera is the "most powerful minority in the restaurant industry" (Royster Jackson, personal interview, June 24, 2003). Under Rivera's leadership, Red Lobster has built an impressive record for hiring more international employees—totaling more than 35 percent of its work force in 2003—than it had in previous years. Rivera believes that management cannot properly respond to customers from different ethnic backgrounds if the majority of its employees are limited to native speakers of English. Closer to the St. Louis area, Whitney Abernathy, manager of Netshop, Inc., a consulting firm, found that contracts from Indonesia increased by 17 percent after she hired Jakarta native Safja Jacoef, who recently graduated from an English program for non-native speakers in Fort Worth, Texas (Adamson, 2003).

Commitment to Ethnic Representation

Many companies already have mission statements on diversity in the workplace that formally acknowledge the importance of multinational employees. The most progressive of those companies, such as Toyota Motor Sales, SBC Communications, and Wal-Mart, promote multinational employees to serve as mentors and interpreters within the company. Such a proactive mentoring program recognizes the leadership abilities of multinational employees within the organization. "Glass ceilings," which in the past have prevented women and ethnic workers from moving up the corporate ladder, are finally being shattered. More and more CEOs are emphasizing recruitment and promotion of non-native speakers of English because of their actual job performance (Liberman, 2003). Carl Lagaigne, human resources director for IT at Southern California Edison in Rosemead, astutely observes, "Not to value diversity in a global field just does not make good business sense" (Solomon, 2002, p. 43).

Following the lead of other innovative U.S. corporations, Sodexho, a Gaithersburg, Maryland, contractor, now ranked as the fifty-seventh largest employer in the United States, recently created the position of vice president of diversity to help establish "an inclusive workplace" ("In Addressing," 2002). Born in Calcutta, Rohini Anand, Ph.D., holds the newly created job. "Our markets are getting more and more diverse," asserts Anand. "In terms of competing for talent, we are—and want to continue to be—the employer of choice. There is a public relations value to leveraging diversity" ("In Addressing," 2002, p. 22).

Promoting and Incorporating Cultural Awareness Within the Company

Cross-Cultural Training

Some companies are creating cultural awareness programs for international employees as well as native speakers to learn about other cultures. Both employees and employers profit: employees find it easier to work with someone whose values and beliefs they understand, while employers benefit from effective on-the-job collaboration. One of the most successful cultural sharing programs is conducted by American Express, whose work force represents more than twenty different nations. According to Moira Valdez, "culturally diverse employees have an opportunity to reach their maximum potential while still maintaining their cultural identities" (2003). Extel Communications, with its large percentage of Hispanic and Vietnamese employees, offers several workshops on those two cultures each year. Similarly, United Parcel Service (UPS) has developed a program whereby employees volunteer to work on a project with someone from another cultural group, with both parties gaining invaluable insights in problem solving and communicating. Shin Nguyen, a UPS employee since 1999, claims that her multicultural experience with Ann Nfara-Kahn was one of the most rewarding experiences of her job (Miller, 2003).

U.S. firms also need to be cautious about severing international workers' cultural ties—a delicate balance. Multinational employees do not like to be singled out because of their differences, yet successful U.S. businesses still must express a sincere response to and respect for their workers' cultures. When management actively promotes bonds among employees with similar identities, workers are less fearful about losing their cultural identity and becoming "token" employees (Raatikainen, 2002). The Amoco Corporation

8

offers networking to its employees, and Chase Manhattan Bank mobilizes culturally similar groups by introducing workers of homogeneous backgrounds to one another (Gabriel & Bentzman, 1999). For instance, employees from Chase Manhattan's New York City office who are of Turkish background lunch twice a month with fellow Turkish-born employees from the Newark branches. Chase Manhattan hosts the business luncheons and in return receives from those workers a bimonthly written evaluation of its Turkish and Middle Eastern policies.

Cultural education must go both ways, though. Both sides have things to learn about doing business in a global environment and working with one other. The United States, too, has social conventions in the business world, and few international employees want to ignore them, but someone needs to tell them what those conventions are (Adamson, 2003). Perhaps one problem with U.S. businesses is that we assume everyone knows how we do things and how we think—it never occurs to us to explain ourselves. Problems often stem from simple misunderstandings. Native speakers are typically comfortable within a space of 1.5 to 4 feet for general personal interactions. But Asians prefer a much greater conversational distance, and so a worker from China or Korea may feel uncomfortable if his or her desk is less than a few feet away from another employee's workspace (Tomoeda & Bayles, 2003).

The Impact of 9/11

Underscoring the need for cultural understanding, the terrorist attacks of 9/11 set off a devastating chain of events that heightened national security and that also have had a profound impact on businesses with multinational employees. Multinational employees became a valuable resource in helping companies to familiarize themselves firsthand with different value systems. Moreover, these multinational workers have helped stamp out stereotypes that can lead to prejudice. Jameela Habib, a senior accounts manager in Manhattan, offered the following moving testimony: "I was born in Damascus, and I celebrate my Syrian roots. Like all of my co-workers, I deplore the terrorism of 9/11 and uplift the heroism of the New York police, firefighters, and medical personnel. I am honored to be a part of a company that brought relief to the victims of 9/11" (personal communication, April 9, 2003).

Promotion of Cultural Sensitivity

Company efforts to validate different cultures might include the recognition, and even celebration, of a non-Western ethnic group's holidays or memorable historical events. Techsure, Inc., an Illinois software firm, allows Muslim employees to change their work schedules to accommodate Ramadan, Islam's holy month of fasting (Michael Saradayan, personal communication, May 28, 2003). Corporations with a Hispanic work force might honor National Hispanic Heritage Month, which coincides with the independence celebrations of five Latin American countries (U.S. Department of Equal Employment Opportunity [USEEO], 2002). GRT Electronics sends New

9

Year's greetings at Waisak (the Buddhist Day of Enlightenment) to its Chinese employees and to Indian workers at Rama Dipawli. Chemeka Taylor, GRT's general manager, wisely points out: "We send native-born employees Christmas cards; why shouldn't we honor our international work force, too?" (personal communication, May 10, 2003). Finally, Techsure and GRT have rethought vacation schedules so that their multinational employees can visit relatives during times more appropriate according to their cultural calendars. Figure 4 provides an example of a multicultural calendar for December.

In recent years, U.S. firms have been sensitive to the special needs of the country's changing work force. Flexible scheduling, telecommuting options, day care, and preventive health programs have become part of corporate plans to take care of employees. An international work force presents additional opportunities for management to respond with sensitivity to its employees. For example, company cafeterias could easily accommodate the particular dietary restrictions of workers who are vegetarian or who abstain from certain meats, such as beef or pork. At Ameritech, Inc., soybean and fish entrées are always available (Stone, 2003). Moreover, adding new ethnic items sends a powerful message of cultural awareness as well as contributes to networking and cultural sensitivity.

Day care raises critical issues for all working parents, non-native as well as native speakers of English. By providing day care that is sensitive to children's culturally diverse needs, companies give their multinational work force greater peace of mind and better equip them for their jobs. DEJ Computers, which offers one of the best on-site day-care programs in the Northwest, insists that at least two or three of its day-care workers must be fluent in Korean or Hindi (Parker, 2003). Another culturally sensitive employer, Angelica Nurseries in Kennedyville, Maryland, assisted its Hispanic work force by hiring bilingual day-care workers and also by serving foods the children eat at home. Angelica also helps Hispanic children enroll in school and arranges with local churches for free instruction in English (Morgan, 2002).

Making Business Communication More Understandable for Multinational Employees

Translation of Written Communications

All employees must be able to read and respond to business communications that directly affect them and their jobs. Among the most essential business documents that may cause trouble for multicultural readers are company handbooks, insurance and health care documents, and OSHA and EPA regulations (Hamilton, 2002). To ensure maximum understanding by a multinational work force, companies should provide a translation or at least a plain-English version of those and other crucial business documents. U.S. firms can solicit the help of employees who are fluent in the non-native English speaker's language as well as contract with professional translators

10

Figure 4
A Multicultural Calendar

December 2003

1	2	3	4	5	6	7
Advent (Christian) Hanukkah continues (Jewish)	Lailat ul Qadr (Islam)			Descubrimient o de la Hispaniola (Haiti, Dominican Republic)	Eid ul Fitri (Islam)	Christmas (France)
8 Bodhi Day (Rohatsu-Buddhist)	**9**	**10**	**11**	**12** Feast day— Our Lady of Guadalupe (Hispanic Catholic)	**13**	**14**
15	**16** Las Posadas begins (Mexico)	**17**	**18**	**19**	**20**	**21**
22	**23** Emperor's Birthday (Japan)	**24**	**25** Christmas (Christian)	**26** Kwanzaa begins (ends Jan. 6) (Interfaith)	**27**	**28** O-shogatsu (Japan)
29	**30**	**31** New Year's Eve				

Some Information about December's Daily Observances
Nov. 29–Dec. 6 Hanukkah: Eight-day celebration commemorating the rededication of the Temple of Jerusalem
Dec. 1 Advent: Christian time of preparation to celebrate Christmas
Dec. 2 Lailat ul Qadr: Islamic Night of Destiny
Dec. 6 Eid ul Fitri: Three-day Islamic fast marking end of Ramadan
Dec. 8 Bodhi Day: Buddhists celebrate Prince Gautama's vow to attain enlightenment
Dec. 12 Feast of Our Lady of Guadalupe: (Mexico) Catholic Christian holiday honoring appearance of the Virgin Mary near Mexico City in 1531
Dec. 7 & 25 Christmas: Christians celebrate birth of Jesus
Dec. 26 Kwanzaa: African American and Pan-African celebration of family, community, and culture. Seven life virtues are presented.
Dec. 28 O-shogatsu: Eight-day celebration of New Year's involving festive meals, music, and spring cleaning

Source: Parker, 2003.

11

to prepare documents that are readily understandable to a growing multinational work force.

Workplace signs in particular, especially safety messages, need to take into account the language needs of international workers. It is in a company's best interest and safety to translate signs into the languages represented in the workplace and/or to post signs that use global symbols, like those shown in Figure 5. Unquestionably, companies must avoid signs that workers would find difficult or impossible to decipher (Stone, 2003). For example, a large Ⓟ for "parking" or a **?** for "questions are answered here," or an H for "hospital" might be unfamiliar to non-native speakers of English.

Exchange of Language Learning

Providing English language instruction for employees who need it also has obvious advantages for the workplace of the new millennium. Unskilled multinational workers may even require instruction in their native language, including tutoring in literacy, basic mathematics, and technology (Adamson, 2003). Companies that cannot provide in-house language training might easily reimburse employees for appropriate courses, language books, tapes, and software, thus encouraging workers to communicate better. At the very least, every business could make available an audio library of specific vocabulary and phrases commonly used on the job as well as multilingual dictionaries or phrase books with relevant technical terms. Furthermore, businesses could invite religious and civic groups to participate in conversation groups and other language programs.

Hiromi Naguchi, a senior analyst at PowerUsers Networking, testified to the value of the English language training she received on the job. Although Naguchi had twelve years of courses in English in the Osaka (Japan) school system and graduated from a language institute in the United States, she needed regular practice in conversation to develop her listening and speaking skills. As a result of her diligence and the initiative of PowerUsers, Naguchi was recognized as her company's "Most Valuable Employee for 2002" (Hiromi Naguchi, personal communication, June 9, 2003). The president of PowerUsers called attention in particular to Naguchi's articulate interpersonal skills.

But language training has to be reciprocal—for native as well as non-native speakers of English—if international communication is to succeed in the global marketplace. Many international workers are trilingual, and several world cultures have two or more national languages. In Canada, for instance, people who speak both English and French have the advantage over those who speak only one of those languages; in India and South Africa the average person uses three or more national languages every day, all essential to conduct business (Demruajian, 1999). Dozens of companies specialize in foreign language instruction for U.S. businesspeople (e.g.,

12

Figure 5
**Safety Messages with Translations
for Multinational Employees**

Danger: Radioactive	Caution: Wet floor	For your protection wear safety glasses
Peligro! Radiactivo (Spanish)	Precaución! Mojado Suelo (Spanish)	Pour votre protection, verres de sûreté d'usure (French)
Dhamki! Jauhari Tawaanaa'i! (Urdu)	Khabar darrkarna! Aabi farsh (Urdu)	Paheñna áasim chashmah (Urdu)
Keikoku: Houshasei busshitsu (Japanese)	Yuka ga nureteiru (Japanese)	Anzen megane wo chakuyoo shitekudasai (Japanese)

Source: Stone, 2003.

Atkins International, Lingua Service Worldwide). An Internet directory for foreign language training companies can be found at *http://www.selfgrowth. com/foreignlanguage.html.* Such instruction can include ways to engage in friendly business conversation and introductions. Instruction can be industry-specific as well.

Conclusions

Because of a competitive world market, U.S. businesses must incorporate cultural diversity into the workplace. Policies and programs should provide new opportunities for the growing and essential multicultural work force. Technologically educated and experienced multinational workers will be in greater demand in the next twenty years. In fact, U.S. embassies in Indonesia, Nigeria, and Turkey encourage highly trained workers in those countries to apply for U.S. visas. U.S. organizations that do not recruit and recognize this vital group of employees will surely suffer in the international marketplace. Adeola Oduwole, head of Diversity Practices for SCENDIS, Inc., appropriately forecasts, "As demographics continue to transform the composition of the marketplace and the workforce, diversity will become an increasingly important part of the strategic corporate strategy" (2003). Equal opportunities, diversity training, and attention to communications issues will keep U.S. businesses globally competitive. Ultimately, businesses in the

13

United States, the most culturally diverse country in the world, can expand only by making a commitment to learn about and respect other cultures and their ways of life.

Recommendations

To be competitive in the global economy, RPM Technologies must attract and retain highly skilled international employees in the new millennium. As this report has shown, both hiring and training policies need to be adjusted to accommodate the cultural—linguistic, social, and religious—needs of a new wave of immigrants. By implementing the following recommendations, RPM Technologies can succeed in its recruitment and training efforts.

1. Recruit multinational students more effectively at campuses both in the United States and in other countries.
2. Help multinationals by working closely with the Immigration and Naturalization Service (INS) to hire and to retain qualified employees.
3. Establish a mentoring program to identify leadership abilities in multinational employees.
4. Form cultural sensitivies and networking groups to ensure the dissemination of cultural information.
5. Provide relevant translations and plain-English versions of company handbooks, manuals, and codes.
6. Reassess day-care facilities to take into consideration the needs of the children of multinational employees.
7. Develop educational materials for employees who are native speakers of English about the cultures of their multinational co-workers.
8. Assist multinational workers in completing language training, as needed, and/or any professional certification or licensure requirements.

14

References

Adamson, R. (2003, February). Challenges ahead for American business. *National Economics Review, 11*, 45–46.

Appel, J. M. (2001). Fulbright scholars discuss immigration. Education Update Online. Retrieved June 24, 2003, from http://www.educationupdate.com/may01/fulbright.html

Brown, P. (2003, January 20). History of U.S. immigration. Retrieved May 2, 2003, from http://immigration.ucn.edu

Business Help. (2002). Foreign language training information. Retrieved July 16, 2002, from http://www.selfgrowth.com/foreignlanguage.html

Demruajian, P. (1999). *Linguistic diversity in business.* Hillsdale, NJ: Erlbaum.

Francis, D. R. (2002, June 20). Despite soft economy, a call for foreign tech workers. *Christian Science Monitor,* p. 21.

Gabriel, B., & Bentzman, J. (1999, July). The 50 best companies for Latinas to work for in the U.S. *Latina Style, 50,* 1.

Hamilton, B. E. (2002, May 15). Diversity is the answer for today's work force. *The New Business Journal, 10*(38), 35–37.

In addressing diversity: Sodexho does "right thing." (2002). *Food Service Director, 15*(5), 22.

Johnson, V. M. (2003). Growing multinational diversity in business sparks changes. *Business Across the Nation, 23*(7), 43–48.

LaJoya, R. (Director). (2002, April 21). *Noticias por la gente* [Television program]. Miami's Extra TV. (Transcript available from Merganser Communications, 61 Woodlawn Street, Miami, FL 33166.)

Levanthall, M. (2000). New York! New York! Most popular spot to immigrate. *All Around New York, 10*(13), 14–17.

Liberman, V. (2003). Tough issues. *Across the Board, 39*(3), 22–30.

Martin, P. (2003). Migration news. Retrieved July 20, 2002, from http://www.migration.ucdavis.edu

Miller, D. (2003). UPS diversified and loving it. *Business, 45*(103), 34–45.

Morgan, O. (2002, July). We say talk the talk. *N Pro.* Retrieved June 24, 2003, from http://bsipublishing.com

Oduwole, A. (2003). Can diversity budgets withstand the recession? *Diversity Central.* Retrieved July 17, 2003, from http://www.diversityhotwire.com/diversity_practitioners/research.html

Parker, M. (2003, May). Immigration facts. Retrieved June 21, 2003, from http://immigration.org

15

Raatikainen, P. (2002). Contributions of multiculturalism to the competitive advantage of an organization. *Singapore Management Review, 24,* 81–89.

Robinson, E., & Hickman, J. (1999, July). The diversity elite. *Fortune, 18,* 62– 63.

Shih, P. (2003). Asian America in the Silicon Valley. APAs are exploding myths to shape Silicon Valley and change the image of Asians in business. *Asian American Village Online.* Retrieved June 15, 2002, from http://www.imdiversity.com/villages/asian/Article

Solomon, M. (2002). Create diversity in culture, ideas. *Computerworld, 36*(19), 42–44.

Stone, B., & Conway, R. (2001, May). Laid off, with no place to call home. *Newsweek, 20*(137), 36–38.

Stone, E. (2003, March 30). Serving up culture. Retrieved June 21, 2003, from http://www.culture.org

Tomoeda C. K., & Bayles, K. A. (2003). Cultivating cultural competence in the workplace, classroom, and clinic. *The Asha Leader Online.* Retrieved July 7, 2003, from http://professional.asha.org/news/020202d.cfm

Union Bank Web site. http://www.ubca.com

U.S. Bureau of Labor Statistics. (2003). Employment status of the civilian noninstitutional population by age, sex, and race. Retrieved June 30, 2003, from http://www.bls.gov

U.S. Chamber of Commerce. (2003, April). Chamber, labor leaders renew call for immigration reform. USChamber.com. Retrieved June 18, 2003, from http://www.uschamber.com/Press+Room/2003+Releases

U.S. Department of Equal Employment Opportunity. (2002). *Hispanic employment program report for 2002* (EEO Publication No. B56.2245). Washington, DC: U.S. Government Printing Office.

U.S. Office of the Census Bureau. (2000). *Immigration figures* (OCB Publication No. A 82-[995]). Washington, DC: U.S. Government Printing Office.

U.S. Office of Employment Projections. (2000). *Employment outlook: 2000–2010* (OEP Report No. 12-632). Washington, DC: U.S. Government Printing Office.

Valdez, M. (2003, Spring). Cultural diversity in the workplace. (From <Business 2000>[SIRS Researcher CD-ROM Spring 2003], Art. No. 35, Boca Raton, FL: SIRS, Inc. [Producer and Distributor].)

✓ Revision Checklist

❏ Concentrated on a major problem—one with significant implications for my major, neighborhood, city, or employer.

❏ Did sufficient research—in the library, on the Internet, through interviewing, from personal observation and/or testing—to convince my readers that I am knowledgeable about this problem, its scope and effects, and likely solution.

❏ Made sure I understand what employer/instructor is looking for.

❏ Followed company's/instructor's guidelines for the format and documentation.

❏ Divided and labeled the parts of long report to make it easy for readers to follow and to show careful plan of organization.

❏ Supplied a one-page letter of transmittal or cover letter informing readers why the report was written and describing its scope and findings.

❏ Supplied an abstract that leaves no doubt in readers' minds about what report deals with and why.

❏ Designed attractive title page that contains all the basic information—title, date, for whom the report is written, my name—readers require.

❏ Gave readers all the necessary introductory information about background, problem, purpose of report, and scope.

❏ Included in body of report the weight of all my research—the facts, statistics, and descriptions—that my readers need in order to know that I have done my homework on the topic well.

❏ Wrapped up report in succinct conclusion. Told readers what the findings of my research are and accurately interpreted all data.

❏ Supplied a recommendations section (if required) that tells readers concretely how they can respond to the problem using the data. Recommendations make sense—are realistic and practical and related directly to the research and topic. Ensured that recommendations are persuasive.

❏ Included in the final copy of report all the parts listed in table of contents.

Exercises

1. What kinds of research did the student do to write the long report in Figure 9.2?

2. Study Figure 9.2 and answer the following questions based on it.
   a. How has the writer successfully limited the scope of the report?
   b. Where does the writer use internal summaries especially well?
   c. Where and how has the writer adapted her technical information for her audience (a general reader)?

d. What visual devices does the writer use to separate parts of the report and divisions within each part?

e. How does the writer introduce, summarize, and draw conclusions from the expert opinions she cites in order to substantiate the main points?

f. What are the ways in which the writer documents information she has gathered?

g. What functions does the conclusion serve for readers? Cite specific examples from the report.

h. How do the recommendations follow from the material presented in the report?

3. Come to class prepared to discuss at least two major problems that would be suitable topics for a long report. Consider an important community problem—traffic, crime, air and water pollution, transportation—or a problem at your college. Then write a letter to a consulting firm, or other appropriate agency or business, requesting a study of the problem and a report.

4. Write a report outline for one of the problems you decided on in Exercise 3. Use major headings and include the kinds of information discussed in the Front Matter section of this chapter (pp. 262–263).

5. Have your instructor look at and approve the outline you prepared for Exercise 4. Then write a long report based on the outline, either individually or as part of a collaborative writing team.

CHAPTER 10

Making Successful Presentations at Work

Almost every job requires employees to have and to use carefully developed speaking skills. In fact, to get hired, you have to be a persuasive speaker at your job interview. And to advance up the corporate ladder, you will have to continue to be a confident, well-prepared, and persuasive speaker. This chapter's goal is to help you be a more successful speaker.

Types of Presentations

On the job you will have numerous presentation responsibilities that will vary in the amount of preparation they require, the time they last, and the audience and the occasion for which they are intended. Here are some frequent types of presentations you may have to make as part of your job:

- sales appeals to prospective customers
- evaluations of products or policies
- progress reports to your boss
- reports to superiors about your job accomplishments
- justifications of your position or even your department
- appeals and/or explanations before elected officials
- presentations at professional conferences
- explanation of a procedure, decision, or plan before a community/civic group (chamber of commerce or local PTA)

Whatever type of oral presentation you are called on to deliver, this chapter gives you practical advice on how to become a better, more assured communicator in both informal briefings and formal speeches.

Informal Briefings

If you have ever given a book report or explained laboratory results in front of a class, you have given an informal briefing. Such semiformal reports are a routine part of many jobs. Here is a list of some of the typical informal briefings you may need to deliver at work:

- a status report on your current project
- an update or end-of-shift report, like those nurses and police officers give
- an explanation of a policy to co-workers
- a report on a conference you attended
- a demonstration of new equipment or software
- a follow-up session on equipment or procedures
- a summary of a meeting you attended

Such informal presentations are usually short (one to seven minutes, perhaps), and you won't always be given advance notice. When the boss tells you to "say a few words about the new Web site" (or the new programming procedure), you will not be expected to give a lengthy formal speech.

Guidelines for Preparing Informal Briefings

Follow these guidelines when you have to make an informal briefing.

- Make your comments brief and to the point.
- Keyboard a few bulleted items you plan to cover.
- Highlight key phrases and terms you need to stress.
- Include in your notes only the major points you want to mention.
- Arrange your points in chronological order or from cause to effect.

Figure 10.1 is an informal outline with key facts used by an employee who is introducing Diana J. Rizzo, a visiting speaker, to a monthly meeting of safety directors.

Formal Presentations

Whereas an informal briefing is likely to be short, generally conversational, and intended for a limited number of people, a formal presentation is much longer, far less conversational, and intended for a wider audience. Therefore, it involves more preparation.

Avoid speaking "off the cuff." The professional speechmaker may be comfortable with this approach, but for most of us, the worst way to make a presentation is to speak without any preparation whatsoever. You only fool yourself if you think you will have all the necessary details and explanations in the back of your head. Once you start talking, generally everything does not fall into place smoothly. Without preparation, you are likely to confuse important points or forget them entirely. Mark Twain's advice is apt here: "It takes three weeks to prepare a good impromptu speech."

FIGURE 10.1   Some notes for an informal briefing to introduce an engineer to a group of safety directors.

- Diana J. Rizzo, Chief Engineer of the Rhode Island State Highway Department for twelve years

- Experience as both a civil engineer and safety expert

- Consultant to Secretary Habib, Department of Transportation

- Member of the National Safety Council and author of "Field Test Procedures in Highway Safety Construction"

- Designed specially constructed aluminum posts used on Rhode Island highway system

- Received "Award for Excellence" from the Northeastern Association of Traffic Engineers in May 2002

Expect to spend several days preparing your presentation. You cannot just dash it off. You will need time to

- research the subject
- interview key resource individuals
- prepare your visuals
- coordinate your talk with presentations by co-workers or your boss
- rehearse your presentation

Many of us are uncomfortable in front of an audience because we feel frightened or embarrassed. Much of that anxiety can be eased if you know what to expect. The two areas you should investigate thoroughly before you begin to prepare your presentation are (1) who will be in your audience and (2) why they are there.

Analyzing Your Audience

The more you learn about your audience, the better prepared you will be to give them what they need. Just as you do for your written work, for your oral presentation you will have to do some research about the audience, emphasizing the "you attitude" and establishing your own credibility.

Consider Your Audience as a Group of Listeners, Not Readers

While audience analysis pertains both to readers of your work and to listeners of your presentation, there are several fundamental differences between these two groups. Unlike a reader of your report, the audience for your presentation

- is a captive audience
- has only one chance to get your message
- has less time to digest what you say
- has a shorter attention span
- can't always go back to review what you said or jump ahead to get a preview
- is more easily distracted—by interruptions, chairs being moved, people coughing, and so on
- cannot absorb as many of the technical details as you would include in a written report

Take all of these differences into account as you plan your presentation and assess your audience.

Who Is Your Audience?

Here are five key questions you need to ask when analyzing the audience for a formal presentation.

1. **How much do they know about your topic?**

   - consumers with little or no technical knowledge
   - technical individuals who understand terms, jargon, and background

2. **What unites them as a group?**

   - members of the same profession
   - customers using the same products
   - employees of the company you work for

3. **What is their interest in your topic?**

   - highly motivated
   - neutral—waiting to be informed, entertained, or persuaded
   - hostile—opposed to your opinion
   - uncooperative and antagonistic, likely to challenge you

4. **What do you want them to do after hearing your presentation?**

   - learn more about your topic
   - buy a product or service
   - adopt a plan
   - change a schedule

5. **What questions are they likely to raise?**

The Parts of Formal Presentations

As you read this section, refer to Marilyn Claire Ford's outline in Figure 10.2 (pp. 298–303). Note that her speech outline uses some PowerPoint presentation techniques (see pp. 305–306) to convince a potential client, GTP Systems, to purchase a service contract provided by World Tech, her employer. Her talk uses images and text.

The Introduction

The most important part of a presentation is your introduction, which should capture the audience's attention by answering these questions: (1) Who are you? (2) What are your qualifications? (3) What specific topic are you speaking about? and (4) How is the topic relevant to us?

Your first and most immediate goal is to establish rapport with your audience, win their confidence, and elicit their cooperation. Since your audience is probably at their most attentive during the first few minutes of your presentation, they will pay close attention to everything about you and what you say. Seize the moment and build momentum.

An effective introduction should be proportional to the length of your presentation. A ten-minute speech requires no more than a sixty-second introduction; a twenty-minute speech needs no more than a two- or three-minute introduction.

How to Begin

You can begin by introducing yourself, emphasizing your professional qualifications and interests. (A self-introduction is unnecessary if someone else has introduced you or if you know everyone in the room.)

Give Listeners a Road Map

Give listeners a "road map" at the beginning of your presentation so that they will know where you are, where you are going, and what they have to look forward to or to recall. Indicate what your topic is and how you have organized what you have to say about it.

> My presentation today on Digital Business software will last about 20 minutes and is divided into three parts. First, I will outline briefly recent software changes. Second, I will give a detailed review of how those changes directly affect our company. Third, I will show how our company can profitably implement those changes. At the end of my presentation, there will be time for your questions and comments.

The most informative presentations are the easiest to follow. Restrict your topic to ensure that you will be able to organize it carefully and sensibly—for example, a tasty diet under 1,000 calories a day or a course in learning Java or another software package.

FIGURE 10.2   Outline of a formal presentation.

Outline for a Presentation Promoting
Desktop Videoconferencing to a Potential Customer

Audience: Executives of GTP Systems

Purpose: To convince management to invest in videoconferencing technology

Speaker: Marilyn Claire Ford, World Tech Telecommunications

Introduction

I. World Tech Desktop Videoconferencing can increase the efficiency of GTP's
communications by 50 to 100 percent—and dramatically cut costs.

   A. GTP spent more than $350,000 for business travel last year (much more
than necessary) so that its employees from various branches could meet
and confer.

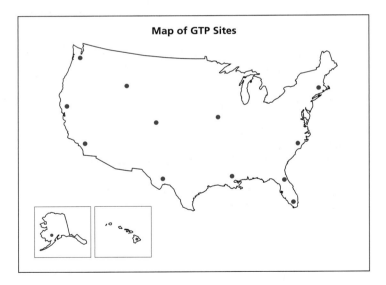

Continued

FIGURE 10.2   (Continued)

2

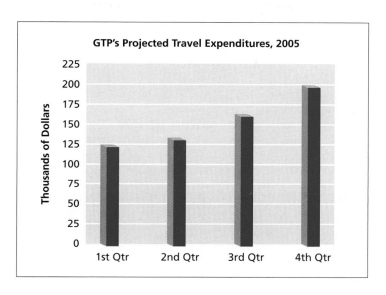

GTP's Projected Travel Expenditures, 2005

B. Conducting staff meetings among branch offices poses several problems:
   1. It entails extensive preparation.
   2. Often there are scheduling conflicts.
   3. Travel delays can adversely affect the success of the meeting.

C. Desktop Videoconferencing solves those problems:
   1. Employees at different sites interact as if in the same room.
   2. Such an arrangement will give GTP a competitive edge.

D. Desktop Videoconferencing transforms existing computers into interactive, multimedia conference rooms.

Continued

FIGURE 10.2   (Continued)

3

Body

II. World Tech's technology for Desktop Videoconferencing is easy to use and cost-effective.

    A. Desktop Videoconferencing is as simple as a telephone call.
        1. Arrange a meeting time with colleagues at other sites.
        2. Use your computer to access World Tech's Microlink.
        3. Dial in to the conference (see and hear all participants access the Microlink).
        4. Talk directly with all participants by telephone.

© Steve Chenn/CORBIS

    B. Reap great benefits with an inexpensive or existing computer system.
        1. Technology is based on a Pentium processor with 128 MB of memory; if new, cost ranges from $900 to $1,500.

Continued

FIGURE 10.2 (Continued)

4

    2. Existing computer system can be upgraded quickly for less than the cost of a new computer
    3. Cost of additional equipment (software, camera, modem, video and sound card) is under $1,400.

C. Integrated service data network (ISDN)—a dedicated phone line that transfers digital data—costs only $900/year to rent.

D. Desktop Videoconferencing can cut data processing costs by 60 percent or more.

III. Desktop Videoconferencing is a strategic weapon in the post–9/11 marketplace.

> ## The Benefits of Videoconferencing in a Post–9/11 Marketplace
>
> - Accelerates global sales
> - Provides low-cost networking
> - Consolidates communication networks
> - Creates interactive, multimedia conference space

A. Competitive businesses are information-driven, not product-driven.
    1. GTP can accelerate global sales via the Internet.
    2. Desktop Videoconferencing provides flexible, low-cost networking.

Continued

FIGURE 10.2   (Continued)

5

    B. Telecommunications is transforming the traditional office.
        1. Desktop Videoconferencing consolidates your communications network into a single point of contact for all types of information—data, image, voice, and video.
        2. For less than the cost of a personal computer, GTP can create an interactive, multimedia conference room.

IV. World Tech Telecommunications offers three communication benefits.
    A. Desktop Videoconferencing enhances employees' collaboration and interaction.
        1. Communication improves when employees can see each other's facial expressions and body language.
        2. World Tech's "whiteboard" allows employees to work simultaneously on a document (they see each other's revisions while sharing ideas on the telephone).

    B. Desktop Videoconferencing will increase GTP's productivity.
        1. Employees transmit both audio and video information, sharing more data with more people—from 50 to 100 percent more effectively.
        2. Employees interact directly, streamlining collaborative projects by 35 to 45 percent.
        3. Employees work more efficiently in their own workspaces.

    C. Desktop Videoconferencing makes better use of time and saves money.
        1. Schedules meetings quickly and avoids conflicts.
        2. Brings the right people together, no matter where they are.
            a. Important discussions will no longer depend on one person's travel schedule.
            b. Schedule emergency meetings quickly when problems arise.

Conclusion

V. World Tech Telecommunications can bring the communication benefits of Desktop Videoconferencing to GTP Industries.
    A. Desktop Videoconferencing will save GTP both time and money.

Continued

FIGURE 10.2   (Continued)

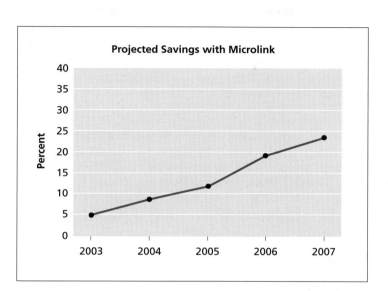

6

Projected Savings with Microlink

B. Desktop Videoconferencing will enhance the professional performance/ achievement of GTP's employees.

C. World Tech Telecommunications will tailor Desktop Videoconferencing to GTP's needs, ensuring a competitive advantage in today's complex business world.

Capture Audience's Attention

Use any of the following strategies to get your audience to "bite the hook."

- Ask a question. "Do you know how much actual meat there is in a hot dog?"
- Start with a quotation. Winston Churchill said, "We get things to make a living but we give things to have a life." (Consult *Bartlett's Familiar Quotations* on-line at *http://www.bartleby.com.*)
- Give an interesting statistic. "In 2006, two million heart attack victims will live to tell about it."(Go to the *World Almanac and Book of Facts* to find something relevant to your presentation topic.)
- Relate an anecdote or story. Be sure it is relevant and in good taste; make your audience feel at ease and friendly toward you by establishing a bond with them.

Be careful about using humor in a business talk. It could backfire—the audience may not get the point or even be offended by it.

The Body

The body is the longest part of your presentation, just as it is in a long report. Make it persuasive and relevant to your audience by (1) explaining a process, (2) describing a condition, (3) solving a problem, (4) arguing a case, or (5) doing all of these. See how the body of Marilyn Claire Ford's speech outline in Figure 10.2 is organized around the customer benefits of GTP's desktop videoconferencing.

To get the right perspective, recall your own experiences as a member of an audience. How often did you feel bored or angry because a speaker tried to overload you with details or could not stick to the point?

Ways to Organize the Body

Here are a few helpful ways you can present and organize information in the body of your presentation. In writing a report, design your document to help readers visually, supplying headings, underscoring, bullets, necessary white space, and headers and footers. In a speech, switch from those purely visual devices to aural ones, such as the following:

1. **Give signals (directions) to show where you are going or where you have been.** Enumerate your points: *first, second, third.* Emphasize cause-and-effect relationships with *subsequently, therefore, furthermore.* When you tell a story, follow a chronological sequence and fill your speech with signposts: *before, following, next, then.*

2. **Comment on your own material.** Tell the audience if some point is especially significant, memorable, or relevant. "This next fact is the most important thing I'll say today."

3. **Provide internal summaries.** Spending a few seconds to recap what you have just covered will reassure your audience and you as well.

> We have already discussed the difficulties in establishing a menu repertory, or the list of items that the food service manager wants to appear on the menu. Now we will turn to ways of determining which items should appear on a menu and why.

4. **Anticipate any objections or qualifications your audience is likely to have.** Address the issues with relevant facts about costs, personnel, and/or equipment in your presentation.

The Conclusion

Plan your conclusion as carefully as you do your introduction. Stopping with a screeching halt is as bad as trailing off in a fading monotone. An effective conclusion leaves the audience feeling that you and they have come full circle and accomplished what you promised. Notice how Marilyn Claire Ford ends her presentation by persuading GTP Systems that they will gain a competitive edge, the point with which she began (see pp. 302–303).

What to Put in Conclusion

A conclusion should contain something lively and memorable. Never introduce a new subject or simply repeat your introduction. A conclusion can contain the following:

- a fresh restatement of your three or four main points
- a call to action, just as in a sales letter—to buy, to note, to agree, to volunteer

- a final emphasis on a key statistic (for example, "The installation of the stainless steel heating tanks has, as we have seen, saved our firm 32 percent in utility costs, since we no longer have to run the heating system all day.")

End your presentation, as Marilyn Claire Ford did, with a concise summary of the main points and urge listeners to invest company money in your product or service—for example, World Tech Telecommunications Desktop Videoconferencing system.

Mean It When You Say, "Finally"

When you tell your audience you are concluding, make sure you mean it. Saying, "In conclusion," and then talking for another ten minutes frustrates listeners and makes them less receptive to your message.

Using Visuals

The more successful a presentation, the greater the chances that the speaker has effectively incorporated visuals into it. Many listeners judge a presentation by the quality of the visuals presented. As we saw in Chapter 6, visuals have numerous benefits for speakers and their audiences.

You may use a variety of visuals during your presentation: photographs; maps; dry-erase boards; foamboards; diagrams; transparencies; slides; and computer displays that take advantage of text, sound, animation, and even virtual reality.

Keep in mind that visuals in any presentation must be constructed even more carefully than for a written report. Unlike a reading audience, a listening audience may not be able to refer to a visual again or have time to study the visual in detail. Keep your visuals clear, simple, and memorable.

PowerPoint Presentations

More and more business talks use computer graphics, especially PowerPoint and Corel Presentation. Using these graphics packages is a crucial skill your employer will expect you to have. You do not need much technical know-how to run Power-Point. It is essentially an electronic slide show that can be created on any computer that has Windows 2000 or XP. Thanks to PowerPoint, you can design or import visuals, display them first on your computer screen, and then transfer them to a specially equipped overhead projector for your audience to see. Projected on the screen, images created with this software are clear, professional looking, and give you maximum flexibility. You can also present simple text messages.

With the software you can determine how and where to introduce a visual in your talk, control how long it stays on the projector, and when it fades (dissolves) from the screen. PowerPoint allows you to create a variety of visuals—graphs, tables, drawings, bars, clip art, animations, even video clips. (Note the diversity of graphics—map, line graph, photograph, bar chart—Marilyn Claire Ford uses in her presentation in Figure 10.2.) Before you attempt to integrate PowerPoint into your presentation, though, make sure you know how the software works. A mistake can mar your entire talk.

Guidelines for Using PowerPoint

Here are some guidelines that, if followed, will help you succeed with PowerPoint.

1. Make sure all your slides are in the right order and in sync with your talk.
2. Allow enough time between images for the audience to process the information you are presenting visually. For example, don't rush through, in two or three seconds, the most important visuals of your talk. Allow those images to stay on the projector longer.
3. Adjust the number of slides to the length of your presentation and your audience's needs. Don't go overboard and include 20 slides for a five- to six-minute presentation.
4. Use slides that will project large enough for your audience to see them easily. For a text message consider using 14- to 16-point type (see Chapter 6, pp. 165–168).
5. Don't clutter your slides. Use no more than five lines of text per slide and double-space between text messages. A PowerPoint screen is not the place to use large chunks of prose, like a paragraph or two.
6. Bullet or number important items in text slides as Marilyn Ford does in Section III. A. of her outline in Figure 10.2 (p. 301).
7. Keep your presentation simple and businesslike. Avoid the temptation to put on a "light show" with a series of erratic fades, zooms, cuts, dissolves, and dancing animations.
8. If you use a photo or another visual, project it clearly without competing clutter. Use just text for a text screen, and show the visual alone without accompanying text.
9. Be prepared for technical glitches. Print copies of your entire presentation so that everyone in your audience will have a hard copy if something goes wrong.

Guidelines for Using Visuals

Regardless of whether you use computerized or noncomputerized visuals, follow these guidelines for your presentations.

1. Make sure visuals are visible. Make sure your visuals are large and easy-to-read, even from the back row or from the far corner of a long conference table. If they cannot be seen clearly from a distance and understood at once, they are not very useful. With any text, stay away from fonts that are difficult to read such as Gothic or script.

2. Make your visuals easy to understand. Each visual should be clear and simple, easy to understand the first time an audience sees it. If you suspect that your audience may have trouble, even momentarily, understanding what your visual is or why and how it works, redesign it or delete it. Using technical (or excessively complex) computer flow charts may detract from rather than add to your presentation if the audience does not recognize what the charts show.

3. Make your visuals self-explanatory. Don't make the mistake of taking five minutes to explain the content of one visual; the visual itself should explain the content of your talk.

4. Make sure your visuals are relevant. Be careful that each visual relates directly to your topic and that it does not interfere with your message. Will it lead an audience off on a tangent or contradict your message? If so, delete or revise it.

5. Make sure your visuals are correct. Double-check for accuracy and be especially on the lookout for any typographical errors, mistakes in math, and inconsistencies with other visuals.

6. Determine how many visuals to use. Use visuals only when your audience needs them, not just for decoration. Their purpose is to clarify (or supplement)—not compete with—what you say.

7. Never substitute a visual for the commentary or analysis the reader needs. Don't think the visual alone will sell your product or service and make all your points. Your visual must work in conjunction with your written text.

8. Be especially cautious with a slide projector. Never stand in front of it and obstruct your audience's view of your visuals. Always stand to the side and make sure you are far enough away from any extension cords so that you do not trip on them during your presentation.

Rehearsing and Delivering Presentations

Don't skip rehearsing your talk thinking it will save you time. It will actually help you become more familiar with your topic and overall message, building your confidence. Rehearsing will also help you to acquire more natural speech rhythms—pitch, pauses, and pacing. Here are some strategies to use as you rehearse your speech.

- Speak in front of a full-length mirror for at least one rehearsal to see how an audience might view you.
- Talk into a tape recorder to determine whether you sound friendly or frantic, poised or pressured. You can also catch and correct yourself if you are speaking too quickly or too slowly. A rate of about 120 to 140 words a minute is easy for an audience to follow.
- Time yourself so that you will not exceed your allotted time or fall far short of your audience's expectations.
- Practice with the PowerPoint software, visuals, or equipment you intend to use in your speech for valuable hands-on experience.
- Monitor the type of gestures (neither too many nor too few) you can use for clarity and emphasis in your talk.
- Videotape your final rehearsal and show it to a colleague or instructor for feedback.

A poor delivery can ruin a good presentation. You will be evaluated by your style of presentation just as you are in your written work. When you speak before an audience, you will be evaluated on the image you project: how you look, how you talk, and how you move (your body language). Do you mumble into your notes, never looking at the audience? Do you clutch the lectern as if to keep it in place? Do you shift nervously from one foot to the other? All those actions betray your nervousness and detract from your presentation.

In business presentations, it is crucial to make a good first impression. Research shows that people decide what they think of you in the first three or four minutes of your presentation. The way you dress is crucial but so is your body language. In fact, seventy-five percent of your audience's impressions are influenced by your body language. The nonverbal signals you send affect how your audience will regard your leadership abilities, your sales performance, even your sincerity. Pay attention to gestures, movement of your hands, how you stand, and so on. No matter how many hours you have worked to get your message ready, if your nonverbal presentation is misleading or inappropriate, the impact of what you say will be lost.

The following suggestions on how to deliver a presentation will help you to be a well-prepared, poised speaker.

Settling Your Nerves Before You Speak

Don't let your nerves stand in your way of delivering a highly successful talk. Here are some ways you can calm yourself before you deliver your presentation.

- Give yourself plenty of time to get there. The more you have to rush, the more anxious you will be.

- Don't bring anything with you that is likely to spill, such as coffee or a soft drink.

- Avoid caffeine for a few hours before your talk if it makes you jittery.

- Take some deep breaths, which can help by slowing your heart rate and lowering your blood pressure.

- Remind yourself that you have spent hours preparing. Your hard work will pull you through.

- Try to chat with one or two members of the audience ahead of time and relax. See your audience as friends—people who can help your career.

Making Your Presentation

Everyone is nervous before a talk. Accept that fact and even allow a few seconds for "panic time." Then put your nervous energy to work for you. Chances are, your audience will have no idea how anxious you are; they cannot see the butterflies in your stomach. Again, see your audience as friends, not enemies. Remember to do the following.

1. Establish eye contact with your listeners. Look at your audience to establish a relationship with them. Never bury your head in notes or keep your eyes fixed on a monitor. You will signal your lack of interest in the audience or your fear of public speaking. Some timid speakers think that if they look only at some fixed place or object in the back of the room, the audience will regard this as eye contact. But that kind of cover-up does not work.

2. Adjust to audience feedback. Watch your listeners' reactions and respond appropriately—nodding to agree, pausing a moment, paraphrasing to clarify a confusing point.

3. Use a friendly, confident tone. Speak in a natural, conversational voice, but avoid verbal tics ("you know," "I mean") and fillers ("um," "ah," "er") repeated several times each minute. Such nervous habits will make your audience nervous and your speech less effective. Use pauses instead.

4. Vary the rate of your delivery. Use your natural speaking voice. Use your rate to help you emphasize key points and make transitions. Talk slowly enough for your audience to understand you, yet quickly enough so that you don't sound as if you are belaboring or emphasizing each word.

5. Adjust your volume appropriately. Talking in a monotone, never raising or lowering your voice, will lull your audience to sleep or at least inattention! Talk loudly enough for everyone to hear, but be careful if you are using a microphone. Your voice will be amplified, so if you speak loudly, you will boom rather than project. Every word with a *b, p,* or *d* will sound like an explosive in your listener's ear. Watch out for the other extreme—speaking so softly that only the first two rows can hear you.

6. Watch your posture. Don't shift from one foot to another. But do not slouch or look wooden either. If you stand motionless, looking as if rigor mortis has set in, your speech will be judged cold and lifeless, no matter how lively your words are. Be natural yet dynamic; move, and let your body react to what you are saying. Smile, nod your head, move your arms, point at an object, stand back a little from the lectern.

7. Use appropriate body language. Be natural and consistent. Do not startle an audience by suddenly pounding on the lectern for emphasis. Avoid gestures that will distract or alienate your audience. For example, don't fold your arms as you talk, a gesture that signals you are unreceptive (closed) to your audience's reactions. Also, avoid the nervous habits that can divert the audience's attention: clicking a ballpoint pen, scratching your head, rubbing your nose, twirling your hair, pushing up your glasses, fumbling with your notes, tapping your foot, or drumming your fingers on a desk.

8. Dress professionally. Do not wear clothes or clanking jewelry (such as necklace or bracelet charms) that call attention to themselves. Be conservative and dress formally. Wear clothes that are the business norm—know your company's dress code. Women should wear a businesslike dress or suit; men should wear a dark business suit, white shirt, and a tasteful tie.

Evaluating Presentations

A large portion of this chapter has given you information on how to construct and deliver a formal speech. As a way of reviewing that advice, study Figure 10.3 (p. 310)—an evaluation form similar to those used by instructors in communications classes. Note that the form gives equal emphasis to the speaker's performance or delivery and to the organization and content of the presentation.

FIGURE 10.3   An evaluation form for an oral presentation.

Name of speaker_____ Date of presentation _____

Title of presentation _____ Length of presentation _____

PART I: THE SPEAKER (circle the appropriate number)

1. Appearance: 1   2   3   4   5
                    sloppy   well groomed

2. Eye contact: 1   2   3   4   5
                     poor   effective

3. Voice: 1   2   3   4   5
                   monotonous   varied

4. Posture: 1   2   3   4   5
                     poor   natural

5. Gestures: 1   2   3   4   5
                   disturbing   appropriate

6. Self-confidence: 1   2   3   4   5
                    nervous   poised

PART II: THE PRESENTATION (circle the appropriate number: 1 = poor;
5 = superior)

1. Speaker's knowledge of the subject—carefully researched; factual errors;
   missing details:
              1   2   3   4   5

2. Relevance of the topic for audience—suitable for this group:
              1   2   3   4   5

3. The speaker's language—too technical; filled with clichés or slang
   expressions; or crisp and descriptive:
              1   2   3   4   5

4. The speaker's visuals—easy to read, large, relevant, carefully ordered:
              1   2   3   4   5

5. Presentation easy to follow—speaker gave the audience signs where
   he or she had been and where he or she was going:
              1   2   3   4   5

6. Speaker's conclusion—clearly identified major points:
              1   2   3   4   5

✓ Revision Checklist

- ❏ Anticipated audience's background, interest, potential resistance, and questions about message.
- ❏ Prepared introduction to provide "road map" of presentation and to arouse audience interest.
- ❏ Started with interesting and relevant statistics, a question, an anecdote, or similar "hook" to capture audience attention.
- ❏ Limited body of presentation to main points.
- ❏ Arranged main points logically and made connections among them.
- ❏ Used supporting examples and illustrations appropriate to audience.
- ❏ Made sure conclusion contains summary of main points of my presentation and/or specific call for action.
- ❏ Prepared outline and identified and corrected any weak or redundant areas.
- ❏ Designed visuals that are clear, easy-to-read, and relevant for audience.
- ❏ Experimented successfully with PowerPoint technology and applications before including in a presentation.
- ❏ Rehearsed presentation thoroughly to become familiar with its organization and visuals.
- ❏ Monitored volume, tone, and rate to vary delivery and emphasize major points.
- ❏ Rehearsed gestures to make them relevant and nonintrusive.
- ❏ Timed presentation, complete with visuals, so as to run close to allotted time.

Exercises

1. Prepare a three- to five-minute presentation explaining how a piece of equipment that you use on your job works. If the equipment is small enough, bring it with you to class. If it is too large, prepare an appropriate visual or two for use with your talk.

2. You have just been asked to talk about the students at your school. Narrow the topic and submit an outline to your instructor, showing how you have limited the topic and gathered and organized evidence. Use two or three appropriate visuals (tables, photographs, charts, or even videos) or offer a PowerPoint presentation. Follow the format of the outline in Figure 10.2.

3. Prepare a ten-minute presentation on a controversial topic that you would present before a civic group—the PTA, the local chapter of an organization, a post of the Veterans of Foreign Wars, a synagogue, a mosque, or a church club. Submit

an outline similar to that in Figure 10.2 to your instructor, together with a one-page statement of your specific call to action and its relevance for your audience.

4. Using the evaluation form in Figure 10.3, evaluate a speaker—a speech class student, a local politician, or a co-worker delivering a report at work. Specify the time, place, and occasion of the speech. Pay special attention to any visuals the speaker uses.

5. Deliver a formal presentation (fifteen to twenty minutes) on the various uses and advantages of the Internet for individuals in your chosen career. Use at least three visuals with your talk. Submit an outline to your instructor first.

A Writer's Brief Guide to Paragraphs, Sentences, and Words

To write successfully, you must know how to create effective paragraphs, write and punctuate clear sentences, and use words correctly. This guide succinctly explains some of the basic elements of clear and accurate writing.

Paragraphs

Writing a Well-Developed Paragraph

A paragraph is the basic building block for any piece of writing. It is (1) a group of related sentences (2) arranged in a logical order (3) supplying readers with detailed, appropriate information (4) on a single important topic.

A paragraph expresses one central idea, with each sentence contributing to the overall meaning of that idea. The paragraph does that by means of a *topic sentence*, which states the central idea, and *supporting information*, which explains the topic sentence.

Supply a Topic Sentence

The topic sentence is the most important sentence in your paragraph. Carefully worded and restricted, it helps you to generate and control your information. An effective topic sentence also helps readers grasp your main idea quickly. As you draft your paragraphs, pay close attention to the following three guidelines.

1. Make sure you provide a topic sentence. In their rush to supply readers with facts, some writers forget or neglect to include a topic sentence. The following paragraph, with no topic sentence, shows how fragmented such writing can be.

> No Topic Sentence: Sensors found on each machine detect wind speed and direction and other important details such as ice loading and potential metal fatigue. The information is fed into a small computer (microprocessor) in the nacelle (or engine housing). The microprocessor automatically keeps the blades turned into the wind, starts and stops the machine, and changes the pitch of the tips of the blades to increase power under varying wind conditions. Should any part of the wind turbine suffer damage or malfunction, the microprocessor will immediately shut the machine down.

Only when a suitable topic sentence is added—"The MOD-2 wind turbine is designed to be operated completely by computer."—can readers understand what the technical details have in common.

2. Put your topic sentence first. Place your topic sentence at the beginning—not the middle or end—of your paragraph because the first sentence occupies an emphatic position. Burying the key idea in the middle or near the end of the paragraph makes it harder for readers to comprehend your purpose or to act on your information.

3. Be sure your topic sentence is focused. If restricted, a topic sentence discusses only one central idea. A broad or unrestricted topic sentence leads to a shaky, incomplete paragraph for two reasons.

- The paragraph will not contain enough information to support the topic sentence.
- A broad topic sentence will not summarize or forecast specific information in the paragraph.

The following example of a carefully constructed paragraph contains a clear topic sentence in an appropriate position (highlighted in color) and adequate supporting details.

> Fat is an important part of everyone's diet. It is nutritionally present in the basic food groups we eat—meat and poultry, dairy products, and oils—to aid growth or development. The fats and fatty acids present in those foods ensure proper metabolism, thus helping to turn what we eat into the energy we need. Those same fats and fatty acids also act as carriers for important vitamins A, D, E, and K. Another important role of fat is that it keeps us from feeling hungry by delaying digestion. Fat also enhances the flavor of the food we eat, making it more enjoyable.

Three Characteristics of an Effective Paragraph

Effective paragraphs have **unity, coherence,** and **completeness.**

Unity

A unified paragraph sticks to one topic without wandering. Every sentence, every detail, **supports, explains,** or **proves** the central idea. A unified paragraph includes only relevant information and excludes unnecessary or irrelevant comments.

Coherence

In a coherent paragraph all sentences flow smoothly and logically to and from each other like the links of a chain. Use the following three techniques to achieve coherence.

1. Use transitional words and phrases. Some useful connective words, along with the relationships they express, are listed in Table A.1.

> Paragraph with Connective Words: Advertising a product on the radio has many advantages over using television. *For one thing,* radio rates are much cheaper. *For example,* a one-time 60-second spot on television can cost $750. *For that money,* advertisers can purchase nine 30-second spots on the radio. *Equally attractive* are the low production costs for radio advertising. *In contrast,* television advertising often includes extra costs for models and voice-overs. *Another* advantage radio offers advertisers is immediate scheduling. *Often* the ad appears during the same week a contract is signed. *On the other hand,* television stations are *frequently* booked up months in advance, so it may be a long time

TABLE A.1 Transitional, or Connective, Words and Phrases

Addition	again	besides	moreover
	additionally	first, second, third	next
	along with	furthermore	together with
	also	in addition	too
	and	many	what's more
	as well as	moreover	
Cause/effect	accordingly	consequently	on account of
	and so	due to	since
	as a result	hence	therefore
	because of	if	thus
Comparison/ contrast	but	in contrast	on the other hand
	conversely	in the same way	similarly
	equally	likewise	still
	however	on the contrary	yet
Conclusion	all in all	in brief	on the whole
	altogether	in conclusion	to conclude
	as we saw	in short	to put into perspective
	at last	in summary	to summarize
	finally	lastly	
Condition	although	granted that	provided that
	depending	if	to be sure
	even though	of course	unless
Emphasis	above all	for emphasis	of course
	after all	indeed	surely
	again	in fact	to repeat
	as a matter of fact	in other words	unquestionably
	as I said	obviously	
Illustration	for example	in other words	that is,
	for instance	in particular	to demonstrate
	in effect	specifically	to illustrate
Place	across from	below	over
	adjacent to	beyond	there
	alongside of	here	under
	at this point	in front of	where
	behind	next to	wherever
Time	afterward	formerly	previously
	at length	hereafter	soon
	at the same time	later	simultaneously
	at times	meanwhile	subsequently
	beforehand	next	then
	currently	now	until
	during	once	when
	earlier	presently	while

before an ad appears. *Furthermore*, radio gives advertisers a greater opportunity to reach potential buyers. *After all*, radio follows listeners everywhere—in their homes, at work, and in their cars. *Although* television is very popular, it cannot do that.

2. Use pronouns and demonstrative adjectives. Words like *he, she, him, her, they*, and so on, contribute to paragraph coherence and increase the flow of sentences.

Paragraph with Pronouns:

Traffic studies are an important tool for store owners looking for a new location. These studies are relatively inexpensive and highly accurate. They can tell owners how much traffic passes by a particular location at a particular time and why. Moreover, they can help owners to determine what particular characteristics the individuals have in common. Because of their helpfulness, these studies can save owners time and money and possibly prevent financial ruin.

3. Use parallel (coordinated) grammatical structures. Parallelism means using the same *kind of* word, phrase, clause, or sentence to express related concepts.

Orientation sessions accomplish four useful goals for trainees. First, they introduce trainees to key personnel in accounting, data processing, maintenance, and security. Second, they give trainees experience logging into the database system, selecting appropriate menus, editing core documents, and getting off the system. Third, they explain to trainees the company policies affecting the way supplies are ordered, used, and stored. Fourth, they help trainees understand their responsibilities in sensitive areas such as computer security and use.

Parallelism is at work on a number of levels in the preceding paragraph, among them:

- The four sentences about the four goals start in the same way grammatically ("... they introduce/give/explain/help ...") to help readers categorize the information.
- Within individual sentences, the repetition of *present participles* (logg*ing*, select*ing*, edit*ing*, gett*ing*) and of *past participles* (order*ed*, us*ed*, stor*ed*) helps the writer to coordinate information.
- Transitional words—*first, second, third, fourth*—provide a clear-cut sequence.

Completeness

A complete paragraph provides readers with sufficient information to **clarify, analyze, support, defend,** or **prove** the central idea expressed in the topic sentence. The reader feels satisfied that the writer has given necessary details.

Skimpy Paragraph:

Farmers can turn their crops and farm wastes into useful, cost-effective fuels. Much grown on the farm can be converted to energy. This energy can have many uses and save farmers a lot of money in operating expenses.

Fully Developed Paragraph:

Farm crops and wastes can be turned into fuels to save farmers on their operating costs. Alcohol can be distilled from grain, sugar beets, potatoes, even blighted crops. Converted to gasohol (90 percent gasoline, 10 percent alcohol), this fuel can run farm equipment such as irrigation pumps, feed grinders, and tractors. Similarly, through a biomass digestion system, farmers can produce methane from animal or crop wastes as a natural gas for heating and cooking. Finally, cellulose pellets, derived from plant materials, become solid fuel that can save farmers money in heating barns.

Sentences

Constructing and Punctuating Sentences

The way you construct and punctuate your sentences can determine whether you succeed or fail in the world of work. Your sentences reveal a lot about you. They tell readers how clearly or how poorly you can convey a message. And any message is only as effective and as thoughtful as the sentences of which it is made.

What Is a Sentence?

A sentence is a complete thought, expressed by a subject and a verb that can make sense standing alone.

> subject   verb
>
> Web sites   sell   products.

The Difference Between Phrases and Clauses

The first step toward success in writing sentences is learning to recognize the difference between phrases and clauses. A **phrase** is a group of words that does not contain a subject and a verb; phrases cannot make sense standing alone. Phrases cannot be sentences.

in the park	No Subject: Who is in the park?
	No Verb: What was done in the park?
for every patient in intensive care	No Subject: Who did something for every patient?
	No Verb: What was done for the patients?

A **clause** does contain a subject and a verb, but *not every clause is a sentence.* Only **independent** (or **main**) **clauses** can stand alone as sentences. Here is an example of an independent clause that is a complete sentence.

> subject   verb   object
>
> The president closed the college.

A **dependent** (or **subordinate**) **clause** also contains a subject and a verb, but it does not make complete sense and cannot stand alone. Why? A dependent clause contains a subordinating conjunction—*after, although, as, because, before, even though, if, since, unless, when, where, whereas, while*—at the beginning of the clause. Such conjunctions subordinate the clause in which they appear and make the clause dependent for meaning and completion on an independent clause.

$$\left.\begin{array}{l}\text{After}\\\text{Before}\\\text{Because}\\\text{Even though}\\\text{Unless}\end{array}\right\}\quad\text{the president closed the college}$$

"After the president closed the college" is not a complete thought but a dependent clause that leaves us in suspense. It needs to be completed with an independent clause telling us what happened "after."

dependent clause	independent clause		
	subject	verb	phrase
After the president closed the college,	we	played	in the snow.

Avoiding Sentence Fragments

An incomplete sentence is called a **fragment.** Fragments can be phrases or dependent clauses. They either lack a verb or a subject or have broken away from an independent clause. A fragment is isolated: It needs an overhaul to supply missing parts to turn it into an independent clause or to glue it back to an independent clause to have it make sense.

To avoid writing fragments, follow these rules. *Note that incorrect examples are preceded by a minus sign, corrected revisions by a plus sign.*

1. Do not use a subordinate clause as a sentence. Even though it contains a subject and a verb, a subordinate clause standing alone is still a fragment. To avoid this kind of sentence fragment, simply join the two clauses (the independent clause and the dependent clause containing a subordinating conjunction) with a comma—*not* a period or semicolon.

- Unless we agreed to the plan. (What would happen?)
- Unless we agreed to the plan; the project manager would discontinue the operation. (A semicolon cannot set off the subordinate clause.)
+ Unless we agreed to the plan, the project manager would discontinue the operation.
- Because safety precautions were taken. (What happened?)
+ Because safety precautions were taken, ten construction workers escaped injury.

Sometimes subordinate clauses appear at the end of a sentence. They may be introduced by a subordinate conjunction, an adverb, or a relative pronoun (*that, which, who*). Do not separate these clauses from the preceding independent clause with a period, thus turning them into fragments.

- An all-volunteer fire department posed some problems. Especially for residents in the western part of town.
+ An all-volunteer fire department posed some problems, especially for residents in the western part of town. (The word *especially* qualifies posed, referred to in the independent clause.)

2. Every sentence must have a subject telling the reader who does the action.

– Being extra careful not to spill the solution. (Who?)
+ The technician was being extra careful not to spill the solution.

3. Every sentence must have a complete verb. Watch especially for verbs ending in -*ing*. They need another verb (some form of *to be*) to make them complete.

– The machine running in the computer department. (Did what?)

You can change that fragment into a sentence by supplying the correct form of the verb.

+ The machine *is running* in the computer department.
+ The machine *runs* in the computer department.

Or you can revise the entire sentence, adding a new thought.

+ The machine running in the computer department processes all new accounts.

4. Do not detach prepositional phrases (beginning with *at, by, for, from, in, to, with,* and so forth) **from independent clauses.** Such phrases are not complete thoughts and cannot stand alone. Correct the error by leaving the phrases attached to the sentence to which they belong.

– By three o'clock the next day. (What was to happen?)
+ The supervisor wanted our reports by three o'clock the next day.

Avoiding Comma Splices

Fragments occur when you use only bits and pieces of complete sentences. Another common error that some writers commit involves just the reverse kind of action. They weakly and wrongly join two complete sentences (independent clauses) with a comma as if those two sentences were really only one sentence. Such an error is called a **comma splice.** Here is an example.

– Gasoline prices have risen by 10 percent in the last month, we will drive the car less often.

Two independent clauses (complete sentences) exist:

+ Gasoline prices have risen by 10 percent in the last month.
+ We will drive the car less often.

A comma alone lacks the power to separate independent clauses.

As the preceding example shows, many pronouns—*I, he, she, it, we, they*—are used as the subjects of independent clauses. A comma splice will result if you place a comma instead of a semicolon between two independent clauses where the second clause opens with a pronoun.

– Maria approved the plan, she liked its cost-effective approach.
+ Maria approved the plan; she liked its cost-effective approach.

However, relative pronouns (*who, whom, which, that*) are preceded by a comma, not a period or a semicolon, when they introduce subordinate clauses.

– She approved the plan. Which had the cost-effective approach.
+ She approved the plan, which had the cost-effective approach.

Four Ways to Correct Comma Splices

1. Remove the comma separating two independent clauses and replace it with a period. Then capitalize the first letter of the first word of the new sentence.

+ Gasoline prices have risen by 10 percent in the last month. We will drive the car less often.

2. Insert a coordinating conjunction (*and, but, or, nor, for, yet*) after the comma. Together, the conjunction and the comma properly separate the two independent clauses.

+ Gasoline prices have risen by 10 percent in the last month, and we will drive the car less often.

3. Rewrite the sentence (if it makes sense to do so). Turn the first independent clause into a dependent clause by adding a subordinate conjunction; then insert a comma and add the second independent clause.

+ Because gasoline prices have risen by 10 percent in the last month, we will drive the car less often.

4. Delete the comma and insert a semicolon.

+ Gasoline prices have risen by 10 percent in the last month; we will drive the car less often.

Of the four ways to correct the comma splice, sentences 3 and 4 are equally suitable, but sentence 3 reads more smoothly and so is the better choice.

The semicolon is an effective and forceful punctuation mark when two independent clauses are closely related, that is, when they announce contrasting or parallel views, as the two following examples reveal.

+ The union favored the new legislation; the company opposed it. (contrasting views)
+ Night classes help the college and the community; students can take more credit hours to advance their careers. (parallel views)

*How **Not** to Correct Comma Splices*

Some writers mistakenly try to correct comma splices by inserting a conjunctive adverb (*also, consequently, furthermore, however, moreover, nevertheless, then, therefore*) after the comma.

– Gasoline prices have risen by 10 percent in the last month, consequently we will drive the car less often.

Because the conjunctive adverb (*consequently*) is not as powerful as the coordinating conjunction (*and, but, for*), the error is not eliminated. If you use a conjunctive adverb—*consequently, however, nevertheless*—you still must insert a semicolon or a period before it, as the following examples show.

+ Gasoline prices have risen by 10 percent in the last month; consequently, we will drive the car less often.
+ Gasoline prices have risen by 10 percent in the last month. Consequently, we will drive the car less often.

Avoiding Run-on Sentences

A **run-on sentence** is the opposite of a sentence fragment. The fragment gives the reader too little information, the run-on too much. A run-on sentence forces readers to digest two or more grammatically complete sentences without the proper punctuation to separate them.

Run-on: The Internet is unquestionably a major source of information and students and other researchers are right to call it a virtual library this library is not like the collections of books and magazines that are carefully shelved always waiting for students to check and recheck them too often a Web site disappears or changes considerably and without a back-up file or a hard copy the researcher has no document to quote from and no exact citation to prove that he or she consulted an authentic source.

Revised: The Internet is unquestionably a major source of information. Students and other researchers are right to call it a virtual library, although this library is not like the collections of books and magazines that are carefully shelved, waiting for students to check and recheck them out. But too often a Web site disappears, is under construction, or changes considerably. Without a back-up file or a hard copy of the site, the researcher has no document to quote from and no exact citation to prove that he or she consulted an authentic source.

As the revision shows, you can repair a run-on by (1) dividing it into separate, correctly punctuated sentences and (2) by adding coordinating conjunctions (*and, but, yet, so, or, nor*) between clauses.

Making Subjects and Verbs Agree

A subject and a verb must agree in number. A singular subject takes a singular verb, whereas a plural subject requires a plural verb.

Singular Subjects   Plural Subjects
the engineer calculates   engineers calculate
a report analyzes   reports analyze
a policy changes   policies change

You can avoid subject-verb agreement errors by following several simple rules.

1. Disregard any words that come between the subject and its verb.

Faulty: The customer who ordered three parts want them shipped this afternoon.
Correct: The customer who ordered three parts wants them shipped this afternoon.

2. A compound subject (two parts connected by *and*) **takes a plural verb.**

Faulty: The engineering department and the safety committee prefers to develop new guidelines.
Correct: The engineering department and the safety committee prefer to develop new guidelines.

3. When a compound subject contains *neither . . . nor* or *either . . . or,* the verb agrees with the subject closest to it.

Faulty: Either the residents or the manager are going to file the complaint.
Correct: Either the residents or the manager is going to file the complaint.
Correct: Either the manager or the residents are going to file the complaint.

4. Use a singular verb after collective nouns (such as *committee, crew, department, group, organization, staff, team*) **when the group functions as a single unit.**

Correct: The crew was available to repair the machine.
Correct: The committee asks that all recommendations be submitted by Friday.

BUT

Correct: The staff were unable to agree on the best model. (The staff acted as individuals, not a unit, so a plural verb is required.)

5. Use a singular verb with indefinite pronouns (such as *anyone, anybody, each, everyone, everything, no one, somebody, something*).

Each of the programmer_s_ has completed the seminar.
Somebody usually volunteer_s_ for that duty.

Similarly, when *all, most, more,* or *part* is the subject, it requires a singular verb.

Most of the money is allocated.
Part of the equipment was salvageable.

6. Words like *scissors* and *pants* are plural when they are the true subject.

Faulty: A pair of trousers were available in his size. (*Pair* is the singular subject.)
Correct: The trousers were on sale.

7. Some foreign plurals (such as *curricula, data, media, phenomena, strata, syllabi*) **always take a plural verb.**

The data conclusively _prove_ my point.
The media _are_ usually the first to point out a politician's weak points.

8. Use a singular verb with fractions.

Three-fourths of her research proposal was finished.

Writing Sentences That Say What You Mean

Your sentences should say exactly what you mean, without doubletalk, misplaced humor, or nonsense. Sentences are composed of words and word groups that influence each other.

Writing Logical Sentences

Sentences should not contradict themselves or make outlandish claims. The following examples contain errors in logic; note how easily the suggested revision handles the problem.

Illogical: Steel roll-away shutters make it possible for the sun to be shaded in the summer and to have it shine in the winter. (The sun is far too large to shade; the writer meant that a room or a house, much smaller than the sun, could be shaded with the shutters.)

Revision: Steel roll-away shutters make it possible for owners to shade their living rooms in the summer and to admit sunshine during the winter.

Using Contextually Appropriate Words

Sentences should use the combination of words most appropriate for the subject.

Inappropriate: The members of the Nuclear Regulatory Commission saw fear radiated on the faces of the residents. (The word *radiated* is obviously ill-advised in this context; use a neutral term.)

Revision: The members of the Nuclear Regulatory Commission saw fear reflected on the faces of the residents.

Writing Sentences with Well-Placed Modifiers

A **modifier** is a word, phrase, or clause that describes, limits, or qualifies the meaning of another word or word group. A modifier can consist of one word (a *green* car), a prepositional phrase (the man *in the telephone booth*), a relative clause (the woman *who won the marathon*), or an *-ing* or *-ed* phrase (*walking three miles a day,* the student was in good shape; *seated in the first row,* we saw everything on stage).

A **dangling modifier** is one that cannot logically modify any word in the sentence.

− When answering the question, his calculator fell off the table.

One way to correct the error is to insert the right subject after the *-ing* phrase.

+ When answering the question, he knocked his calculator off the table.

You can also turn the phrase into a subordinate clause.

+ When he answered the question, his calculator fell off the table.
+ His calculator fell off the table as he answered the question.

A **misplaced modifier** illogically modifies the wrong word or words in the sentence. The result is often comical.

− Hiding in the corner, growling and snarling, our guide spotted the frightened cub. (Is our guide growling and snarling in the corner?)
− All travel requests must be submitted by employees in red ink. (Are the employees covered in red ink?)

The problem with both of those examples is word order. The modifiers are misplaced because they are attached to the wrong words in the sentence. Correct the error by moving the modifier to where it belongs.

+ Hiding in the corner, growling and snarling, the frightened cub was spotted by our guide.
+ All travel requests by employees must be submitted in red ink.

Misplacing a relative clause (introduced by relative pronouns such as *who, whom, that, which*) can also lead to problems with modification.

− The salesperson recorded the merchandise for the customer that the store had discounted. (The merchandise was discounted, not the customer.)

– The salesperson recorded the merchandise that the store had discounted for the customer. (The salesperson recorded for the customer; the store did not discount for the customer.)

+ The salesperson recorded for the customer the merchandise that the store had discounted.

Always place the relative clause immediately after the word it modifies.

Correct Use of Pronoun References

Sentences will be vague if they contain a faulty use of pronouns. When you use a pronoun whose **antecedent** (the person, place, or object the pronoun refers to) is unclear, you risk confusing your reader.

Unclear: After the plants are clean, we separate the stems from the roots and place them in the sun to dry. (Is it the stems or the roots that lie in the sun?)

Revision: After the plants are clean, we separate the stems from the roots and place the stems in the sun to dry.

Unclear: The park ranger was pleased to see the workers planting new trees and installing new benches. This will attract more tourists. (The trees or the benches or both?)

Revision: The park ranger was pleased to see the workers planting new trees and installing new benches, because the new trees and benches will attract more tourists.

Words

Spelling Words Correctly

Your written work will be judged in part on how well you spell. A misspelled word may seem like a small matter, but on an employment application, e-mail, incident report, letter, or short or long report it stands out to your discredit. A spelling mistake will look careless or, even worse, uneducated to a client or a supervisor. Readers will inevitably question your other skills if your spelling is incorrect.

The Benefits and Pitfalls of Spell-checkers

Computer **spell-checkers** can be handy for flagging potential problem words. But beware! Spell-checkers recognize only those words that have been listed in them. Moreover, a spell-checker will not differentiate between homonyms (soundalikes) such as *too* and *two, there* and *their, sea* and *see,* or *through* and *threw.* A spell-checker identifies only misspelled words, not misused words. In short, do not rely exclusively on spell-checkers to solve all your spelling and word-choice problems.

Consulting a Dictionary

Always have a dictionary handy. Two on-line dictionaries to consult are *Merriam-Webster On-line* at *http://www.m-w.com* and *The American Heritage Dictionary of the English Language* at *http://www.bartleby.com/61/.*

Using Apostrophes Correctly

Apostrophes cause some writers special problems. Basically, apostrophes are used for four reasons: (1) contractions, (2) possessives, (3) plurals, and (4) abbreviations. The following guidelines will help you to sort out those uses.

1. In a **contraction,** the apostrophe takes the place of the missing letter or letters: *I've = I have; doesn't = does not; he's = he is; it's = it is.* (*Its* is a possessive pronoun (the dog and its bone), not a contraction. There is no such form as *its'*.)

2. To form a **possessive,** follow these rules.

a. If a singular or plural noun does not end in an *-s,* add *'s* to show possession.

Mary's locker   the woman's jacket
children's books   the women's jackets
the staff's dedication   the company's policy

b. If a singular noun ends in *-s,* add *'s* to show possession.

The class's project   the boss's schedule

c. If a plural noun ends in *-s,* add just the *'* to indicate possession.

employees' benefits   computers' speed
lawyers' fees

d. If a proper name ends in *-s,* add *'s* to form the possessive.

Jones's account   Keats's poetry
the Williams's house   James's contract

e. If it is a compound noun, add an *'* or *'s* to the end of the word.

brother-in-law's business   Ms. Allison Jones-Wyatt's order

f. To indicate shared possession, add just *'s* to the last name.

Warner and Kline's Computer Shop   Juan and Anne's major

g. To indicate separate possession, add *'s* to each name.

Juan's and Tia's transcripts   Shakespeare's and Byron's poetry

3. To form the plural of numbers and capital letters used as nouns, including abbreviations without periods, just add *s*. To avoid misreading some capital letters, however, you may need to add the apostrophe.

during the 1980s   all perfect 10s
his SATs   several local YMCAs
the 3 Rs   straight A's

4. For abbreviations with periods and for lowercase letters used as nouns, form the plural by adding *'s.*

his *p*'s and *q*'s   Ph.D.'s

Using Hyphens Properly

Use a hyphen (- as opposed to a dash –) for

- **compound words**

  four-part lecture   heavy-duty machine   hand-held PC

- **most words beginning with self**

  self-starting   self-defense   self-regulating   self-governing

- **fractions used as adjectives**

  at the three-quarter level   two-thirds majority   three-dimensional drawing

Using Ellipses

Sometimes a sentence or passage is particularly useful, but you may not want to quote it fully. You may want to delete some words that are not really necessary for your purpose. These omissions are indicated by using an *ellipsis* (three spaced dots within the sentence to indicate where words have been omitted). Here is an example.

Full Quotation: "Diet and nutrition, which researchers have studied extensively, significantly affect oral health."
Quotation with Ellipsis: "Diet and nutrition . . . significantly affect oral health."

Using Numerals versus Words

Write out numbers as words rather than numerals

- **to begin a sentence**

  Nineteen ninety-nine was the first year of our recruitment drive.

- **to list the first number when two numbers are used together**

  The company needed eleven 9-foot slabs.

Use numerals, not words,

- **with abbreviations, percentages, symbols, units of measure, dates**

17%	11:30 a.m.	70 ml
Dec. 3, 2003	$250.00	50K

- **for page references**

  pp. 56–59

- **for large numbers**

3,000,000	23,750	1,714

Use both numerals and words when you want to be as precise as possible in a contract or a proposal.

We agreed to pay the vendor an extra twenty-five dollars ($25.00) per hour to finish the job by the 18th of May.

Using Italics or Underscoring

Use italics or underscoring for the titles of books, newspapers, magazines, journals, and films.

<u>The Ten Best Investment Strategies</u>

The New York Times

<u>Newsweek</u>

<u>Journal of Economic Growth</u>

The Alamo

Matching the Right Word with the Right Meaning

The words in the following list frequently are mistaken for one another. Some are true homonyms; others are just similar in spelling, pronunciation, or usage. The part of speech is given after each word.

accept (v) to receive, to acknowledge: *We accept your proposal.*
except (prep) excluding, but: *Everyone attended the meeting except Neelou.*

access (v) to gain entrance, to search: *Gandi was able to access the new program.*
excess (n) abundance, too much: *They had an excess of last year's models.*

advice (n) a recommendation: *I should have taken Juan's advice.*
advise (v) to counsel: *Our lawyers advised us not to sign the contract.*

affect (v) to change, to influence: *Does the detour on Route 22 affect your travel plans?*
effect (n) a result: *What was the effect of the new procedure?*
effect (v) to bring about: *We will try to effect a change in company policy.*

allot (v) to distribute: *The manager allotted the bonuses to the most successful sales staff.*
a lot (n) money, much: *Petra had a lot of work to do before the June 1 deadline.*

all ready (adj) two-word phrase *all + ready;* to be finished, to be prepared: *We are all ready for the inspector's visit.*
already (adv) previously, before a given time: *Our Webmaster had already constructed the sites.*

ascent (n) move upward: *We watched the space shuttle's ascent.*
assent (n) agreement: *She won the teacher's assent.*
assent (v) to agree: *The committee asked the company to assent to the new terms.*

attain (v) to achieve, to reach: *We attained our sales goal this month.*
obtain (v) to get, to receive: *You can obtain a job application via their Web site.*

capital (n) money: *The company had the capital to invest in a new franchise.*
capital (adj) main: *The boss told her new assistant he had a capital idea.*
capitol (n) building: *We took a tour of the capitol last week.*

cite (v) to document: *Please cite several examples to support your claim.*
site (n) place, location: *They want to build a parking lot on the site of the old theater.*
sight (n) vision: *His sight improved with bifocals.*

coarse (a) rough: *The sandpaper felt coarse.*
course (n) subject of study: *Sharonda took a course in calculus this fall.*

complement (v) to add to, to enhance: *Her graphs and charts complemented my proposal.*
compliment (v) to praise: *The customer complimented us on our courteous staff.*

continually (adv) frequently and regularly: *This answering machine continually disconnects the caller in the middle of the message.*
continuously (adv) constantly: *The air conditioning is on continuously during the summer.*

council (n) government body: *The council voted to increase salaries for all city employees.*
counsel (n) advice: *She gave the trainee pertinent counsel.*

discreet (adj) showing respect, being tactful: *The manager was discreet in answering the complaint letter.*
discrete (adj) separate, distinct: *Put those figures into discrete categories for processing.*

dual (adj) double: *A clock-radio serves a dual purpose.*
duel (n) a fight, a battle: *The argument almost turned into a duel.*

eminent (adj) prominent, highly esteemed: *Dr. Felicia Rollins is the most eminent neurologist in our community.*
imminent (adj) about to happen: *A hostile takeover of that company is imminent.*

envelop (v) to surround, to embrace: *A fog enveloped the city.*
envelope (n) a covering for a letter: *Address every envelope using the correct ZIP codes.*

fair (n) convention, exhibition: *The technological fair featured a DVD-CD home theater with five satellite speakers.*
fair (adj) honest: *Their price was fair.*
fare (n) cost for a trip: *She was able to get a discount on a round-trip fare.*
fare (n) food: *They ate East Asian fare.*

foreword (n) preface, introduction to a book: *The foreword outlined the author's goals and objectives in her research study.*
forward (adv) toward a time or place; in advance: *We moved the time of the visit forward on the calendar so we could meet the overseas manager.*
forward (v) to send ahead: *We forwarded her e-mail to her new server.*

imply (v) to suggest: *Mr. Chin implied that the mechanics had taken too long for their lunch break.*
infer (v) to draw a conclusion: *We can infer from these sales figures that the new advertising campaign is working.*

it's (noun + verb) contraction of *it* and *is*: *Do you think it's too early to tell?*
its (adj) possessive form of *it*: *That old printer is on its last legs.*

knew (v) (past tense of *know*): *She knew the new regulations.*
new (a) never used before: *The subwoofer was new.*

lay/laid/laid (v) to put down: *Lay aside that project for now. He laid aside the project. He had already laid aside the project twice before.*
lie/lay/lain (v) to recline: *I think I'll lie down for a while. He lay there for only two minutes before the firefighter rescued him. She has lain out in the sun too often.*

lean (adj) skinny, not fat: *He ordered a lean cut of meat.*
lien (n) a debt against: *Because the gate fees were not paid, the condo association put a lien against his unit.*

lose (v) to misplace, to fail to win: *Be careful not to lose my calculator. I hope I don't lose my seat on the planning board.*
loose (adj) not tight: *The printer ribbon was too loose.*

miner (n) individual who works in a mine: *His uncle was a miner in West Virginia.*
minor (n) someone under legal age: *The law forbids the sale of tobacco to minors.*

overdo (v) to work too much: *If you overdo, you'll be stressed.*
overdue (adj) past due: *The account was 90 days overdue.*

pare (v) to cut back: *She pared the skin from the apple.*
pair (n) a couple: *They offered a pair of resolutions.*
pear (n) a fruit: *Alphonso ate a pear with lunch.*

passed (v) went by (past tense of *pass*): *He passed me in the hall without recognizing me.*
past (n) time gone by: *We've never used their services in the past.*

personal (adj) private: *The manager closes the door when she discusses personal matters with one of her staff.*
personnel (n) staff of employees: *All personnel must participate in the 401(k) retirement program.*

perspective (n) view: *From the customer's perspective, we are an honest and courteous company.*
prospective (adj) expected, likely to happen or become: *E-mail the prospective budget to district managers.*

plain (adj) simple, not fancy: *He ate plain food.*
plane (n) airplane: *The plane for Dallas leaves in an hour.*
plane (v) to make smooth: *The carpenter planed the wood.*

precede (v) to go before: *A slide show will precede the open discussion.*
proceed (v) to carry on, to go ahead: *Proceed as if we had never received that letter.*

principal (adj) main, chief: *Sales of new software constitute their principal source of revenue.*
principal (n) the head of a school: *She was a high school principal before she entered the business world.*

principal (n) money owed: *The principal on that loan totaled $32,800.*
principle (n) a policy, a belief: *Sales reps should operate on the principle that the customer is always right.*

quiet (adj) silent, not loud: *He liked to spend a quiet afternoon surfing the Net.*
quite (adv) to a degree: *The officer was quite encouraged by the recruit's performance.*

stationary (adj) not moving: *Miguel rides a stationary bicycle for an hour every morning.*
stationery (n) writing supplies, such as paper and envelopes: *Please stop off at the stationery store and buy some more address labels.*

than (conj) as opposed to (used in comparisons): *He is a faster keyboarder than his predecessor.*
then (adv) at that time: *First she called the vendor; then she summarized their conversation in an e-mail to her boss.*

their (adj) possessive form of *they: All the lab technicians took their vacations during June and July.*
there (adv) in that place: *Please put the printer in there.*
they're (noun + verb) contraction of *they* and *are: They're our two best customer service representatives.*

waist (n) circumference: *He wore a 34 waist size.*
waste (v) to squander: *Justin wasted 2 hours looking in the wrong place for the files.*

waive (v) to exempt, to forgo, to cancel: *They waived the late fee this time.*
wave (n) surf: *The waves were 12 feet as the storm surged.*
wave (v) to gesture: *The child waves to his mother.*

who's (noun + verb) contraction of *who* and *is: Who's up next for a promotion?*
whose (adj) possessive form of *who: Whose idea was that in the first place?*

you're (noun + verb) contraction of *you* and *are: You're going to like their decision.*
your (adj) possessive form of *you: They agree with your ideas.*

Proofreading Marks

Mark	Example	Corrected
⌢o	Correct a typo.	Correct a typo.
r⌢/m⌢/⌢o	Correct more than one typo.	Correct more than one typo.
t	Insert a letter.	Insert a letter.
or words	Insert a word.	Insert a word or words.
◌/	Make a deletion.	Make a deletion.
◌̃	Delete and close up space.	Delete and close up space.
◠	Close up extra space.	Close up extra space.
#	Insert proper spacing.	Insert proper spacing.
#/◠	Close up and insert space.	Close up and insert space.
eq #	Regularize proper spacing.	Regularize proper spacing.
tr	Transpose letters indicated.	Transpose letters indicated.
tr	Transpose as words indicated.	Transpose words as indicated.
tr	Reorder shown as words several.	Reorder several words as shown.
[[	Move text to left.	Move text to left.
]]	Move text to right.	Move text to right.
¶ [	Indent for paragraph.	Indent for paragraph.
no ¶ [	No paragraph indent.	No paragraph indent.
// //	Align type vertically.	Align type vertically.
run in	Run back turnover lines.	Run back turnover lines.
⌐	Break line when it runs far too long.	Break line when it runs far too long.
⊙	Insert period here.	Insert period here.
ʌ	Commas commas everywhere.	Commas, commas everywhere.
˅	Its in need of an apostrophe.	It's in need of an apostrophe.
˅ / ˅	Add quotation marks, he begged.	"Add quotation marks," he begged.
;	Add a semicolon don't hesitate.	Add a semicolon; don't hesitate.
:	She advised "You need a colon."	She advised: "You need a colon."
?	How about a question mark.	How about a question mark?
(/)	Add parentheses as they say.	Add parentheses (as they say).
lc	Sometimes you want Lowercase.	Sometimes you want lowercase.
caps	Sometimes you want upperCASE.	Sometimes you want UPPERCASE.
ital	Add italics instantly.	Add italics *instantly*.
bf	Add boldface if necessary.	Add **boldface** if necessary.
wf	Fix a wrong font letter.	Fix a wrong font letter.
sp	Spell out all 3 terms.	Spell out all three terms.
˅	Change x to a subscript.	Change $_x$ to a subscript.
˄	Change y to a superscript.	Change ^{y} to a superscript.
stet	Let stand as is.	Let stand as is. (To retract a change already marked.)

Index